Trevor Foster
The life of a rugby league legend

Trevor when he signed for Bradford Northern in 1938
(Photo: *Telegraph & Argus*)

Simon Foster, Robert Gate & Peter Lush

London League Publications Ltd

Trevor Foster
The life of a rugby league legend

Front cover photos: Trevor Foster holding the Challenge Cup in 1944 after Bradford Northern had beaten Wigan (photo: Courtesy Trevor Foster); Trevor Foster holding the Challenge Cup after Bradford Bulls victory in 2000 at Murrayfield (Photo: David Williams). Back cover photos: Trevor Foster and Ernest Ward (courtesy Robert Gate) Trevor Foster with young supporters at Odsal (*Telegraph & Argus*).

Photos as credited. All photographs copyright to the photographer. We have not intentionally breached any copyright. If any photographer believes this is the case, please contact the publishers.

A CIP catalogue record for this book is available from the British Library.

First published in Great Britain in March 2005 by:
London League Publications Ltd, P.O. Box 10441, London E14 8WR

ISBN: 1-903659-18-3

Cover design by: Stephen McCarthy Graphic Design
                     46, Clarence Road, London N15 5BB

Layout: Peter Lush

Printed and bound by: Biddles Ltd, Kings Lynn

All Trevor's profits from the sales of this book will be donated to cancer charities in West Yorkshire.

This book is dedicated to the game of rugby league and all those involved in it.

Foreword

I am delighted to be able to write this forward to Trevor's book. It has certainly been a long time in coming and I know it is one that everyone in rugby league is waiting to read.

I have known Trevor since I was about seven or eight years old, when he was the school 'Boardman'! I think they are called Education Welfare Officers now, but in my days they were 'the Boardman!! I can't begin to tell you how many times he was knocking on my front door while I was making a quick exit through the back! I can tell you it was quite scary to see a man that big coming down your garden path!

But eventually he got me to join the Police Boys Club in Manningham, Bradford, where I lived and it was a life changing experience for me. In those days, if you lived in Manningham, you either joined the Police Boys Club or became a criminal! Fortunately I joined up with Trevor and it was through him that I started playing rugby, signed for Bradford Northern and began the career that I am enjoying now.

Trevor is iconic in Bradford, not just at the Bulls, but in the community as a whole. I have attended many meetings with him and listened in awe of what he has had to say. He is inspirational, has great clarity of vision and is enthusiastic about everything he becomes involved with. His work for CHAS and other charities in the city is legendary and he cares as passionately about that work and his Catholic faith as he does about his rugby.

At the time of the change from Bradford Northern to the Bulls many 'Northern diehards' looked to Trevor to lead their campaign against the change but Trevor embraced it wholeheartedly and was very positive towards it. He has been a very big part of the Bulls in the 10 years of Super League and has enjoyed the success we have achieved in the past decade.

Trevor's story is a tremendous one and he has undertaken to tell it, just like he has with everything he has done in his life, with great enthusiasm. I am sure you will enjoy reading it.

Brian Noble

Photo: Honorary Doctorates: Brian Noble and Trevor at the ceremony when they were both awarded Doctorates by the University of Bradford in July 2002. Brian Noble's was in recognition of his contribution to the success of the Bradford Bulls, Trevor's was for his community work and contribution to the city of Bradford. (Photograph: Ede & Ravenscroft)

Introduction: Trevor John French Foster

Here is a man who has been honoured by the Pope, the Queen, the Rugby Football League, the Welsh Sports Hall of Fame, the City of Bradford, the University of Bradford, and many others. He has acted the part of Jesus Christ, captained Wales and scored decisive tries in two Wembley Challenge Cup finals. He is revered and loved in sporting spheres, in charitable spheres, in educational spheres, in the sphere of community affairs and, in his chosen habitat, Bradford, his achievements and memories of him will live on long after he has left the scene.

If there was any real justice the Queen would confer a knighthood or an earldom on him, never mind an MBE, and Bradford would rename Forster Square Trevor Foster Square. There is no doubt about it, Trevor has in many ways been a genuine paragon, a fine example to us all.

My dealings with Trevor have been within the world of rugby league and usually of an historical nature. He has always been approachable, knowledgeable, modest and humble. I would think it impossible for Trevor to be in any way offensive. He does actually reek of most of the virtues anyone admires and yet he has achieved so much in so many areas of human endeavour.

As a rugby player Trevor conducted himself in a manner all sportsmen should seek to emulate. He was a brilliant exponent of both codes of rugby – arguably the best forward in both league and union in those strange days during the Second World War, when some lucky men were allowed to play both games. Trevor had the strength, the fitness, the stamina and the ability to soak up punishment required of a forward at top level in both games. He also, had the ball skills, the pace and the instinct to be in the right place at the right time which sets apart the great from the merely very good. That he preferred the rugby league style of forward play with its requirements for running, handling and athleticism and lack of rucks and mauls, proves he also had good sense and taste! Trevor's total of 142 tries in first-class rugby league is an eloquent testimony to his value to the teams in which he appeared at club and representative levels. However, it is equally evident that he would always place the team's benefit before his own.

Rugby league has produced a number of exemplary players for whom no one has a bad word, men who played the game as it should be played, men who are held up as role models for children and aspiring young players. Some who spring to mind are heroes such as Douglas Clark, Willie Horne, Roger Millward, Geoff Gunney, Alan Hardisty, Johnny Whiteley and the late Roy Powell. All played at the highest level for many years and were targets for the hard cases of the game. Provocation seldom, if ever, got the better of such men. They just got on with their business, rose above the mayhem and are honoured and remembered not just as good or great rugby players but as true sportsmen. Trevor Foster certainly ranks as one of these special men. He was never sent off or, as far as is recorded, even received a referee's caution. Chivalrous may be an unusual term to apply to a rugby league forward but it appears to be appropriate in Trevor's case. If anyone ever played rugby in a chivalrous manner, that man was Trevor.

Of course, Trevor's contribution to rugby league has far exceeded his playing record, fantastic as that is. Any player who has represented Wales and Great Britain, toured Australasia as a Lion and won all the game's major domestic honours can happily and deservedly rest on his laurels. Trevor's contribution to his sport continued well past the day he hung up his boots in 1955 and continues even now, when he has entered his 91st year. It may surprise those who have been brainwashed into thinking that coaching only properly began with the arrival of Super League that Trevor, in his role as director of coaching to the RFL in the late 1940s and early 1950s, had pioneered much of what passes for rocket science in the modern era. Naturally, anyone who knows anything about the game is familiar with Trevor's magnificent contribution to his beloved Bradford Northern/Bulls, a relationship which has now endured for 67 years. He has done almost everything imaginable at Odsal – played, coached, worked on the ground staff, worked in the office, led the campaign to install floodlights, led the fight to resurrect the club in the dismal days of the early 1960s, been president of the Supporters Club and is currently the club's official time-keeper, among other things. Some of us wonder what he will do next.

But, when all is said and done, he is, like the rest of us, human. He did make a few knock-ons, he did stray off-side occasionally and he once told me a fib. When I interviewed him for my book *Gone North* in 1986, he told me he was born on 3 December 1916, a fallacy which I have subsequently repeated on more than one occasion. He was in fact born on 3 December 1914 and appears to have been employing a traditional wheeze, used by sportsmen from time immemorial, i.e. knocking a couple of years off their age in order to make them seem a better prospect for potential employers. Remarkably, Trevor maintained this for the greater part of the 20th century and persuaded other interviewers, such as Bill Bowes, the great Yorkshire bowler and *Yorkshire Post* journalist, in the 1940s, and, much more recently in the 1990s, the estimable Raymond Fletcher, also of the *Yorkshire Post*, that he was two years younger than he is. At least that puts me in good company and I can certainly forgive Trevor for his fib.

Trevor's real age was revealed when his son Simon told me that London League Publications intended to bring out a biography of Trevor to mark his 90th birthday in December 2004. The sums, of course, did not add up. Anyway, I am glad that we got that sorted out at last!

In these days of spin, hype, image and cynicism it is salutary and refreshing to be confronted with the antidote, a distillation of the virtues of Trevor Foster - a man to be counted on, a man to be trusted, a man of honour. A simple man, in that word's best and truest sense.

Robert Gate

Thank you: We would like to thank everyone who was interviewed for the book, wrote pieces or lent us photographs or programmes for it; Dave Farrar, Michael O'Hare for sub-editing, Steve McCarthy for the layout of the cover; David Williams for providing photographs. Sam Grundy for his work on the 1963-64 chapter; also Gary Baker; Bradford Bulls RLFC; Stuart Duffy; Newport RFC; Jack Bower; Charlie Ebbage; Harry Edgar for providing photographs; Bev Risman; Tony Collins; Tony Hannan for transcribing and editing tapes of interviews; the *Telegraph & Argus* for permission to use photographs; the Rugby Football League for permission to reproduce Challenge Cup final programmes and other documents and the staff at Biddles Ltd.

About the authors:

Simon Foster is currently employed as marketing manager and lecturer at East Riding College in Beverley, following a career in teaching. He lives in Beverley with his wife Nicola, daughter Hannah and son Michael. Simon is a sports enthusiast, a keen cricketer and, not surprisingly, has a passion for rugby league. He remembers watching his father playing at Odsal for the first time in 1955 and has supported the Bradford Club ever since.

He qualified as a rugby league coach at Lilleshall under the tutorship of Albert Fearnley and Laurie Gant. He was proud to be involved in the pioneering days of rugby league development when the Midlands and South West Amateur Rugby League Association (MASWARLA) was formed in the early 1980s. He has always had an ambition to produce a book about his father's extraordinary life - Trevor has been an inspiration to so many people.

Robert Gate continues to write books and articles on rugby league history, against his better judgment and to the detriment of his garden and wife's pocket, because he cannot shake off his life-long fascination for the game's past. He is presently working with Neil Fox on a biography of that great centre three-quarter, after which he will attempt to write books on Jim Sullivan and Douglas Clark. Also in the pipe-line are a Dictionary of biography of Great Britain Players, the complete and utter book on Welsh rugby league players, the entire history of British international and test rugby league matches, a play, a novel and a gardening book.

Peter Lush with Dave Farrar founded London League Publications Ltd in 1995. Since then, they have published 22 books on rugby league, and launched the magazine *Our Game*. Peter was joint author of *Touch & Go, From Fulham to Wembley, I wouldn't start from Here!* and the *Rugby League Grounds Guide*, and joint editor of *Tries in the Valleys*. He has written regularly for *Our Game*, and for the London Broncos and London Skolars match programmes. He was introduced to rugby league by Dave Farrar in 1980, and has followed the game ever since. He is also a West Ham United season ticket holder, and Middlesex CCC member. He works as a freelance consultant in the social housing and voluntary sectors.

Sam Grundy is the current chairman of Bradford Independent Supporters Association (BISA). He is a civil servant and has been following rugby league, especially Bradford, for 25 years. He is a keen writer on rugby league for the BISA magazine and has contributed work to several other rugby league books and publications.

Historical notes

Rugby league scoring: During the whole of Trevor's playing career in rugby league, a try was worth three points, and all goals, including drop-goals, were worth two points.
W. T. H. Davies: Trevor's distinguished Bradford, Wales and Great Britain colleague was called Billy by his playing colleagues, rather than Willie which was often used in press reports. To avoid confusion, we have used Billy in this book, but have not changed direct quotations from press reports.
Rugby League and rugby union: Since 1995, when rugby union went 'open' and accepted professionalism, players have been able to play both codes at any level, and switch between them. However, before 1995, professionalism was banned in rugby union, and any player who had played rugby league as a professional was banned from playing rugby union again. This ban was lifted in services rugby during the Second World War.

Bibliography:

Books & pamphlets:
The Headingley Story 1955-1979 (Volume Two – Rugby) by Ken Dalby (Leeds CFA Ltd, 1979)
One hundred years of Newport Rugby by Jack Davis (The Starling Press Ltd, 1974)
Bradford Rugby League – Bradford, Northern and Bulls by Robert Gate (Tempus Publishing, 2000)
Gone North (Volumes 1 & 2) by Robert Gate (R. E. Gate, 1986 & 1988)
The Struggle for The Ashes by Robert Gate (R. E. Gate, 1986)
The History of Royal Air Force Rugby 1919-1999 by John Mace (The Royal Air Force Rugby Union, 2000)
Fields of Praise – Official history of the Welsh Rugby Union 1881-1981 by David Smith & Gareth Williams (University of Wales Press, 1980)
England to Australia and New Zealand by Eddie Waring (F. Youngman, 1947)
1905 and All That by Gareth Williams (Gomer Press, 1991)
Bradford Northern - The History 1863-1989 by Nigel Williams (self published, 1989)
Trevor Foster Souvenir Brochure (Committee of the Trevor Foster Testimonial Fund, 1955)

Newspapers and journals:
Rugby Leaguer
Rugby League Gazette
Rugby League Review
South Wales Argus (Newport, Gwent)
Telegraph & Argus (Bradford, West Yorkshire)
The Courier & Guardian (Halifax, West Yorkshire)
The Times
The Yorkshire Observer (Bradford, West Yorkshire)
The Yorkshire Post

Contents

This book was very much a team effort. However, the initial work on chapters 1, 6 and 11 was done by Simon Foster, chapters 4, 5, 7 and Appendix 1 by Robert Gate, chapter 10 by Sam Grundy and the other chapters by Peter Lush.

1.   Early years in Newport

Newport has a great rugby tradition, and it was here that Trevor John French Foster was born at The Church House Inn, 14 Portland Street on 3 December 1914. He was the youngest of six children. This was the year that Sir John French, a Field Marshal in the First World War, was made a Viscount, and Trevor's mother, Mabel, expressed her admiration by giving her son the names of the famous soldier.

The Church House, in the Pill district of Newport, was said to be the most interesting public house in the town and was listed by the Ministry of Housing and Local Government as being of outstanding historical and architectural importance.

Trevor's father Richard had a distinguished military career. In 1885 at the age of 15, he enlisted in the 41st Foot (now the Welsh regiment) and served with them for 26 years, reaching the rank of Colour-Sergeant. For his services during the Boer War he was awarded the Distinguished Service Medal and the Queen's and King's South African medals. Later, at a presentation ceremony in Aber-Bargoed he received from Field Marshall Montgomery the Meritorious Service Medal, which was awarded in recognition of long service in the army. In 1910 Richard Foster became licensee at the Church House Inn, which had previously been kept by his wife's mother and would soon become Trevor's home throughout his early years. Trevor's father was also a rugby footballer. He partnered the famous Gwyn Nicholls in the Cardiff team between 1894 and 1896, and then joined Llwynypia, in the Rhondda club's heyday, when his team mates included the celebrated Willie Llewellyn, Dick Hellings, Rob Jones and Jack Evans.

Richard had a great influence on his son's character and ambition. For a number of years before his death aged 79, he was blind, but his long service in the army had left its stamp on him, and he remained a soldier in outlook and bearing. His discipline, strength in adversity, commitment and duty to his family were values Trevor inherited. Richard Foster had a military funeral with a guard of honour and a Union Jack escort.

Trevor shared his Church House birthplace with the famous Tramp Poet William Henry Davies. Born in 1871, Davies wrote prolifically of his time in Newport before setting off to London and later America. He walked the streets at night to discover what he called "the beggar's experience of the worst side of life". This inspired him to write more than 700 poems published in 20 books before his death in 1940. In his lifetime Davies was a truly popular poet and he became the Poet Laureate.

There are some interesting similarities between William Henry and Trevor, who both shared a great love for Newport and its people. In very different ways they committed a large part of their lives to enable others to enjoy life a little more. William Henry loved being around people as much as Trevor does. They also much preferred to walk rather than own a motor car.

Trevor recalls: "I remember a special ceremony being held at The Church House Inn just before I left Newport to join Bradford Northern in 1938. The Lady Major of Newport unveiled a plaque to commemorate the Tramp Poet's birthplace. William Henry Davies attended in his very last public appearance. He was a lovely gentleman, very endearing. I asked him what he would like to drink; he said a nice pint of beer would be fine. He was delighted to visit his birthplace and walked all around the house - despite having lost a foot when jumping from a freight train in Canada - recalling memories in the different rooms. He had a big smile on his face. I remember a poem he wrote about The Church House: 'This little house where I was born, and where my early childhood lies, was built with solid blocks of gold, and all its walls have diamond eyes'."

Trevor has happy memories of his early childhood in Newport: "Our family pub was the focal point for the Pill district community and there was a great deal of poverty. The neighbourhood was very close to the docks and most of our customers and friends worked in the local area. There was a strong sense of respect and responsibility for others and their property. Despite the docklands area, Newport has a lot of natural beauty. As children, with my two brothers and three sisters, we climbed Stow Hill for the Mayor's annual procession and often walked to Christchurch to admire the view over the ships and islands in the channel. The most beautiful part is Allt-yr-yn, known as the 'green country', which has a clear canal coming down lock-by-lock with Twm Barlwm mountain in the distance. Standing on the hillside road you could see down into a wonderful green valley.

The Church House Inn was used by the locals as a place to relax, have the odd pint of beer and enjoy one another's company. It was also the place where everyone came to celebrate a birth or a marriage and to gather to pay respects after a death. It had that warm and welcoming family feeling and an open-house appeal."

Trevor's first schooling was at a private fee-paying Catholic convent, St Josephs on Stow Hill, which was run by nuns. His mother was keen to see he received a good early education and worked hard to ensure there were a few extra pennies available to support his needs. At the age of eight, Trevor transferred to Holy Cross Elementary School, in the middle of Newport High Street, where he spent the rest of his schooldays. Holy Cross was noted for rugby football and had an ethos which encouraged all pupils to achieve their potential in academic studies and importantly in sport.

Trevor recalls: "The head teacher was Sister Aquinous, a strict disciplinarian, a great organiser and one who loved her rugby football. Rugby was very strong in the Welsh schools system at that time. There was an abundance of fixtures arranged between local schools. She encouraged our rugby team 100 per cent and even handed out packets of sweets to all the players at Monday morning assembly if we had won our match on the Saturday. However, my greatest influence when starting to play rugby was the enthusiastic Father Honan, an Irish priest who visited the school every week to take rugby training. The Latin motto on the team jerseys 'In hoc signo vinces' translated as 'in this sign we shall conquer'. Whenever we ran out on to the field to play a match the whole team would shout the word 'vinces', like a war cry.

Sister Aquinous allowed all the rugby players certain privileges, including attending afternoon training sessions with Father Honan in normal school class time. I was first chosen to play for the team when I was aged 11 or 12. Our team captain was the late Alec Givvons, who went on to play for Cross Keys and then joined Oldham Rugby League Club. We later played together in the Wales rugby league team. With Father Honan's coaching ability - he had played rugby in his younger days - and Alec at scrum-half and leader on the field, we were very successful. There was a tremendous local following for the team, particularly from parents and friends of the school. I played full-back and enjoyed the freedom and space to run. Tackling and kicking were very important too. One highlight when I was 13-years-old was to play in a cup final against Newport Grammar School. The final was played at the Newport rugby ground, Rodney Parade. We were a year younger than the grammar school lads, but lo-and-behold we won the cup. We walked back to school after the match, carrying the cup, and were greeted by hundreds of people. It was a great day for Holy Cross School, where I learned the basics of rugby football.

The Newport club was quite a good team at the time and we were given free passes to watch them, every other Saturday afternoon. Jack Morley, who later joined Wigan, was the star player and a Welsh international. There was always a great rivalry between Newport and Cardiff. The Cardiff team were very strong and would usually beat Newport. There were always big crowds when the two sides clashed, home and away. Occasionally we would watch Newport County association football team, just for a change of sport."

Trevor's first experience of a Cardiff Arms Park international came courtesy of the priest at his school. "Father Honan, our coach, took four of us down to Cardiff and paid all our expenses. What a wonderful occasion, my first experience of international rugby. It was Wales versus England, on a Saturday with a 1.00pm kick-off. We stood very near the front of the terrace and the people around us lifted us down onto the touchline, close to the pitch. We choked with pride when the red jerseys appeared down the tunnel. We felt 10 feet tall when they scored. I shed a few tears when we sang 'We'll keep a welcome in the hillsides' and *Cwm Rhondda*.

Before I left school I was chosen to represent the Newport Boys team. I remember a cup final game when my mother paid one of her rare visits to watch me. At the end of the match she came onto the field and kissed me. She never did realise it was a man's game."

Trevor left school aged 14, partly owing to his father's increasing blindness and the need to help run the busy family inn. Rugby football was forgotten for nearly four years.

Trevor reflects: "My dad lost his sight after an unusual accident. He went out one afternoon with a regular customer who had a small fruit and vegetable business. They took a small pony and cart to pick apples at an orchard the gentleman had just purchased. My dad slipped and fell awkwardly from a tree. He hit his head hard on the ground and lay unconscious for a few minutes. When he came around he was troubled with poor vision. My mother was very concerned and later took him to visit a Harley Street specialist in London. Unfortunately, there was little they could do and gradually his sight deteriorated until he was completely blind. It was my duty to take him on walks as soon as I arrived home from school.

He loved to walk near our pub, with his white stick guiding him along the railway siding whilst chatting to friends and neighbours. He was still very fit and strong and had a very optimistic outlook on life. Many of his soldier pals from all parts of the valleys would visit the Church House to see him and quite remarkably he remembered their voices and immediately called them by their first name. He enjoyed listening to his portable radio which he carried with him around the house. I remember often getting up in the early hours to listen to cricket test matches and world championship boxing with him."

One particular fight had a profound effect on Trevor and his dad. It was the rematch between Joe Louis and Max Schmeling in 1938. It seemed the whole world was tuned in on that night. The famous fight in the Yankee Stadium in New York was a brutal affair but had international significance. Trevor recalls: "Germany was building its powerful forces under the Nazi regime and was threatening world peace. Max Schmeling was German and the former heavyweight champion of the world and had previously knocked out Louis, the dignified black American, in the latter rounds of a non-title fight in 1936. Schmeling was heralded by the Germans as coming from a 'superior race'. However, Joe Louis took the fight to Schmeling from the first bell and with phenomenal punching power and great accuracy, sensationally destroyed him in just over two minutes. The victory was celebrated all over the world and had a great impact on me. Joe Louis was a class act and my first real sporting hero. He had given the champion such a beating. The Nazi regime had ordered the commentary to be cut off, because Schmeling's cries of pain could be heard live over the radio. I honestly believed that his defeat would put paid to any ideas Germany may have had to conquer the world! My optimism was short lived.

Unemployment was a real issue in Newport. Even on the local docks, jobs were hard to come by. I was fortunate; I got a part-time job as an errand boy with a local baker. It was quite natural that I should become more involved running the pub, particularly as my two brothers started in business on their own. My eldest brother Leslie went into the motor car trade and owned a successful garage on the Cardiff road. Teddy [Edward] became a high class butcher in Port Talbot. Both were keen sports followers. Leslie liked boxing and had a few amateur fights. Teddy played a bit of rugby. They both followed my football career with enthusiasm, as did my sisters Madeline, Freda and Eileen."

Like his brother Leslie, Trevor was also quite useful when wearing boxing gloves. Around the corner from Church House lived Jerry Shea a famous former Welsh rugby union international, Wigan and Pontypridd rugby league player and one-time boxer. After the lunchtime pub closing, Trevor and Leslie cleared the inn's decks, put on the gloves and helped Jerry with his training.

Trevor recalls: "My mum led an extremely busy life. She had to care for my disabled father, run the home and the business. She was a wonderful cook, and always insisted on fresh produce. My sisters and I went down to the open-air market in Dock Street to buy dried fish – it came in huge solid blocks and was relatively cheap. The fishmonger would chop it up and wrap it in newspaper. It provided two or three hearty meals for the family. One Christmas we bought a live goose from Newport market and on the way home it broke loose in Dock Street. With other people trying to catch it, the goose finished up in Portland Street. Still running it found its way to The Church House – with feathers ruffled and looking half-dead. It finally flew up onto the table in the living room. It knew its place. Sunday lunch at home was always a formal occasion. After celebrating mass at the parish church of St. Michael's, all the family sat down to a roast of beef, lamb or pork with all the trimmings."

Trevor's mother spoke fluent French; she had spent some of her early years in France, and often acted an interpreter for the local council when French dignitaries visited Newport.

Trevor remembers: "As children we were never at a loss for something to do, we had to make our own fun. With very little money, sport was the main pastime and street games were played all the time and until late into the night. We always had cats and dogs around the house. My sisters loved animals.

One day a group of gypsies who used to call selling their wares brought a monkey to our house. The girls were smitten and so we kept him. He was called Micky and proved to be a very popular addition to the family and had a lively personality. He was fed on all the pub leftovers. Everyday local children on their way to school would stop and talk to him as he ran along the high wall behind the house. He performed somersaults and other acrobatics. There was a complaint from the school because some of the pupils were regularly late for classes.

The teacher came around to the house one lunchtime and complained: 'Your boy Micky is making our pupils late for school'. My mother told him: "He's not a boy, he's a monkey" and the teacher laughed and saw the funny side. Micky was a great friend and stayed with us for two years before returning to the gypsies."

The Foster family annual holiday was a day trip to the seaside at Barry Island which was just a short distance down the Welsh coast. They also went to Porthcawl for an occasional afternoon outing.

Trevor recalls: "My favourite haunt as a schoolboy was the local lighthouse on the river Usk. We would pitch a tent for the weekend, swim and watch the shipping pass by. There were some wooden buildings facing the sea that contained shops, novelty stores and small takeaway tea and coffee bars. I think this is where I developed my sweet tooth. In the summer time hundreds of Newportians would visit to sunbathe. My other interest was to joyride on the famous Newport transporter bridge across the river Severn. The bridge was within walking distance of our house and on the other side of the water were some playing fields where I played a lot of baseball with the Newport Hibernians and Pill Harriers. I was backstop and it definitely improved my ball-handling skills for rugby. Baseball was very popular in the Newport and Cardiff area.

On a wet weekend or cold winter afternoon we would visit one of the local cinemas for a matinee. It cost two pennies for a two hour show. Other highlights were the annual sports day at the Newport Athletic Ground [home of the Newport Rugby Club] and the Danters' Fair which was always held on the spare ground between the Shaftsbury Hotel and Newport Castle. There were some amazing rides, which drew kids from all over the district.

A trip to Cardiff was rare, though after I left school I would occasionally travel by train to Ninian Park to watch Cardiff City play. Cardiff were a top First Division team in those days and won the FA Cup for the first time, beating Arsenal at Wembley. As soon as I left Ninian Park at the end of a match I would ring home and the result would be announced to all the waiting customers in the pub."

One of Trevor's Newport contemporaries was 'The Welsh Flyer' – Ken Jones, a Welsh rugby union wingman and an international sprinter. Trevor recalls: "Ken was a very successful athlete and covered the 100 yards in 9.8 seconds at the Empire Games. He doubled up in the 220 yards and finished third before taking up serious rugby."

When Trevor was invited to return to play rugby with Newport Hibernians, a local team of former Holy Cross schoolboys, he didn't need asking twice: "The Hibernians were noted for playing expansive running rugby. They had lots of local support and played in the traditional Irish green jersey with a shamrock motif. I played with them for one season in junior rugby, and was then asked to play for the district club, Pill Harriers. The Harriers had a great history in the Monmouthshire league, and they were recognised as the nursery team for the main Newport club.

The Pill Harriers ground was compact with a small clubhouse full of trophies, including a display cabinet containing international caps and jerseys donated by former players and visiting teams. I felt very proud to pull on the all-white jersey. I played wing-forward and had the knack of catching the high ball at the back of the lineout to start a variety of attacking moves. It was a very competitive league to play in, with tremendous local rivalry with teams around the valleys, and it provided an excellent grounding for anyone progressing into senior rugby. We had an outstanding goalkicker named Herbert Rich. He reminds me of the late and great Terry Price who was so successful with Bradford Northern in the late 1960s, after moving north from the Welsh valleys. They both kicked penalties, conversions and drop goals from long distances all over the park and with seemingly little effort. After a season with Pill Harriers, playing alongside some very gifted teammates, a few of us went along to the Newport trials with the aim of playing for the senior club the following season".

Trevor had played occasionally for Newport's reserve teams in the 1936-37 season, and had been top scorer for Pill Harriers. Newport often recruited from Pill Harriers, but even so, to be asked for trials at one of Wales's top clubs was a great opportunity.

Top: The Church House Inn, Newport.
Bottom left: Field-Marshall the Right Honourable Viscount Montgomery of Alamein presenting
the Meritorious Service Medal to Richard Foster, watched by Bonnie Dean, Trevor's brother in law.
Bottom right: Freda Foster, Trevor's sister, who helped persuade him to sign for Bradford Northern.
(All photos courtesy Trevor Foster)

2.   Playing for Newport 1937-38

Newport are one of the great clubs of Welsh rugby union. Founded in September 1874, they were founder members of the WRU. In the 19th century, they were the first Welsh Cup winners in 1878, contributed more players to the Welsh team than any other club, and provided four Welsh captains. They did not lose a match until 20 November 1879, when they played Blackheath. This defeat, by four goals and eight tries to nil, resulted in a major review of how to play the game.

Their glorious history continued into the 20th century. During the period 1900 to 1914, Newport competed against all the visiting touring sides and were the first club side to defeat the Springboks in 1912. They provided 11 British Lions, including one captain. From 1919 to 1939, Newport were twice Welsh club champions, provided five Welsh captains and supplied six British Lions during this golden era, which included such great players as Jack Wetter, Harry Uzzell, Vincent Griffiths, Jack Morley (who moved to rugby league with Wigan in 1932) and Bunner Travers, 'The prince of hookers'.

The economic slump of the 1930s hit all sport in South Wales hard, particularly the amateur rugby union code. Many quality players headed north to rugby league to be rewarded financially for their endeavours on the pitch, and others left the area to look for work. Gareth Williams outlines in *1905 and All That* how rugby union teams in Oxford and the South Midlands also found themselves strengthened by Welsh players who had come to the area for work. Between the wars, 69 Welsh internationals headed north to play rugby league. The first player featured in Jack Davis's *One Hundred Years of Newport Rugby* is Jerry Shea who, after heroics in rugby union, headed north to play for Wigan, and then played rugby league for the short-lived Pontypridd team in 1926 and 1927.

Trevor was recruited to a club who had been through an uneven spell in the 1930s. Davis describes the 1929-30 season as "not up to the usual standards", and during the next season, 18 matches were lost – the club's biggest ever number of defeats. In 1931-32, Jack Morley became captain, and things improved, with 30 wins from 43 matches. But the next year was "the most melancholy season ever" with, for the first time, more matches being lost than were won. Morley signed for Wigan, and went on to play for Wales and Great Britain in rugby league, becoming a British Lion in both codes. Raymond Ralph, another star, missed much of the season through injury and the club's gates slumped. He then also went north, joining Leeds. The team improved, but the next two seasons were "not especially distinguished". Their campaign in 1934-35 was not helped by another three first teamers going north: Stan Mountain to Huddersfield, Mel Meek to Halifax and Bill Johnson, who had joined Newport from Pill Harriers, also signed for Huddersfield.

In 1935-36, the club had one of their best seasons since the immediate post-war period, and finished third in the unofficial Welsh championship. Bunner Travers joined the club, and was to become one of their great stars, as well as being capped by Wales before and after the war, and for the British Lions in South Africa in 1938.

The next season, 1936-37, saw 14 games lost, but the attack improved, with more than 400 points being scored for the first time in five years. Despite this, Davis comments that "Newport's rugby had begun to be dull and support was dwindling". The problem of falling crowds was not restricted to Newport. Dai Smith and Gareth Williams, in their history of the Welsh Rugby Union (WRU), *Fields of Praise*, outline: "With club games becoming unimaginative and unattractive, and with rival professional codes attracting the crowds away from rugby union, fitful attempts were made to restore creativity to the game. Indeed, at Eric Evans's instigation, a sub-committee was established in May 1938: 'to discover and consider fully the true causes of the decline in the interest taken in Welsh rugby and… the serious financial state of the Welsh clubs'.""

The economic slump had hit clubs hard. Some clubs had collapsed; others had sought financial support from the WRU to continue. Smith and Williams comment that: "international occasions attracted a full house, but club rugby languished".

Another problem that Newport faced was that they had recruited widely among the police. However, the contemporary growth of police rugby meant that some of these players were obliged to play for police teams, missing Newport matches and training, and causing divided loyalties. Davis says that there was an "unmistakable decline in the morale of the club".

Trial matches

At the start of the 1937-38 season, Trevor was invited to play in trial matches for Newport. In the *South Wales Argus*, the report of the trial game said: "With so many players seeking the limelight as individuals, the forward play was ragged, but several good men were noted, such as… T. Foster (Pill Harriers) a lively winging forward".

Newport opened their season with a match against Pill Harriers. Trevor and B. Gough were playing for Pill, having been in Newport's trial matches, and the *South Wales Argus* said they were being "seriously considered" by the senior club. The report of the match, which Newport won 24-9, commented that "there was much to admire in the unyielding spirit of T. Foster and F. C. Emms, who were going as strongly as ever when their side were 15 points behind".

The next week, the paper reported that the "Newport rugby team have selected T. Foster of Pill Harriers to fill the vacancy in their pack for their match with Penarth at the Newport Athletic Ground on Saturday. Foster takes the place of Leslie Evans who has not yet recovered from the effects of a shaking received in the opening match of the season against Pill Harriers. A dashing loose-forward, Foster played occasionally for Newport United [the club's reserve team] last season, but he never appeared in Newport's first team. Last season Foster gained a big reputation with Pill Harriers and was regarded as one of the most promising young forwards in Monmouthshire." The report of the match said Trevor was "a very useful third man in the back row". Newport won 41-3. Trevor kept his place for the midweek match with Cross Keys. The report said of Newport's forwards: "Their best efforts, in which Evans, Chatwin and Foster, as back-row men generally took the lead, came only spasmodically".

Trevor then played a couple of games for the Newport United side. The report of the second match, against Tredegar, commented: "Foster is a forward with the quality of impetus which made Jehoida Hodges great, and with a little improvement in handling should shine in first class football". Newport United won 19-5. David Smith and Gareth Williams, in their excellent official history of the Welsh Rugby Union, say that Hodges was "a club player who took on fresh powers in an international. It was said of him that 'he could do everything a Rugby player should be able to do, whether he is a full-back, threequarter, half-back or forward'." Hodges played for Newport and won 23 Welsh caps from 1899 to 1906, so for Trevor as a young player with virtually no experience in senior rugby union to be compared to him is a remarkable compliment.

One of the highlights of Newport's season was their fixtures with Cardiff. These fixtures often attracted big crowds. Trevor recalls: "Being next door to each other and with all the outstanding players at Cardiff, the house full notice went out hours before kick-off. I remember Cardiff had Wilf Wooller playing for them. He was an outstanding centre threequarter and a Glamorgan cricketer; also Cliff Jones at half-back with amazing trickery and electric pace. Cliff was the most difficult man to pin down and tackle I ever encountered in rugby union. He reminds me very much of the modern-day players Henry and Robbie Paul. They have very similar style and skills, great athleticism and tremendous determination to put the ball down over the whitewash". Trevor was selected to play against Cardiff. Newport won a memorable victory over their local rivals, 6-5, to end Cardiff's unbeaten record. The *South Wales Argus* said it was "one of the most remarkable upsets of current form of recent years". The next week, Trevor scored his first try for Newport in a 26-11 victory over Blackheath. The report of the match said "Foster scored because of an almost ridiculous mistake by J. W. G. Davies who had ample time to touch down... The whole Newport pack deserves the highest praise for a rousing display". Two weeks later, when Newport lost 6-3 at home to Swansea, the headline was "Wily Willie Davies beats Newport". The report said that Trevor was the most effective loose-forward on either side.

Trevor scored again against Oxford University and, in a 3-3 draw with Neath, "...had another splendid day, proving an ideal partner in the back row of the scrum for Leslie Evans, another brilliant forward..." Against Aberavon Newport's team was weakened as five of their players were in a trial match for the Welsh team. The match report again said that Trevor was the best loose-forward, and "in fact was more like an extra threequarter, but the pity of it was that nearly all his excellent opening work was nullified by hesitation in running and haphazard passing by the backs".

In the return match with Cardiff on 13 November, Newport drew 3-3. Again Trevor was prominent, with the report saying: "Only rarely could Cardiff emulate the driving power of the loose rushes made by Newport, with Evans, Foster, Law and Jerman generally at the head". By now, Trevor was established in the Newport first team. After a tremendous 8-5 win at Gloucester on a frozen pitch on 18 December, the *South Wales Argus* said that "Foster is unquestionably developing into one of the most promising forwards in Wales". The next week, Trevor had to play as a threequarter with fellow forward Evans because of injuries. But he was back in the pack the next day against Bridgend, the match report saying that he 'gained a lot of ground'.

Newport opened the New Year with a 0-0 draw with Old Merchant Taylors. But Trevor was otherwise engaged, playing for the Possibles against the Probables in the Welsh international trial match at Swansea. The Probables won 32-11, and the *South Wales Argus* said that the "Possibles forwards, despite their extra incentive to attract attention, were beaten in every phase of play by the Probables".

Newport's unbeaten run came to an end when Llanelli won 19-6 at the Athletic Ground on 22 January. The match report said that "for more than a month they have been beset by all sorts of team building difficulties and week by week the attack has had to be reshuffled. ... In no sense were the Newport forwards to blame for the defeat". Trevor played in that game, but on 26 January, the WRU announced an unchanged Wales team to play Scotland.

Newport then beat Bristol 16-7, with Trevor having to play on the wing in the second half following an injury to Hopkins. The team then made a short visit to the west country, beating Plymouth Albion, and then winning 23-0 against Devonport United Services. Trevor scored two tries, and the report said his play "at winging forward was always enterprising". Against Leicester the following weekend, Trevor was "in fine form". His colleague Leslie Evans and Trevor were the best loose forwards in Newport's 14-0 win.

For Newport's match at Cardiff, the Welsh selectors were represented, preparing to pick the team for the match against Ireland. Newport lost 11-3, but their forwards were overwhelmingly superior. The *South Wales Argus* said: "But even more striking was the play of Foster, as blind-side winger, for undoubtedly he was the finest forward of the game, up with every move of Newport's and back to help check every move of Cardiff's".

Trevor made a rare trip to London the following week for Newport's match at Blackheath. Newport lost 7-5 in a disappointing display, but the match report outlined: "Only two features of the play will be remembered with pleasure by Newport's large company of followers. They were Legge's fine all round display and Foster's magnificent try [in the second half]. In these days Foster is a forward and a half. He had been an outstanding figure before he made that wonderful run from near half-way and scored a try after beating nearly a dozen opponents with swerves and sheer impetus. Only these two, of the Newport team, can look back on a disappointing game with full satisfaction of knowing they played their parts without a flaw."

Newport lost again the next Saturday to Cardiff, but again, "Foster did excellent work". At Cross Keys, in a 14-0 win, "Leslie Evans and Foster broke away in their usual, dashing style on a number of occasions". On 23 March, Trevor was selected for Monmouthshire. The county side beat Herefordshire and Worcestershire 24-8. Trevor was one of the best Monmouthshire forwards, and "was always quick in following up and was a sound tackler".

In April, Trevor played in Newport's 10-8 triumph over Pontypool. Once again, the *South Wales Argus* praised his efforts: "In Foster, Evans and Travers they [Newport] had men with sure hands and a driving power when in possession that made them dangerous in attack and invaluable in defence. Foster was clearly the best loose-forward of either side. He had an uncanny knack of being in the right position as well as an instinctive sense of when to make his supreme efforts... Foster's opportunism won him a splendid try after Pontypool had heeled a scrum and the ball had beaten both Tucker and Hawkins."

On Easter Tuesday, the prestigious Barbarians came to Newport and were beaten 8-0. Trevor "made a terrific dash for the line" and it was Newport's forwards who were the foundation for the victory. The season finished with a 14-9 defeat at Abertillery, and then a match at Risca, a local junior club, to help their funds. Trevor shone for Newport.

Overall, Newport were inconsistent in Trevor's one full season at the club, finishing with a record of 22 wins, four draws and 16 defeats, scoring 438 points, but conceding 308. Trevor finished as top scorer with 12 tries in 34 matches, and was the only try-scorer in double figures. Davis says of Trevor: "This ex-Pill forward made his mark on the game at once. Although operating on the blind side of the scrum, he was sensationally effective in attack... Unfortunately for Newport and the amateur game generally, Foster went north after playing one game in the following season, and in a wonderful career in the professional game he proved one of the greatest personalities, as player, coach and legislator, the Rugby League has ever known."

Trevor was playing in a very strong pack, recognised as the best in Wales, led by captain Vivian Law, and including Bunner Travers, Leslie Evans, Bill Jones, Alf Bale, Jack Jerman and Ernie Coleman. However, Newport suffered from continual team changes in the backs. Davis outlines: "Newport had to call on as many as 50 players, most of them backs, and often the back play seemed too bad to be true."

"It was great to wear the black and amber jersey," recalls Trevor. "As a wing forward I was in my element, scoring 12 tries in that campaign. It was unusual for a forward to head the scoring list. It was rough and tough in the forwards. I managed to keep reasonably clear of the rucks and mauls and avoided being pulled into the set pieces too much. I felt that players continually piling in on top of one another was pretty negative at times. I was on the fringes as a wing-forward and capitalised on the tenacious scrummaging of my team-mates".

Vivian Law, a Welsh international front-row forward, was our captain. Bunner Travers, the son of the famous Newport and Wales legend Twyber Travers, was our hooker. I looked up to Bunner as the master. He was the outstanding figure in the Newport team, and had also played with Pill Harriers. He received many offers to go to rugby league. Whenever the big matches were on involving Newport, there were scouts in attendance from the north of England trying desperately to get Bunner's signature. The Travers family was steeped in the history and traditions of Welsh rugby; he had no desire to turn professional. If he had, he would have been a sensation in rugby league. He was an outstanding member of the British Lions tour to South Africa where some of the greatest players in the world were in opposition. Bunner could have held his place in any forward position during that period. He had so much enthusiasm and made a real impact in every game he played. There was one incident when the outstanding figure of the Australian rugby league, Harry Sunderland, who was then the Wigan manager, made a visit to Bunner's home, very close to where I lived, and offered him a large signing-on fee. Mr Sunderland was met at the door, by his sister, given short shift and chased away from his house.

I also remember a try which Bunner scored at Rodney Parade against Cardiff. He suddenly shot away from the middle of a ruck with a characteristic burst of speed and left defenders scattered around him like fallen soldiers." Bunner did Trevor the honour of attending a *This is Your Life* event hosted by television commentator John Helm, at the University of Bradford in 1988 to celebrate Trevor's 50th anniversary with Bradford Northern.

As well as playing in the Welsh trial and for Monmouthshire, Trevor toured the South West of England with Captain Crawshay's Welsh XV and was selected as travelling reserve for Wales versus Ireland at Swansea. Captain Crawshay's invitation XV included the top players from the services and Welsh clubs. Most were full internationals.

Trevor remembers: "We were captained on one occasion by Billy Davies, the Welsh stand-off half, who later joined me at Bradford Northern and on another occasion by Haydn Tanner, the Welsh scrum-half. Billy and Haydn were cousins, but not too friendly towards each other. We played at places like Gloucester, Redruth and Camborne. It was 'Barbarian'-style rugby, we were told to express ourselves and whenever possible play with imagination and freedom. I learned a great deal on that tour and particularly how important it was to follow the man with the ball to gain the maximum advantage from breaks and half breaks".

Rugby league

The question of turning professional and going north to rugby league was always present for prominent Welsh rugby union players at this time. But even to be seen talking to a rugby league scout could cause problems for a player. This season, Newport lost one of their wingers, Bill (W. H.) Hopkin, to rugby league in unusual circumstances. According to Davis, he was "being pestered by rugby league agents to go north". To stop this, he signed a form saying that if he ever did go to rugby league, he would join a particular club. The WRU found out about this and declared him a 'professional', despite Hopkin assuring them he had no intention of playing rugby league. He refused to appeal, and played association football for Newport County reserves. Eventually, seeing no prospect of reinstatement, he went north to play rugby league.

Trevor always took an interest in stories reported in the *South Wales Argus* about Welsh rugby union players who had gone north to play league and how they were progressing from week to week. He recalls being approached for the first time when playing for Pill Harriers: "I was genuinely alarmed when a Wigan agent named Arthur Fairfax called at my home to see my mum and dad. He asked me if I would consider going to Wigan to play rugby league and be paid good money. He said I should go up for a trial. I dismissed his approach completely, very worried his visit may find its way into the local paper. I had no intention, no ambition and no desire whatever to go north. My mind was set on one thing only, to play for Newport and then win a Welsh cap".

But as Trevor became established in the Newport first team, it was inevitable that the rugby league scouts would return. Once at Newport, it wasn't long before the 13-a-side code came calling again.

"Halfway through the season we were playing Cardiff on a Saturday afternoon at Rodney Parade," Trevor remembers. "There was a big crowd, around 18,000. After the match, two men stopped me while I was on my way home and crossing the Newport Bridge. They said, "Trevor can we talk to you please, we're from Wigan". It turned out they were directors of Wigan Rugby League Club. I was quite frightened to acknowledge them, knowing that you could be in trouble if you were seen talking to people from rugby league.

They said they would like to talk to me and asked if it would be possible for them to come and meet with me at my house. I was a bit ill at ease and told them I was catching the bus. They asked where my house was and followed me home.

When I got home, some 10 minutes later, they arrived and my mum and dad greeted them. They went into the sitting room, spoke to my parents and said they wanted me to come north and play for Wigan, saying I could earn good money. They offered me £300 if I went to play for them." Trevor was fully aware of all the other players who had left Welsh rugby union and travelled north, such as Jim Sullivan. Yet while being well up-to-date on what he still calls "the great game of rugby league" and despite Wigan being the top club in the country, Trevor was still eyeing that first Welsh cap.

Having travelled to Swansea as a reserve for the international match, he recalls: "I felt that I was really close to getting a full cap and it might even come the following season. I wanted more than ever to represent my country of birth. The press certainly thought I should be picked for Wales. I'm not sure about the selectors. Wales had a system whereby 'the big five' would choose the national side and they ran Welsh rugby generally. These five men were gods in Welsh sporting eyes. They were the people who gave up their time and money to become legislators. I never met them as such; they were very remote people really.

Towards the very end of that season, when we were playing the Easter matches, I had visitors from Bradford," Trevor remembers. "There was the chairman, Mr Harry Hornby, and a gentleman with him, Len Rees, who did the scouting for the club in Wales and was a brother of the Bradford Northern manager Dai Rees. Mr Hornby, right out of the blue, came to the Church House and said he had come down to Wales to watch the Easter matches.

The big clubs always played one another over Easter. That was also the time when the Barbarians toured and they visited South Wales. Mr Hornby had come down to follow the Newport, Cardiff, and Neath matches, just scouting. He said they were interested in signing me. They came and stayed for an hour, discussing terms. Mr Hornby told us he would write a letter confirming the visit. Bradford was building up a great club, he said."

Trevor was impressed with Harry Hornby, whom he considered to be an honourable man: "He was calm, quiet and business-like, a person, I was sure, who could be trusted. The letter he promised arrived, the following week, saying that they would return to see me at the beginning of the next season. In August, I got another letter to say they were travelling down and would like to make me an official offer to sign for Bradford Northern. I had started training in early August, and kept thinking that I might go to rugby league, but never with any great conviction."

Trevor played in Newport's opening match of the season on 10 September against Pill Harriers, his former club. Once again, he was forced by injury to a colleague to play on the wing in the second half. Even there, the *South Wales Argus* said that he "was as dangerous a man to the Pill defence as any". He did not know it was to be his last peacetime game of club rugby union.

Trevor recounts: "Training was held on Tuesday and Thursday evenings between 6.30pm and 9.30pm. When I came home on the Thursday evening prior to the first major match of the season against Penarth, there outside our public house was a big black Buick car. It was Mr Hornby and Len Rees. I went in through the front door of the bar and my mum said: 'Mr Hornby is in there from Bradford'. The bar was pretty well packed. I said, 'Oh, I'm not going Mum, I'm not interested'. She answered: 'Well, act the man and go and say so'.

I walked into the sitting room where Mr Hornby, Len Rees and my dad were sitting down having a glass of beer. I remember Mr Hornby so vividly, with his horn-rimmed glasses, big bushy eye brows and Homburg hat. I told Mr Hornby that I was not signing and that I didn't want to go to Bradford. He went very quiet and then burst out, 'What? I've come all the way from Bradford, all this way and you're not coming? Why is that? What has changed your mind? Here, there's £100. He slammed it on the table. £200. £300. £400. You're not going to take that? What has made your decision? Why have you said no?' "

Typically, Trevor was thinking of his blind father and his mother who would have to run the family business if he left home and how close he was to being awarded his first Welsh cap. Harry Hornby thought he had lost his man.

Trevor continues: "I told him that I wanted a Welsh cap, that's all. He said: 'Well go and buy yourself half-a-dozen caps'. Unexpectedly, at that very moment, my elder sister Freda came into the room and said: 'Mam tells me that you're not going to go and play for Bradford'. I said, 'No, I have no desire. I want a Welsh cap'. She said 'What if you break your leg next Saturday? You may never again get such a chance in your life. I'll look after Mum and Dad'. I picked up the pen and signed, just like that. There was £400 on the table. I handed the money over to my mother to keep for me and she put it in the post office. The following Monday, Mr Hornby returned to drive me to the city of Bradford. Freda's words had changed my mind, and I never ever regretted my decision to go north."

On Saturday, 17 September 1938, the *South Wales Argus* had a front page report headed: "Foster refuses to go north." The article said: "Rugby league agents are again active in Monmouthshire and South Wales, and Trevor Foster the Newport forward has been approached by Bradford Northern and Wigan. Foster however, turned down their offer and he told a reporter that he has no intention of turning professional since he is well satisfied with his present prospects in Newport. Foster would not divulge the terms, but he said that both clubs made 'good offers'."

Trevor missed that weekend's Newport match because of a severe chill, but also because he knew he would be finalising his move to Bradford Northern the next day.

Just two days later the paper reported: "Foster signs for Bradford - Biggest fee ever paid for a Welsh forward." The report quoted Trevor's father as saying it was a "magnificent offer". The fee was not divulged, "because it is so large it might embarrass any future negotiations by the club in Wales". Trevor also said that he had been offered a choice of jobs in Bradford, and the club were even prepared to find a pub for his parents to manage in Bradford if they wanted to move as well. However, they preferred to stay in Newport. Clearly, Harry Hornby was determined to get his man. Trevor said that Bradford Northern's representatives had told him that, on his present form, he would be considered for a place in the end-of-season rugby league tour to Australia.

Understandably, given his raw years and the culture shock that was to come, Trevor had his doubts at first. "I wondered whether I had done the right thing," he says. "I wondered what would happen. I had no qualifications for a job, I was going to be a long way from home, where I had a happy family life, and was leaving my brothers and sisters. But I loved the game of rugby football and just thought: 'Well, here goes'. I promised myself I would do my best.

The journey north was a very memorable one. I had never been so far away from Newport in my life and on the journey via Birmingham and through Halifax, all the buildings seemed to be so different. I remember seeing all the chimney stacks when we were travelling into Bradford and, of course, the stadium itself. It was about 6pm when we arrived at Odsal Stadium. I was given a look around, but the place was empty. We then drove across the city to the home of my two lovely landladies, Miss Norcliffe and Miss Hainsworth, where I was put into digs just a stone's throw away from Mr Hornby's house. I was ready to start life in Bradford and experience rugby league football, I was very excited indeed.

There was a wonderful welcome for me in Bradford. Wherever I went I was greeted with warmth and friendliness. The early days in Bradford left a great impression on me. There was a real affinity between Welsh rugby players and the people. In the north, the supporters almost lived with you on the field of play and they gave you all the wonderful greetings before and after a match, whatever the result. The world of rugby league was similar to South Wales."

A letter from Charles Driscoll, the secretary of Newport Hibernians RFC, his first club, to Trevor in September 1950 shows what rugby union meant to Trevor. Trevor had donated £2.00 to the club funds. The reply to Trevor said: "When I read your letter to the lads at our last meeting, tears of joy came to their eyes, especially the older men now acting in official capacities in the club, who were your colleagues in the old days. It is nice to know that you still have that sporting spirit, that was always predominant in your nature when you were back in your home town, keep up the good work Trev, and I am sure you are just as beloved amongst your colleagues in the North as you were down here, so once again, thanks for everything, and best wishes from all the lads in the Hibs."

Holy Cross Rugby Union team. Trevor is in the back row, one in from the left. The captain, holding the ball, is Alex Givvons, who later played rugby league for Oldham and Wales.
(Photo: Courtesy Trevor Foster)

A Newport RFC XV 1938 – Trevor is in the back row, fourth from the left.
(Photo: Courtesy Newport RFC)

Trevor with Bunner Travers, his former Newport RU playing colleague at a 'This is Your Life' for Trevor, to celebrate 50 years in Bradford, held in 1988 at Bradford University.
(Photo: Courtesy Trevor Foster)

Bradford Northern 1938-39. Trevor is in the back row on the right.
(Photo: Courtesy Trevor Foster)

3. Playing for Bradford Northern 1938-39

Today, Bradford Bulls are one of the game's top clubs. But the club Trevor joined in 1938 had not won a trophy for more than 30 years, and had to go back to before the First World War for their last cup final appearance, when they were losing finalists in the Yorkshire Cup in 1913-14.

After the war, Bradford struggled. As club historian Nigel Williams points out, from 1919 to 1934, they won just under 23 per cent of their league, Challenge Cup and Yorkshire Cup matches, finished bottom of the league table five times, in penultimate place six times and twice more in the bottom five. The club was wracked by financial problems, and their ground at Birch Lane was regarded as one of the worst in the league.

Their move to Odsal in 1934 was a turning point. Although the club required financial help from the Rugby Football League to build a basic stand, the club's first match at Odsal, the first home game of the 1934-35 season, was seen by around 20,000 people. Bradford lost 31-16 to Huddersfield, and only won 11 games all season, although the campaign finished with a flourish: a 51-17 victory over St Helens Recs.

Around the time the club moved to Odsal, Harry Hornby became a director. He had a vision for Odsal as a multi-sports stadium, especially outside the rugby league season. This was not unusual in this period, when greyhound racing and speedway often shared stadiums with football or rugby league. Hornby soon became a driving force at the club.

In July 1936, after a slight improvement on the pitch in the 1935-36 season, Dai Rees became team manager. He had played for Halifax and Wales, and was to give remarkable service to Bradford Northern. He had a shrewd understanding of tactics, good man-management skills, and was able to build a team with Harry Hornby's support. Some of the players who had already been signed by the club fitted his plans: full-back George Carmichael and hooker Vincent Dilorenzo. Another fine recruit in 1934 was New Zealander Ted Spillane, and prop Len Higson was signed in 1935. But maybe Rees's best signing was made just 13 days into his reign at Odsal: he recruited Ernest Ward, one of rugby league's most famous players, on his 16th birthday. In 1937, another Kiwi, George Harrison, who had come to England to play for Streatham & Mitcham, and then joined Wigan, came to Odsal. Also recruited in the autumn of 1937 were stand-off or centre Ernest Pollard and half-back George Bennett, also from Wigan, for a club record fee of £1,000. Bradford also looked overseas for the first time for players. Mike Gilbert and Robert Hohaia came to Odsal from New Zealand.

This recruitment and the work of Dai Rees gradually saw Bradford rise up the league table. From 25th (out of 28 clubs) in 1934-35 they rose to 19th (out of 30 clubs) in 1935-36 to 15th in 1936-37, their highest position since 1907-08. The next season, Bradford finished 11th. But in November, after a great run of nine straight wins and a draw, they had briefly been top of table, the first time they had been in this position since March 1905.

As the team improved, so did the crowds. More than 24,000 saw a narrow defeat against Wakefield Trinity in the Challenge Cup in 1936. And in September 1937, a new Odsal record was set with 28,843 paying to see a Yorkshire Cup match against Leeds. However, approximately a further 5,000 got into the ground free after climbing in over a wall. Six months later, 31,317 paid to see Bradford lose in the Challenge Cup against Halifax.

The improved gates also meant that the club's financial position was stronger. The local council paid for a programme of improvements for Odsal in the summer of 1938. These included a new stand, and new terracing built from wooden railway sleepers. New drainage for the pitch had also been installed in 1937.

So the club Trevor joined was going in the right direction. The new signings by the astute Dai Rees would perform well for a long time. Three months after signing Trevor, Rees and

17

Hornby captured another former Welsh rugby union player who would play a crucial role for the club - giant prop Frank Whitcombe from Broughton Rangers.

'Forward', writing in the *Telegraph & Argus*, recognised the importance of Northern's new signing, saying that in South Wales Trevor was regarded "as the finest constructive forward in that country" and had been certain to win a Welsh rugby union cap. He was also "in demand" by various rugby league clubs, and had promised "first refusal" to Northern last season.

One of the first players Trevor met at Odsal was Bill Smith: "Bill welcomed me to Odsal with his arm in a sling. He was from Cumbria and a lovely chap. He told me that the game was very tough and warned me to be wary. Bill took me around the ground before we started training and became a good friend. He had a reputation as a very strong, no-nonsense prop forward".

Trevor had to settle into his new life at Odsal very quickly and the personnel at the club, including team manager Dai Rees, helped him do so: "Dai had been a top-class player in his time and had toured Australia. He was a very astute man, extremely positive with a good football brain. He had also been through the same experiences that I was now going through when he came up from Wales and signed for Halifax years earlier. Dai guided me like a father figure and, after a few training sessions, told me I would be playing on Saturday against Hull as a loose-forward, I was ready.

There were plenty of great players at Bradford at that time including Ernest Ward and his brother Donald, also Vic Darlison and Frank Whitcombe. Frank Whitcombe came from Cardiff and we got on like a house on fire. Another team mate, Des Case, had previously played a match for Newport on the wing. Vincent Dilorenzo was a celebrated hooker who always demanded the ball as first receiver. I played with Dillo in Egypt towards the end of the war. Tom Winnard, was a well-known Lancashire lad who came to Odsal and made a great name for himself, while Sandy Orford, a fine upright man and an imposing forward, was also there."

It didn't take long for Trevor to realise that his new rugby code and his still-beloved rugby union had their differences. "The biggest difference was the play-the-ball. In rugby union, scrummages were a big part of the game. In rugby league, with six forwards and the play-the-ball and everybody automatically moving back five yards after a tackle, I found there was a lot more space and room to move. This suited my style of play. The mauls in rugby union were semi-stoppages compared with standing back at rugby league, where you were one-on-one. You were tackled by your opposite number and had to play the ball as quickly as you could and move it along the line. That was one of the finest things for me as a forward. It was much more positive than going into rucks for the ball, getting pulled down and out of the next play.

My new team-mates were very friendly. Their attitude was outstanding and there was lots of help and advice from the veterans of rugby league. They taught me where to stand, some basic positional play and how best to use my weight in the scrum. In the dressing room they were also very keen to see that I had settled in."

In many ways, Trevor's arrival at Bradford Northern could not have come at a better time. Harry Hornby and Dai Rees were in the process of steadily building a team that would challenge all-comers and the crowds were flocking back to Odsal Stadium. Trevor soon got a job at the club on the ground staff which he thoroughly enjoyed, though he was a part-time employee, with time to fill away from match days. Trevor recalls: "I went on to have 12 years working at Odsal in various departments, mostly in the dressing room, and on the ground and then in the office. Odsal meant everything to me and soon became my second home".

Trevor always had a great regard for Harry Hornby, who had brought him to Bradford. The mutual respect is shown by a letter Harry Hornby sent to Trevor's parents in 1942: "As parents of a lovely family, you have enjoyed a blessing, denied to my dear wife and I, probably we have been blessed in other ways, and one certainly is the extreme pleasure we get from the loyalty and consideration shown to us by these boys we have brought to our club from South Wales. Bringing them in the first place for purely football motives, Trevor and Emlyn [Walters], particularly Trevor has so endeared himself, that I feel that had we a son I should not wish him to be different to Trevor in any way. As you know I am in hospital at present, but hope to be going home in a few days.

What the future holds for us, none can tell, but if I am spared, my endeavour and pleasure will certainly be to do all I can to be worthy of the loyalty that Trevor has shown to both the club and myself.

He is one of the most popular players in RL football today, without an equal as a second row forward – honours won't spoil him – he's too big a man – and I hope I live to see him play and leave a name that will last in history, as one of the greatest football players that ever lived."

Trevor was included in the Bradford squad for the home match against Halifax on 24 September, but did not play because he had not yet learnt enough about his new code. He made his debut the following week, in the 'A' team at Odsal against Huddersfield's 'A' team. He was then in the first team squad for the next two matches, and finally made his first-team debut at Odsal against Hull on 29 October. Bradford were missing Carmichael, Ernest Ward and Pollard, and lost 14-20. Trevor played at loose-forward, and 'Forward' wrote that his "display as loose-forward had promising features without, however, being satisfactory owing to lack of experience". Trevor remembers: "My first game against Hull felt very strange. With no mauls it felt completely new but I found a lot of space around the middle of the field with only six forwards as against eight in Union. I remember getting a pass under my own goal post and I kicked the ball around 60 yards into touch. The crowd clapped and clapped and gave the impression that they thought this chap knew what rugby league was all about. It was just a spontaneous thing. We lost the match, but the newspaper critics wrote: 'This lad looks good, he is well built and will be a very useful player'."

Trevor missed the next match, a 9-0 defeat at Batley, but returned the next week against Oldham at Odsal. Bradford won 9-2; Trevor scored his first try for Bradford and tackled magnificently, but was injured.

Trevor returned to action on 10 December, in an 11-3 win over Warrington at Odsal, and "was prominent with powerful dashes". He was now established in the first team, and on Boxing Day scored his first hat-trick in rugby league – against Bramley. He scored again in the return match, Northern winning 11-5. But Northern's inconsistency was shown again with a 7-5 defeat at home to Salford on New Year's Eve. Trevor missed the 22-0 win over Wakefield at the start of the New Year with a cold, and was then rested for the trip to Hull, missing a 21-0 defeat. According to 'Forward', Bradford's forwards lacked the power of the Hull pack.

Bradford's match with Huddersfield scheduled for 14 January was postponed, with 10 inches of snow on the Odsal pitch. However, there were complaints from supporters that the club had not done enough to try to clear the pitch, because Bradford Park Avenue had managed to play an association football match in the city. Bradford were expected to win at struggling York the next week. Trevor returned to the action, but Bradford lost 10-7, their opponents York scoring twice in the last few minutes. But 'Forward' said that Bradford had not been as aggressive or penetrative as York, although he felt that the muddy ground had handicapped Northern more than their hosts.

Bradford lost again the next week – a 3-0 lead against Castleford at Odsal ending in an 11-3 defeat. This prompted a letter in the *Telegraph & Argus* from a Bradford supporter saying that they had been playing so poorly recently, he had gone to watch Leeds versus Halifax instead, and claimed to have met dozens of Northern's supporters there. He said three or four places in the team needed strengthening. And the club's cause was not helped when Ernest Pollard announced his retirement from the game. He had injured his knee in October, and had been advised that he could not play again.

Trevor now had his first experience of the Challenge Cup. Cumberland amateurs Seaton were due at Odsal on Saturday 4 February, but snow caused the match to be postponed on the Friday, to save the amateurs missing a morning's work unnecessarily. Once again there were complaints from supporters that straw had not been used to protect the pitch. The game was staged the following Wednesday, and Seaton took an early 5-0 lead. But Bradford recovered to lead 11-7 at half-time, and eventually won 37-7. Incidentally, the Everton football team watched the match – they were training at Harrogate in preparation for an FA Cup tie.

Trevor missed a 23-8 defeat at Hunslet the next week with a cold. However, he returned for the next round of the Challenge Cup at Oldham, and did not miss another game for the rest of the season. Northern trained every night leading up to the game, and finished the week with an outing to the Alhambra theatre to see a pantomime. The extra training paid off with a 2-0 win. 'Forward' said that Bradford "deserved victory over Oldham. Oldham had shot their bolt before the interval and throughout the second half of the game were penned to their half. If only for their amazing stamina, Bradford deserved their win. The second-row men, Harrison and Foster were magnificent. Harrison worked with terrific zeal and Foster was powerful and constructive."

Trevor scored his first try of 1939 against Hull KR the next week at Odsal in a 27-0 triumph. But the following week, Oldham extracted ample revenge for their Cup defeat with a 21-2 league win at Watersheddings. The cup draw had not been kind to Bradford, and sent them to Central Park for their first cup match with Wigan since 1915. It was only Bradford's third visit to Central Park since the war. Bradford lost 7-0, in front of a 20,325 crowd. But 'Forward' felt that they were rather unlucky, and had more try-scoring openings than Wigan.

Bradford's inconsistent form continued for the rest of the season, with six wins and six defeats. Trevor scored in a 14-13 win over local rivals Leeds at Odsal the week after the cup exit, and contributed a try to Northern's 49-point haul on Good Friday against Keighley. He scored again in a 10-5 win at Wakefield on Easter Saturday. And seven days later, he scored a try and a goal against Dewsbury in a 15-0 win at Odsal. This was the only goal that Trevor ever scored for Bradford.

After defeating Dewsbury, Bradford beat Widnes 17-5 at Odsal, but then finished the season with two defeats, at Castleford and Swinton. However, 'Forward' said that at Castleford, Northern's forwards "scrimmaged well and covered a lot of ground in the loose, Foster, Harrison and Smith being an outstanding trio".

Bradford finished 16th in the league table of 28 clubs, with 39 points from 40 matches. It was away from home that the team struggled, with only five wins. However, Trevor could look back on his first season with satisfaction. He had adapted well to rugby league, playing 24 first-team matches for Northern. He scored 11 tries, and that solitary goal, and was the top try scorer for Bradford's forwards, and the only one to reach double figures. But world events would intervene before his rugby league career could develop much further.

4.   Wartime rugby

On 1 September 1939 Nazi Germany invaded Poland. Two days later Britain and France declared war on Germany. Trevor had been at Bradford for less than a year and, like most of his generation, was to see his world turned upside down, although he was luckier than many. For most of the war he was stationed in Yorkshire and engaged in duties which suited him down to the ground. Paradoxically, he would find himself playing rugby all over Britain rather than merely within the counties of Yorkshire and Lancashire and, in sheer volume and variety of matches, he would never experience the same again when peace was declared.

Two more Welsh rugby union players joined Northern just before the war. Neath's Emlyn Walters, a winger, arrived in August 1939 but the most undeniable statement of Northern's intent was the sensational signing of Swansea's Billy (W.T.H.) Davies that same month. Will o' the wisp Davies, a newly-qualified teacher, was the current Wales rugby union fly-half and by any standards a most brilliant performer. The fee had reputedly been a massive £1,500. Oddly, Willie became Billy to his team-mates in rugby league. It was probably preferable to being known by his initials, as he often was in rugby union.

1939-40 season

The season began for Northern on 26 August, when Emlyn Walters scored a hat-trick on his debut, a 29-10 home victory over Castleford. Two days later Trevor was a scorer in an 8-3 success at Dewsbury but was on the losing side at Wakefield on 2 September, his last peace-time game for Bradford until February 1946.

The war, quite obviously, caused significant changes. Initially all sports gatherings were banned until further notice but on 14 September the RFL announced that Yorkshire and Lancashire League competitions would commence on 30 September. Unlike during the First World War, the government positively encouraged the playing of sport, recognising its value as a distraction and morale booster for participants and spectators. However, because of the dangers of bombing, ground capacities were severely slashed, generally to 8,000. Odsal's capacity was the highest in rugby league at 15,000 but it was later raised to 30,000. Players' and officials' wages were also reduced, reflecting the drop in income for the clubs. Trevor must have wondered whether professional rugby was all it was cracked up to be when the RFL announced that players would only receive 10 shillings (50p) expenses, plus fares. Halifax, Huddersfield and Bradford Northern players decided to strike over the issue, but eventually played under protest, Northern holding out longest. On 11 October the RFL decided that players and referees could be paid £1 and eventually there was an agreement that pay should be 25 shillings (£1.25) for a win and 15 shillings (75p) for a defeat.

Bradford enjoyed a good start to the War Emergency League (Yorkshire Section) and were soon engaged in a trial of strength with Huddersfield and Hull as their main rivals. Trevor's form was excellent and when it was announced that an England versus Wales match would be played at Odsal on 23 December, there was little surprise that he was selected for his first Welsh cap. The international was the first of six wartime England-Wales games, all of which were played in aid of Red Cross charities, Trevor playing in the first five.

Trevor regards that game as the most exciting moment of his career. Thirty years later, in an interview for the *Manchester Evening News*, he recalled: "Pulling on that red jersey meant a lot to me. It was a big thrill, playing at my own ground, Odsal, and with men I had only heard or read about. Jim Sullivan was captain. He had a few words before the match and told us, 'I want every last ounce of effort from you. When this match is over I want to see your tongues hanging out'."

The two teams filed on to the field together accompanied by *"Hen Wlad Fy Nhadau"*, the Welsh National Anthem, the crowd rising and standing bare-headed. The teams were then presented to Lord Harewood, who was given a rousing greeting, before the *"God save the King"* was played. England kicked off and Trevor's career as an international rugby player began. The teams were:

England: W. Belshaw (Warrington), E. Batten (Hunslet), A. J. Croston (Castleford), J. Lawrenson (Wigan), O. Peake (Warrington), T. Kenny (Salford), H. Goodfellow (Wakefield Trinity), F. Gregory (Warrington), T. Armitt (Swinton), H. Dyer (Leeds), R. Roberts (Widnes), C. Booth (Hull), E.H. Sadler (Castleford).
Wales: J. Sullivan (Wigan), A. Bassett (Halifax), C. Evans (Leeds), A. J. Risman (Salford), A. S. Edwards (Salford), W. T. H. Davies (Bradford Northern), D. Jenkins (Leeds), F. W. Whitcombe (Bradford Northern), C. Murphy (Leeds), D. M. Davies (Salford), T. J. F. Foster (Bradford Northern), J. Orford (Wakefield Trinity), A. Givvons (Oldham).

Wales, who had beaten England four times running since 1936, quickly gained the ascendancy. Sullivan kicked them into the lead with a penalty after 10 minutes and added a further two before half-time, his second a monster. However, England struck back two minutes before the interval when inspired play from centre Jimmy Croston led to a try from Eric Batten – 6-3 to Wales. The Bradford *Telegraph & Argus* sporting pink report noted that "Foster was constantly in evidence". It was Trevor who put the game out of England's reach in the final quarter. Gus Risman made the initial inroads before releasing Trevor, who "gained the reward of a grand afternoon's work by shaking off three English defenders and crossing the line for a great try, converted by Sullivan". A final try to Cliff Evans, improved by Sullivan, gave Wales a convincing 16-3 victory.

E.G. Blackwell, writing in the *Sunday Chronicle* was much taken by Trevor's performance: "Wales had in Trevor Foster the best forward on the field. Foster gave a great display, and was admirably supported by the front-row men, Whitcombe, also of Bradford Northern, Murphy and Davies (D. M.)". Another reporter, 'Enderley', wrote: "Coming to the forwards, Wales again had an outstanding personality in Trevor Foster, who often broke through in the most delightful fashion before falling to weight of numbers".

In his *News of the World* column, Jim Sullivan wrote: "It must have been with a pang many of the stars of this match realised that, but for the war, they would have been playing themselves into the touring team to go to Australia in April. I think I can name a few players who would have been assured of the trip to Australia. Trevor Foster, the Welsh forward of Bradford Northern, would have been a certainty for the second row. Powerful, fast, and intelligent, he is one of the finest players who ever left my native country. Willie Davies, the Bradford Northern outside-half, is another who would now be preparing his gear. Willie is one of the best our game has ever seen, and, remember, this is his first season as a professional."

Trevor recalled, "My father was at home in Newport listening to Harry Sunderland's commentary on the radio. He was blind and, when I scored, he jumped up throwing his arms about and scattering dishes everywhere".

Meanwhile, Northern won a couple of local derbies against Bramley on Christmas Day and Boxing Day 1939 but then did not play again until March because football and rugby were more or less wiped out by two months of Arctic weather. In the meantime, Trevor and his contemporaries had been to register for military service at the Mechanics Institute, which served as the recruitment centre in Bradford. He was sent to Strensall, near York, in January 1940 and assigned to the King's Own Yorkshire Light Infantry. There, he remembers: "We were put through our basic training. We were up early in the morning, drilling, PT and rifle training. It was a very hard time in your Army career, when they got you fit for whatever was coming. You weren't allowed leave for a couple of months but I enjoyed it and at the end of three months I applied to become a PT Instructor. I was accepted to go into the gymnasium and excused any further military duties. I was keen on physical fitness and spent the next nine months in the gym. After six months I was made a corporal. I was very proud. I was selected to go on a tour to Aldershot and spent a month there under a very strict regime. I finally passed out as a Sergeant-Instructor of the Army Physical Training Corps, a very elite type of military personnel. My first posting was to Harrogate. I was there for six months and really enjoyed it. I was very fit and I loved looking after the new recruits and putting them through their paces – swimming, boxing, wrestling, the lot. Many professional footballers became PTIs and Roy Francis, who came up from Brynmawr to play rugby league for Wigan and then Barrow, Warrington and Hull, was on my course. We were good friends".

When the weather finally abated in March 1940 Trevor was back playing for Bradford, who won 12 of their last 15 league games to win the Yorkshire Section title, three points clear of Huddersfield. He was selected to represent a Yorkshire XIII, which contained five Welshmen, against Lancashire at Barrow on Easter Saturday, 23 March. It was a splendid game, the Tykes coming back from an eight point interval deficit to win 13-10. The *Yorkshire Post* noted: "Harry Beverley, the Halifax loose-forward, was conspicuous in Yorkshire's forward revival, and Booth and Foster backed him up nobly. The distinction of scoring the winning try fell to Foster". Trevor received £1, plus 10 shillings expenses.

On 4 May Trevor played for a 1940 Tour Probables XIII against the 1936 Tourists at Salford in a game for the Red Cross Fund. It had originally been set for 10 February, when Trevor would have been unavailable. The notification to the players from the RFL secretary, John Wilson, told them: "Please bring all the gear you require, except jerseys, pants and stockings, which will be provided. Other items such as garters, laces, belts, knee and ankle bandages, etc. must be brought. You are to make your own arrangements for travelling to and from Salford. As you know, rail and bus facilities have been severely curtailed and you should take steps to ensure that any trains and buses you intend to use are actually running. Rail ticket is enclosed". The Probables won a fast and spectacular game 29-21 and Trevor, playing loose-forward, scored two tries. Frank Whitcombe and Billy Davies were also in the Probables line-up but there was to be no Lions tour for any of the Northern trio for another six years.

The RFL decided that Bradford Northern should play Swinton, the Lancashire Section winners, in a two-legged Championship play-off on 18 and 25 May, allowing Trevor to experience the first major final of his career. The first leg at Swinton was a remarkable game. Swinton's backs played wonderfully well in the first half, which ended somewhat fortuitously 10-8 in Northern's favour. However, "The strain of summer football sapped the energy of some of Swinton's mighty veterans, and the longer the game went on the more emphatic became Bradford's mastery. In such as Whitcombe, a strong man, Foster, a clever youngster, and Smith, a tireless worker, Northern had forwards to compare in the open with the best that Swinton could show in the first half, when the home men's play often touched a high level. In the second half, when Swinton tired, Northern's forwards became more and more aggressive in the loose... Their enthusiasm never flagged: the keen point of their attack sharpened as they drove deeper and deeper into their opponents' ranks". A 21-13 victory looked sufficient to give Bradford the title.

For the second leg at Odsal Trevor moved out to the wing, as Northern struggled to field a representative back division with Billy Davies, Emlyn Walters, Des Case, Stanley Brogden and Ernest Ward all missing. Bradford won comfortably 16-9 (37-22 on aggregate) before a crowd of 11,721. Northern centre Jenkins and Swinton stand-off Frank Bowyer were sent off in the closing stages for fighting, Swinton already having lost winger Bill Hopkin through injury.

23

Swinton's veteran captain Martin Hodgson, the best second-rower of his generation, was magnificent in defeat. He had dropped a goal to give Swinton an early lead and kicked two remarkable penalties in the second half, one truly astounding from a foot or so inside Bradford's half and almost on the touch-line, which "found the mark with astonishing ease". The teams for the first leg were:

Swinton: T. Bartram, W. Hopkins, R. Lewis, T. Shaw, J. McGurk, F. Bowyer, T. Holland, J. Wright, T. Armitt, J. Stoddart, C. Williams, M. Hodgson, F. Garner.
Scorers: Tries: Hopkins, Shaw, McGurk. Goals: Hodgson (2).
Bradford Northern: G. Carmichael, E. Jenkins*, T. Winnard, S. Brogden*, E. Walters, W. T. H. Davies, D. Ward, F. W. Whitcombe, V. Dilorenzo, H. Smith, G. Harrison, T. J. F. Foster, J. Moore. (* Guest players: Jenkins - Keighley, Brogden – Hull)
Scorers: Tries: Brogden, Davies, Whitcombe, Smith, Harrison. Goals: Carmichael (3).

For the second leg, Swinton's team was the same as the first leg, with Hodgson and Williams switching shirts. Their scorers were: Try: Williams. Goals: Hodgson (3). Bradford Northern's team was:

G. Carmichael, T. J. F. Foster, T. Winnard, E. Jenkins, N. Lambert, W. Hayes, D. Ward, F. W. Whitcombe, V. Dilorenzo, H. Smith, L. Higson, G. Harrison, J. Moore.
Scorers: Tries: Winnard (2), Ward, Whitcombe. Goals: Carmichael, Winnard.

Northern's 1940 trophy victories were their first since 1906. The next few years would make up for the last 34 and Trevor would be a major driving force.

1940-41: Two trophies

The war went badly for Britain and her allies in 1940. The Nazis conquered Denmark, Norway, Holland and Belgium and, shortly after Trevor and Bradford's triumphs on the rugby field, the British Army suffered the indignity of the evacuation from Dunkirk. By June, France had capitulated and the British had been defeated in Greece. Britain now stood alone with a seriously weakened army against Hitler and the Axis powers. A coalition government was formed under Winston Churchill and the Home Guard was created to help resist the expected German invasion.

The 1940-41 rugby league season opened as the RAF fought the Luftwaffe to a standstill in the Battle of Britain, only for the Germans to begin the London blitz at the start of September. Against that background the population had to take their pleasures where they found them. The rugby-loving citizens of Bradford were lucky. Northern began with nine consecutive victories, followed by a 2-2 draw at Huddersfield. Trevor missed the last match, but was back for the following match at York on 16 November, which was lost 8-5 to a team which jointly finished bottom of the league. It was, however, the last league match that would be lost during the campaign, Northern finishing top of the Yorkshire Section with a record of 23 wins and a draw from 25 games.

Bradford's success was largely based upon the ability to field an almost unchanged team throughout the season, at a time when many clubs depended upon guest players from other clubs. The Northern side almost picked itself: George Carmichael; Walter Best, Tom Winnard, Ernest Ward, Emlyn Walters; Wilf McWatt, Donald Ward; Frank Whitcombe, Cliff Carter, Len Higson, Laurie Roberts or Bert Smith, Trevor Foster and Jack Moore. Billy Davies, serving in the RAF, missed the entire season but his place was admirably filled by Hull Kingston Rovers' Wilf McWatt and towards the end of the season by the Salford legend Gus Risman. Hooker Cliff Carter took over from Vincent Dilorenzo, whose army service took him overseas for the duration. Dai Rees's policy was to use guests only when absolutely necessary and only when the very best players were available. His policy certainly paid off both in terms of results and the style of football. Wingers Walters with 35 tries and Best with 24 were the league's leading try-scorers, while centres Winnard (18) and Ward (15) also piled up the tries. Trevor scored 13 tries, the best by a forward.

Trevor had missed the drawn game with Huddersfield on 9 November because he was playing loose-forward for Wales against England at Oldham, along with his team-mates, Walters and Whitcombe. Trevor's immediate opponent at loose-forward for England was another team-mate, Jack Moore, who had the potential to become an outstanding forward for years to come. Both Trevor and Jack scored tries in the international. It was Trevor who opened the scoring, full-back Joe Jones converting his try. Moore's try from an inside pass by winger Ossie Peake was the only other score of the first half. There was, however, a good deal of excitement when the game was stopped temporarily in the first half, as the players and 5,000 spectators sought shelter after an air-raid warning was sounded.

The only scores of the second half were a thrilling try by England centre Jack Waring and the conversion by full-back Billy Belshaw, the star turn of the game. It was an afternoon for forward play and the England pack was magnificent in their 8-5 victory. The *Oldham Evening Chronicle* stirringly reported: "No quarter was asked and none conceded. Hard blows were given, taken and forgotten". What a wonderful description of how the game should be played! And Wales had very nearly pulled the game out of the fire, with winger Syd Williams being thrown into touch at the flag by the last tackle of the game.

By April 1941 Bradford had clinched the Yorkshire League title and reached the final of the Yorkshire Cup. Their opponents at Huddersfield's Fartown on 5 April were Dewsbury, who were reinforced by eight guest players, the most notable being Jim Sullivan. Northern's only guest was stand-off Gus Risman. A crowd of 13,316 produced receipts of £939, nine shillings and sixpence – the biggest gate so far taken during war-time rugby league. The final proved a strenuous affair with few patches of brilliance, but it held the fans' attention as Dewsbury tested Northern's resolve to the limit.

Sullivan opened the scoring with a magnificent penalty goal. Northern replied with a try from Best – "a good forcing effort" – and a second from Trevor to lead 6-2. Dewsbury stand-off Frank Tracey bagged an unconverted try to bring the score to 5-6. Shortly before half-time Jim Sullivan astounded everyone on the ground. Tom Winnard was caught offside in front of the posts, allowing Sullivan a chance to give Dewsbury a 7-6 lead, only for the maestro to smack the ball against the post for Northern to regain possession – unbelievable! Having escaped, Bradford gained the upper hand and scored another nine unanswered points in the second half. Trevor claimed a second try and skipper George Carmichael booted three goals for a 15-5 victory. George T. Thompson in the *Yorkshire Observer* wrote: "Bradford's ability to maintain almost constant second half pressure indicated the wisdom of their team manager's insistence on regular team training... Dewsbury's forwards, robust and strong in the loose, with Garner and Bradbury best, lacked the better football touches applied among the other set by Foster and Moore. Foster's remarkable backing-up enabled him to score tries in each half, with Donald Ward and Best playing a leading part in each".

An interesting feature of the game was referee George Phillips's insistence on proper playing of the ball. Several times he made players do it twice. George Thompson was not amused, observing: "The time is now well past when referees should attempt to teach players how to obey this rule". Happily, he also noted: "There was no penalty for rough play".

Bradford Northern: G. Carmichael, W. Best, T. Winnard, E. Ward, E. Walters, A. J. Risman*, D. Ward, F. W. Whitcombe, C. Carter, L. Higson, T. J. F. Foster, H. Smith, J. W. Moore.
(* Guest player: A. J. Risman – Salford).
Scorers: Tries: Foster (2), Best. Goals: Carmichael (3).
Dewsbury: J. Sullivan*, H. Germaine, J. Waring*, T. Kenny*, D. Barnes*, F. Tracey, H. Royal, Thomas*,

G. Jones, S. Crabtree, L. Garner*, G. Kershaw, J. Bradbury*.
(* Guest players: J. Sullivan: Wigan, J. Waring: St Helens, T. Kenny: Salford, D. Barnes: Swinton, F. Tracey: St Helens, G. Jones: Broughton Rangers, L. Garner: St Helens, J. Bradbury: St Helens, Thomas: Broughton Rangers).
Scorers: Try: Royal. Goal: Sullivan.

Northern played off with Wigan, who had been undefeated in the Lancashire Section, for the Championship on 12 and 14 April. The first leg at Wigan effectively settled the issue, Northern winning 17-6. Gus Risman, who scored a try, was the star, but the highlight was a second-half try by Emlyn Walters, which began a few yards from Bradford's posts. Beautiful passing to the right flank stretched Wigan. Walters, the left-winger, followed the chain to the opposite side of the field and when right-winger Walter Best adroitly beat two opponents, Walters took his inside pass to claim a delightful try "with a forceful and spirited finish". Little less outstanding was an effort by Trevor which failed by inches. Trevor and his pack were dominant, another report saying: "The tireless Moore was never subdued, while once or twice by his Herculean efforts Whitcombe must have thought he was still driving his four ton lorry". Northern added other tries through Walters - his second - Higson and Best. Ernest Ward landed the game's solitary goal. Wigan replied with tries by Joe Jones and Johnny Lawrenson.

Two days later at Odsal a crowd of 20,205 paying £1,148 – both new war-time records – turned up to see Northern demolish Wigan 28-9 to complete a remarkable treble haul of trophies within a fortnight. Both hookers, Cliff Carter and Joe Egan, were sent off in the second half, which materially helped Northern, who had been losing the scrums. In the open Bradford's forwards were dominant, one reporter stating: "The forward merit of Moore, Foster and Whitcombe in the loose was undeniable". The teams in the first leg were:
Wigan: J. Jones, G. Aspinall*, J. Lawrenson, J. R. Maloney*, V. Johnson, J. Cunliffe, T. Bradshaw, G. Curran*, J. Egan, K. Gee, J. Bowen, J. Cayzer*, J. Simpson.
(* Guest players: G. Aspinall & J. R. Maloney: Liverpool Stanley, G. Curran: Salford, J. Cayzer: Hull KR).
Scorers: Tries: J. Jones, J. Lawrenson.
Bradford Northern: G. Carmichael, W. Best, T. Winnard, E. Ward, E. Walters, A. J. Risman*, W. Hayes, F. W. Whitcombe, C. Carter, L. Higson, T. J. F. Foster, H. Smith, J. W. Moore.
(* Guest player: A. J. Risman: Salford).
Scorers: Tries: Walters (2), Best, Risman, Higson. Goals: Ward.

For the second leg, Sharratt replaced Cayzer for Wigan. For Bradford Northern, Whitcombe and Higson switched positions, but otherwise the team was the same. The scorers were:
Bradford Northern: Tries: Risman (2), Winnard (2), Walters, Moore. Goals: Ward (5).
Wigan: Tries: Aspinall, Johnson, Bowen.

Trevor's season ended with disappointment, however. Northern looked good for a clean sweep of all the trophies and had reached the Challenge Cup semi-finals. Surprisingly, on 3 May, Leeds held them to a 10-10 draw in the first leg at Headingley and, even more surprisingly on 10 May, before yet another wartime record crowd of 22,500 won the second leg 12-2. Leeds went on to beat Halifax 19-2 in the final at Odsal a week later when the wartime gate figures were again shattered with 28,500 fans paying £1,703.

1941-42: Rugby union

In June 1941 Germany invaded Russia, having conquered Crete and Yugoslavia. And as the war wore on, ever increasing difficulties beset rugby league too. Only four Lancashire teams started the 1941-42 campaign and Broughton Rangers folded in October. The Lancashire Section was disbanded and all remaining 17 teams played in a solitary War Emergency League. Oldham and Wigan were allowed to compete in the Yorkshire Cup, which reverted to its peacetime place in the calendar. In November the Ministry of Transport announced that buses could not take football teams more than 50 miles, so it was fortunate that Hull had already played their away fixtures at St Helens, Wigan and Oldham. Trevor's duties were still allowing him to turn out regularly for Northern, who again enjoyed much success.

On 18 October Odsal hosted the third Red Cross international. Bradford provided Ernest Ward and Len Higson to the England side and Emlyn Walters, Frank Whitcombe and Trevor, as loose-forward, to Wales. The BBC broadcast the second half of a game which was not especially exciting. Weather conditions were bad and the 4,339 spectators were inconspicuous in the great bowl of Odsal. Wales looked likely winners at half time, leading 7-2, thanks to a try by Alan Edwards and two goals from Risman, against a penalty from Belshaw. The *Sunday Chronicle* reported on the "poorness of the game" and said that even the "great Foster did little to enhance his reputation". The England pack regained the initiative in the second half, however, and a 9-9 draw was a fair result, Risman adding a third goal for Wales in the second half against two by Belshaw and a Johnny Lawrenson try.

Trevor played a major role in Bradford's progress in the Yorkshire Cup. In the first round against Batley he scored two tries in each leg and, in the second leg of the semi-final at Odsal, scored Northern's only try in a 9-3 victory over Huddersfield, which overturned a 10-11 defeat at Fartown. The final, at Huddersfield on 6 December, pitted Northern against arch local rivals Halifax. Another dreadful day kept the crowd down to 5,989 and after 36 minutes the game was scoreless, Halifax's defence being ruthless. However, Billy Davies completely changed the course of events a few minutes either side of the interval. Two brilliantly opportunistic tries by the stand-off in the 37th and 41st minutes swept Northern into a 10-0 lead and thoroughly nonplussed Halifax. Davies played one of the games of his life. He was irresistible, for apart from his two tries, he made another, saved a certain Halifax try and always seemed to be on the ball. Trevor played a starring role too, although he sustained a cut thigh. Frank Williams, writing in the *Halifax Courier & Guardian*, had warned before the match that Northern's "forwards, with Foster, Whitcombe and Higson outstanding, are stated to be man-eaters". Williams was not wrong on this occasion. He wrote: "Probably the best try was the one scored by Foster. This came as the result of an effort commenced by Walters inside his own 25, and Foster finished off the movement with a great run from half-way". A 24-0 hammering for Halifax was one of the least expected results imaginable. Interestingly, instead of medals the players received War Savings Certificates. The teams were:

Bradford Northern: G. Carmichael, E. Walters, E. Ward, E. Billington, W. Best, W. T. H. Davies, D. Ward, F. W. Whitcombe, C. Carter, L. Higson, H. Smith, T. J. F. Foster, W. Hutchinson.
Scorers: Tries: Davies (2), Best, Carter, Smith, Foster. Goals: E. Ward (2), Carmichael.
Halifax: H. Lockwood, G. Elias, C. Smith, F. Rule, A. E. Doyle, G. Todd, T. McCue*, G. Baynham, M. A. Meek, H. Irving, H. Millington*, C. Brereton, J. Dixon.
(* Guest players: T. McCue & H. Millington: Widnes).

In 1939 the Rugby Football Union had declared it would lift its ban on rugby league men playing for forces XVs against rugby union club sides during the war, providing such individuals had not played rugby league since enlisting. The Welsh Rugby Union went along with the RFU but the Scottish Rugby Union refused point blank to endorse such an arrangement and stuck to their obstinate stance throughout the war. In the event both the RFU and WRU passed all responsibility for representative rugby to the military authorities and many servicemen from rugby league were able to enjoy playing both codes at a very high level. Trevor was one of those who benefited most, for he became probably the most admired forward in both league and union in the last few years of hostilities. From 1942 onwards he was in demand for practically every representative game of either sport and his seasons became a bewildering mixture of fixtures here, there and everywhere.

In 1943 John Radnor wrote: "In England it has been left to a special committee of the Imperial Services to keep representative Rugby alive. In Wales an emergency committee containing members of the Army and RAF have arranged representative games and picked the teams... A similar committee has functioned in Scotland. The international matches between these three countries now rank as Service internationals and not as matches in the International Championship. As sporting events, however, they have remained outstanding and many a good judge has declared that any lowering in the standards of skill has more than been made up for by the spirit in which the games have been played."

It is interesting to note that while Scotland played England they never played Wales, probably fearing contamination from the many Welsh rugby league players with whom they would have to have contact. They seem to have conveniently failed to notice the presence of men such as Ernest Ward, Stan Brogden, Billy Belshaw, Ned Hodgson, Roy Francis, Johnny Lawrenson, Ernie Ruston, Harry Pimblett, Jimmy Stott, Ted Bedford and Ted Sadler in the England XVs which opposed Scotland. Presumably, they would have had to ban themselves for playing against professionals if they had looked too closely.

On 7 March 1942 Trevor took his place as a flanker in the first rugby union Services International, at Swansea's famous St Helen's Ground. A 20,500 crowd paid £1,959, which went to services charities. England fielded three rugby league men and Wales seven, including Gus Risman, the captain. Risman was a revelation to those Welsh fans who had only heard about him. Trevor could never speak highly enough of Gus, whom he regards as one of the all-time great men and leaders of either code. England led 12-0 at the interval, but were overhauled as Trevor and his fellow packmen slowly wrested control. A penalty from Risman was followed by a try from Alan Edwards, which Gus had instigated. Gus then converted a try from Haydn Tanner, another of Trevor's rugby heroes, to bring the scores to 11-12. Gus edged Wales ahead with a long penalty goal and Billy Davies sealed a 17-12 Welsh victory with a late touchdown.

A week later Trevor scored Bradford's only try in a top-of-the-table clash at Dewsbury, which ended in a 5-5 draw. A stark reminder that there was a war on appeared in the *Yorkshire Observer* on 16 March, however. Trevor's forward colleague Jack Moore, who was serving on HMS *Electra*, was reported missing, when his ship was sunk in the Java sea battle. Another Northern player, Charlie Freeman, had been killed over a year earlier.

On 21 March Trevor had his first experience of captaining a rugby league team. He led Northern Command against a Rugby League XIII at Halifax, the £267 proceeds going to the Northern Command Welfare Fund. Both teams were full of internationals, who provided an excellent spectacle which was, however, decided by a scrambled last gasp try by Castleford scrum-half Tommy Walsh, which gave Trevor's soldiers a scarcely deserved 22-18 win.

Trevor was selected to play league for Yorkshire against Lancashire at Dewsbury on 28 March but the services had priority when it mattered and instead he turned out in the return union Services International at Gloucester. Wales fielded seven league men again, but England's contingent was reduced to Cumbrian forward Ned Hodgson. *The Times* reported that 12,000 saw "a game that produced much excitement if little high-class three-quarter play". The English won most of the possession but Trevor and his forwards killed any good ball for the opposing backs. Risman kicked a penalty but England equalised at 3-3 with a try from their flanker W.T. Reynolds before the interval. Wales triumphed 9-3, however, with further tries from Alan Edwards and Trevor.

He was not so happy at Richmond the following Saturday, when he was a late call-up to replace C.L. Newton-Thompson of Cambridge University in the Army team which lost 14-3 to the RAF. The RAF team included Salford's Alan Edwards, Castleford's Ted Sadler and Bill

Fallowfield from Northampton RUFC, the future secretary of the RFL, who would effectively become Trevor's employer in later years, when Trevor became the RFL's national coach.

Back at Odsal, Northern had finished second to Dewsbury in the league. However, they beat Halifax 15-8 in the Championship semi-final on 11 April, with Trevor bagging a try, putting them into the final against Dewsbury at Headingley. The game drew an excellent crowd of 18,000, but went badly for Bradford from the beginning. Trevor suffered a bad jaw injury in the first minute and Cliff Carter sustained damaged ribs. It was all uphill for the Northern forwards and even Frank Whitcombe was subdued. Of the pack it was noted that "Foster, despite the pain he must have been suffering, was the best". Dewsbury won the second-half scrums 30-6, but it was not until the hour mark that they took the lead with an Alan Edwards drop goal. They eventually won 13-0.

Bradford Northern: G. Carmichael, W. Best, E. Billington, E. Ward, E. Walters, W. T. H. Davies, K. Davies*, F. W. Whitcombe, C. Carter, L. Higson, T. J. F. Foster, W. Smith, W. Hutchinson.
(* Guest player: K. Davies: Kelghley)
Dewsbury: S. Miller*, B. Hudson*, A. S. Edwards*, A. J. Risman*, R. L. Francis*, T. Kenny*, H. Royal, H. Hammond, G. Nicholson, J. Gardner*, G. Kershaw, G. Curran*, G. Bunter*.
(Guest players: S. Miller: Salford, B. Hudson: Salford, A. S. Edwards: Salford, A. J. Risman: Salford, R. L. Francis: Barrow, T. Kenny: Salford, J. Gardner: Salford, G. Curran: Salford, G. Bunter: Broughton Rangers).
Scorers: Tries: Hudson, Francis, Kenny. Goals: Edwards, Risman.

1942-43: Representative rugby

When the new season opened, only 14 teams were left in the War Emergency League, Bramley, Castleford and Hunslet all having given up the ghost temporarily. It was certainly becoming harder to raise teams, because so many men were committed to war work or were in the services. Bradford were no exception and Dai Rees had to compromise heavily on his aversion to using guest players. Northern finished third in the league, but were knocked out of the Yorkshire Cup by Huddersfield in the semi-finals and by Keighley in the second round of the Challenge Cup.

Trevor appeared in 19 of Northern's 31 fixtures, scoring nine tries, but much of his time was spent in playing representative rugby and enhancing his already formidable reputation. On 10 October he skippered Northern Command to a 14-10 win over a Rugby League XIII at Hull. The *Hull Daily Mail* reported: "Foster led his forwards with such relentless energy that he was able to score a couple of tries". The next week he was back in Swansea playing union before a 12,000 crowd representing the Army in their 16-12 win against South Wales, scoring another try, after backing up Gus Risman. Clem Lewis, a former fly-half and captain of Wales before and after the First World War, gave Trevor a ringing endorsement: "Prescott, Graham and Hodgson were great-hearted raiders, but the outstanding forward was Foster, a grand player".

Three weeks later, on 7 November, it was back to Swansea again for the Wales versus England Services International, this time with over 20,000 in attendance. There were six rugby league players in the Welsh XV and five in the English, including Ernest Ward. The Welsh forwards played splendidly and Billy Davies scored the try of the match, a sizzling 40-yarder. Wales won much more easily than the 11-7 scoreline indicated.

On 21 November, Trevor was at Richmond where the Army defeated the RAF 18-0 before "the biggest crowd that has watched a rugby match in London this season", according to *The Times*. Despite the score it was a close game, the Army scoring 10 points late on. *The Times* remarked, "Of the Army forwards, Foster was perhaps the best, but the thinning locks of Prescott and Newton-Thompson were seldom far behind".

29

Christmas Day saw Trevor in Bradford's second-row for an 8-8 draw at Keighley and, in his first engagement of 1943, at Dewsbury on 2 January, he led a Northern Command XIII to a 21-10 victory, scoring the opening try.

On 23 January Trevor had a role in one of rugby's truly historic occasions. That Saturday afternoon a Northern Command Rugby Union XV met a Northern Command Rugby League XV at Headingley, under RU laws, of course. A crowd of 8,000 contributed £470 to services charities. The curmudgeonly Scottish RU tried to throw a spoke in the wheels of fraternisation, demanding that no one who had ever played rugby league should be allowed in the Union XV. The Army and the Yorkshire RFU ignored the Scottish fulminations and the Scots in the XV, who, ironically, were the majority, kept mum. To Trevor fell the honour of captaining the League XV to an 18-11 victory. It was a close-run thing and the Union XV were unfortunate to lose forward Corporal Ronnie Cowe to injury in the second half when they led 11-9. The League XV scored six tries to one, however. *The Times* noted "There was some superb passing by both sets of backs, but the League players carried out their movements more quickly and were more accurate". Unsurprisingly, the Union XV enjoyed more possession. Trevor, Ken Jubb, Bill Chapman and Dai Prosser were the most prominent of the League's forwards. Trevor remembers: "That game thrilled a lot of people. It was a very even contest, with great players from both codes. I well remember having to revert to all those rucks and the close forward play. It was not really my cup of tea any longer. I stood out on the fringe of the mauls. That was one of the things I enjoyed about taking up rugby league – not being caught in the rucks."

The teams on that momentous occasion were:

Northern Command Rugby League XV: Lance-Corporal G. R. Pepperell (Huddersfield), Sergeant-Instructor R. L. Francis (Barrow), Trooper H. Mills (Hull), Private J. Stott (St Helens), Corporal R. W. Lloyd (Castleford), Lance-Bombardier T. H. Royal (Dewsbury), Signalman W. Thornton (Hunslet), Sergeant-Instructor D. R. Prosser (Leeds), Lance Corporal L. L. White (Hunslet), Gunner L. White (York), Corporal K. Jubb (Leeds), Corporal E. Tattersfield (Leeds), Private W. G. Chapman (Warrington), Corporal E. Bedford (Hull), Sergeant-Instructor T. J. F. Foster (Bradford Northern).

Northern Command Rugby Union XV: Corporal J. Bond (Cumberland), Lieutenant T. G. H. Jackson (Cheltenham), Captain M. M. Walford (Oxford University), Lieutenant D. R. MacGregor (Rosslyn Park), Sergeant-Instructor D. F. Mitchell (Gala), Second-Lieutenant L. Bruce Lockhart (Cambridge University), Officer Cadet H. Tanner (Swansea), Major R. O. Murray (London Scottish), Signalman J. D. H. Hastie (Melrose), Corporal J. Maltman (Hawick), Captain R. C. V. Stewart (Moseley), Corporal R. Cowe (Melrose), Second-Lieutenant R. A. Huskisson (Cambridge University), Private A. Crawford (Melrose), Second-Lieutenant R. G. Furbank (Bedford).

A week later Trevor was in Belfast, representing the British Army against an Irish XV before a crowd of 12,000 at Ravenhill. The Irish XV was essentially their international team. The Irish led 11-0 at the interval but Trevor, admirable in the loose, and his pack gradually tamed their opposites and a 70th minute drop goal, worth four points, from fly-half Murdoch won the game for the Army 12-11. On 13 February the Army were not so fortunate, losing 11-3 to the RAF at Leicester, although *The Times* reported: "The forwards had a terrific struggle with Jubb, Tamplin and Prosser ably assisting Foster in the Army pack".

On 27 February Trevor's itinerary took him to Wigan for a league Red Cross International. It was a special day for him as he was awarded the Welsh captaincy for the first time. The *Yorkshire Observer* reported that "the Welsh forwards played well, and many times were the spearhead of the Welsh attack, with Foster outstanding". The 17,000 crowd saw a good game but, well though Trevor performed, his team went down 15-9. England had displayed superior team work and better ability to take chances.

On 20 March Trevor had better luck at Gloucester in the union Services International where Wales crushed England 34-7 before a crowd of 18,000. The Welsh forwards were much too good for England and the latter's cause was not helped by an injury to Ernest Ward. Welsh debutant centre Bleddyn Williams scored a hat-trick.

The business end of the rugby league season developed into a farce. The top six teams, based on a percentage of games won and lost, were Wigan, Dewsbury, Bradford, Halifax, Leeds and Huddersfield. A dispute arose as to when the league season actually ended, because clubs were becoming a bit haphazard at getting their fixtures completed, hence the need for a table based on success percentages. It was decided that the last two places for the top four would be decided by play-offs between the third and the sixth, and the fourth and the fifth-placed teams. Leeds (fifth) withdrew but Northern beat Huddersfield 16-13 to qualify for an away semi-final at Dewsbury on 8 May. Northern scored a famous 8-3 victory, Trevor and Emlyn Walters claiming the tries, and proceeded to the Championship final against Halifax. Or so it seemed.

Dewsbury objected to the RFL's' Emergency Committee that Trevor's fellow Welsh second-rower Sandy Orford, a guest from Wakefield Trinity, had not played the four league games required to qualify for the play-offs and was therefore not eligible to play. The objection was upheld and Northern were booted out of the final. Dewsbury went onto beat Halifax to take the Championship. But the dispute was not over.

On 23 June, a month after the final, Bradford objected that Dewsbury had fielded their own ineligible player in forward Frank Smith, a guest from Castleford, in the semi-final. Like Orford, he had only played in three league games for the club. Northern's objection was upheld, Dewsbury were fined £100 and the Championship was declared null and void.

1943-44

The chaos in rugby league mirrored that of the world at war. By the summer of 1942, Japan was cutting a swathe of bloody destruction through Asia and the Pacific and the Germans had attacked Stalingrad. In North Africa Rommel had reached El Alamein on 1 July and looked likely to defeat the British Eighth Army. But the tide of the war finally turned in favour of Britain and her allies. In October and November Montgomery defeated the Germans in North Africa and in January 1943 the Germans retreated from Stalingrad. Sicily was conquered in the summer of 1943 and, as the 1943-44 rugby season was getting under way, the Allies accepted the surrender of Italy.

Representative calls and military duties restricted Trevor to only 15 appearances for Northern, who played 35 fixtures during 1943-44. In the league, however, Northern played only 19 games, fewer than anyone else – the others were cup ties - and ultimately finished sixth. Trevor scored eight tries, including a hat-trick in a 34-5 home win against Oldham on 11 September. Trevor's absences aside, Northern were less reliant on guest players during this campaign and more able to field settled sides. Notable newcomers were Hunslet's England winger Eric Batten and Jack Kitching, a local centre. Vic Darlison became established at hooker and Billy Hutchinson was successfully integrated at loose-forward.

Trevor's first big engagement was at Swansea on 9 October, when 14,000 gathered to watch the Army beat South Wales 31-10. Among his pack colleagues was Reverend H. C. C. Bowen, an Army chaplain. Rugby league men did most of the Army's scoring, Billy Belshaw landing five conversions and Ernest Ward, with two, and Roy Francis scoring tries. A rare injury caused Trevor to drop out of the Army's union clash with the RAF at Gloucester on 30 October and he was also ruled out of several games for Northern.

He was fit, however, for the Services International at Swansea on 20 November. A huge crowd of more than 25,000 attended, including several thousand American service-men. This clash between England and Wales was arguably the most exciting of all the wartime Services Internationals. John Radnor of the *Sporting & Dramatic* described it as "often a desperate encounter but hardly once too desperate... It made a thrilling spectacle and a fine story. Certainly it was better to watch than many a drab championship affair in the years before the war." Wales won by the skin of their teeth, 11-9. *The Times* reported, "It was a tremendous and unceasing struggle in which the Welsh pack, for all their deficiencies in heeling, were a terrific force in the loose, while behind them at intervals the Welsh backs frequently promised the kind of attack which actually came off only twice".

Haydn Tanner broke his nose in the second half but bravely carried on and Trevor's club mates Billy Davies and Ernest Ward played key roles in the match. Ward landed two penalties for England in the first half, the first a beauty, and Davies scored a try for Wales after a terrific run by Alan Edwards. Alban Davies landed a penalty after the interval to level the scores at 6-6 and then converted a try by Syd Williams for an 11-6 lead. An absolutely superb try by Johnny Lawrenson brought the score to 9-11 but Ward missed the conversion and then failed with a penalty and Wales held out for their narrow victory. Amazingly, league men had scored every point. The *Yorkshire Post's* verdict on Trevor's performance was succinct but sweet, "Always in the thick of the fray, Trevor Foster stood out in a class by himself".

Meanwhile, Bradford had come through three two-legged Yorkshire Cup ties to reach the final against surprise packets Keighley. Trevor had been absent throughout the run but was in the second-row on 27 November when the first leg of the final took place at Odsal. By now Trevor had taken over the Northern captaincy but his first final in charge was a sore trial to the 10,251 spectators present. Trevor played well enough and scored the only try of the game early in the first half, after combining with Hutchinson and Walters in one of the very few open passages of play in the match. The *Halifax Courier & Guardian* described the game as boring and "simply a stopping affair". The scrummaging count was said to be "about 30-30". Keighley were actually probably quite satisfied with the result, 5-2 to Northern. They were unbeaten at Lawkholme Lane and were confident they could overturn the deficit the following Saturday.

There were 8,993 at Keighley for the second leg and they witnessed a much more entertaining affair. The highlight was a fantastic try from their Welsh centre Idris Towill, which opened the scoring. Towill wrong-footed half-a-dozen opponents in a scintillating dash from halfway. Unfortunately for Keighley, another Welshman, Mel De Lloyd missed the easy conversion. Ernest Ward levelled the scores with a try and before half-time hooker Vic Darlison dropped an improbable goal to give Northern the lead. The only score of the second half was a penalty by De Lloyd, the game ending tied at 5-5, with Northern taking the trophy 10-7 on aggregate. Trevor received the Yorkshire Cup from Mrs Popplewell, wife of the Yorkshire Rugby League president. The teams for the first leg were:
Bradford Northern: G. Carmichael, E. Batten, G. L. James, E. Ward, E. Walters, W. H. T. Davies, D. Ward, L. Roberts, V. J. Darlison, L. Higson, F. Murray, T. J. Foster, W. Hutchinson.
Scorers: Try: Foster. Goal: James.
Keighley: L. Jones*, H. Caldwell, I. A. Towill, F. Lamb*, K. Davies, M. De Lloyd*, P. J. Goodall*, H. Jones*, D. Cotton*, J. Miller*, J. Flanagan, F. Farrar, N. Foster.
(* Guest players: L. Jones: Warrington, H. Caldwell: Wigan, F. Lamb: Rochdale Hornets, M. De Lloyd: Warrington, P. J. Goodall: Halifax, H. Jones: Warrington, D. Cotton: Warrington, J. Miller: Warrington).
Scorer: Goal: De Lloyd.

For the second leg, E. Billington replaced James for Bradford, and Murray and Trevor changed positions. For Keighley, K. Davies played at centre in place of F. Lamb, with Castleford's R. Lloyd playing on the wing as a guest. The scorers were:
Keighley: Try: Towill. Goal: De Lloyd.
Bradford Northern: Try: E. Ward. Goal: Darlison.

On 18 December Trevor was in charge of an Army XIII which went down 11-4 to a very powerful Rugby League XIII at Halifax. His team's cause was not helped when Wales international hooker Les White failed to turn up for the kick-off. Batley forward George Brown started instead, but when White arrived 15 minutes later, Brown retired to allow him to play. It was a flagrant breach of the laws of the game but there was a war on! The Army winger Reg Lloyd of Keighley was even more unfortunate with his travelling arrangements, being stuck 15 miles from Thrum Hall when the game ended.

On 8 January, 1944 Trevor had the novel experience of turning out for South Wales against the Army at Cardiff. In a surprise 23-11 triumph, Trevor, Bill Tamplin and Cardiff's Ray Bale were the most effective forwards and Trevor had the satisfaction of forcing his way over for the last try of the game. He took part in another unusual rugby union fixture at Castleford on 22 January, when Northern Command beat a National Civil Defence Services XV 14-11 in a well-contested game containing much good football despite difficult conditions. The Civil Defence were already leading 3-0 before Gus Risman, another victim of war-time travelling problems, turned up. His inspiration helped to turn the game's fortunes and Trevor again got his name among the try scorers just before half-time.

The vicissitudes of wartime rugby were again on show on 29 January, when Trevor appeared for the Army, who lost 11-8 to the RAF, before "one of the largest crowds ever seen on the Richmond Athletic Ground". One person who was not seen was Tommy Armitt, the veteran Swinton hooker, who had toured with Great Britain in 1936. He was supposed to be hooking for the RAF but had fallen asleep in his room after a good lunch at the Russell Hotel. No-one had noticed he was not on the team bus. When he finally came round, he dashed to the Old Deer Park ground instead of Richmond. Bob Weighill, a future Secretary of the RFU, who had just returned from a sortie over France, came out of the crowd to take Tommy's place on the pitch.

On 12 February Trevor was back in Belfast for the British Army's annual clash with the Irish XV. The Army won 15-0 and were acclaimed as one of the best teams seen in Ireland for many years. Trevor was imperious. *The Irish Times* writer, P. D. MacWeeney called him "the hero of the afternoon". He added: "While the home defence could perform wonders in stopping the opposing backs, they just could not cope with an enormous forward who could travel for 20 yards or so as fast as any man on the field, shake off tackles, swerve and sell the dummy. Two of the British tries were scored by Foster all on his own, and on his two appearances at Ravenhill he must rank as high, at least, as any of the great wing-forwards of rugby history".

Trevor's next big occasion soon followed on 26 February, when he played his fifth and final rugby league Red Cross international for Wales at Wigan. A sign of the austerity of the times was visible in the jerseys with missing numbers and the lack of regularity in the players' stockings but it was still a matter of pride for the players to be representing their countries, something Trevor never lost. The game was a good one. Ted Tattersfield, the England loose-forward, was the star man but on the Welsh side Trevor stood out in the pack, with Con Murphy and Bill Chapman. One critic wrote: "Foster was a great player when opportunity was afforded to make progress". There was a touch of controversy when Alan Edwards shot down his wing and the touch-judge momentarily raised his flag. The English defenders undoubtedly slackened their efforts in response but the referee did not see the touch-judge's action and Edwards was allowed to carry on for the try. The game ended in a 9-9 draw, although Trevor could have been forgiven for being disappointed, Wales having scored three tries to one.

Back on 6 November 1943, the Northern Command rugby union side had lost 17-20 to Scottish Services at Galashiels and were eager for revenge, when the Scots came down to Headingley for the return fixture on 14 March. No doubt there were some with whom the official Scottish RU stance on fraternisation still rankled. More than 4,000 turned out to witness the two XVs produce some fast and attractive football. This time, however, the Scots were overrun. Trevor's men led 16-5 at half-time and thereafter it was one-way traffic, Northern Command winning 37-5. The *Yorkshire Post* commented: "Foster handled with the skill and craft of a back. He got a try, he made a try for Risman, and then he scored another try".

One of Trevor's last big engagements of the rugby union season on 8 April was for Wales against England at Gloucester. There were many British and American service personnel, preparing for D-Day, in the 15,000 crowd, who were treated to a spectacular game. Wales, captained by Billy Davies, went down 8-20, England having lost in the previous five encounters. Paradoxically, Wales never got into the lead but until the final quarter had looked the likelier winners. England had led 9-8 at the break, Ernest Ward having contributed two penalties, one from the half-way line. Three tries in the last 20 minutes gave the final scoreline a misleading look, although England were devastating in that period. It was noted in *The Times* that "Travers, Coleman and Foster constantly took the eye by their grand play".

Despite picking up a leg injury at Gloucester, two days later, on Easter Monday, Trevor was in the Bradford team which met Halifax at Odsal in the second leg of the Challenge Cup semi-final. It was a game which attracted huge interest, the attendance of 28,500 equalling the best of the war so far: the 1941 Challenge Cup Final at Odsal. The receipts of £2,080 proved to be the highest in war-time rugby league. Halifax had won the first leg at Thrum Hall 5-2, but the teams were missing their key playmakers, Billy Davies and Tommy McCue, for the second leg. It turned out to be a tremendously tense and nerve-shredding affair, with defences almost impregnable. George T. Thompson wrote: "Bradford battled gallantly on attack until the last ten minutes, in which, tired, despairing and battered, they were forced to withstand a final and terrific Halifax rally". The only scores were two first-half penalties from Ernest Ward and a later try from Eric Batten, giving Northern a 7-0 victory and entry to the final on a 9-5 aggregate. Halifax had a last gasp try near the posts controversially disallowed.

Northern were through to meet Wigan in the final, the first leg set for 15 April at Central Park. As Northern's skipper, it would be a highly significant day in Trevor's career. The Army did not agree, however, and he was instructed that instead he would be playing in a rugby union sevens tournament at Headingley. The Northern Command Sports Board had arranged a similar competition the previous year, which was won by a Rugby League VII. All the proceeds were to go to the Northern Command Sports Board Welfare Funds and "The Golden Trophy" was to be awarded to the winners. Trevor recalls: "I was a little disappointed when in 1944 I was called home to play for the British Army over the same weekend that 'Northern' played Wigan at Central Park in the first leg of the Challenge Cup Final. Happily I was able to play in the second leg at Odsal."

While Trevor played rugby union sevens, despite having his mind on what was happening without him at Wigan, there was no happy ending that afternoon. His Northern Command Welsh VII made the final but went down 13-3 to the Rugby League VII, who thus retained their title. Meanwhile Northern had lost 3-0 at Central Park to a first-half try by second-rower Jimmy Featherstone.

There had been 21,500 at Wigan and for the second leg at Odsal on 22 April there was a new wartime record crowd of 30,000 paying £2,061, most of whom were desperate to see that three points deficit overhauled. The Army allowed Trevor to take his place as Northern's leader. However, there was some controversy before a ball was kicked. Northern and Wigan's colours clashed and, as was the custom for the home team, Wigan, had changed their jerseys in the first leg. Consequently, Northern should have done the same for the Odsal leg. However, there was a heated discussion and the upshot was that Wigan turned out in blue jerseys with

Bradford in their normal colours. Northern were later fined 10 guineas for their infraction and Dai Rees was severely censured for his attitude to the Rugby League chairman and vice-chairman before the match.

Like many Challenge Cup finals, the game as a spectacle failed to live up to expectations. There were few thrills and too much individualism but the contest was a keen one. Wigan's backs were well contained and Vic Darlison beat Joe Egan 44-27 in the scrums, while the penalty count was 14-14. Northern lacked Billy Davies but full-back George Carmichael was probably the best back on the day and their forwards played masterfully. The *Yorkshire Observer* opined: "Foster tried too much and held the ball unwisely at times, but he was all over the field, and Hutchinson and Whitcombe were also prominent in support".

By half-time Northern had levelled the aggregate score with an Eric Batten try. They then took the lead courtesy of a penalty by Carmichael awarded after Ernest Ward had been struck in the face and a few minutes later Frank Whitcombe scored a try. Northern thus won 8-0 on the afternoon and 8-3 on aggregate. Trevor was certainly a proud and happy man when he ascended the steps of the main stand to receive the coveted trophy from Mrs Bob Anderton, wife of the famous Warrington official who was also chairman of the RFL Council. The teams for the second leg were:

Bradford Northern: G. Carmichael, E. Batten, J. Kitching, E. Ward, E. Walters, D. Bennett, D. Ward, F. W. Whitcombe, V. J. Darlison, L. Higson, T. J. Foster, L. Roberts, W. Hutchinson.
Scorers: Tries: Batten, Whitcombe. Goal: Carmichael.
Wigan: J. Jones, J. H. Lawrenson, W. Belshaw*, J. R. Maloney*, E. J. Ashcroft, M. Ryan, H. Gee, K. Gee, J. Egan, J. Blan, J. J. Featherstone, E. Watkins, J. Bowen.
(* Guest players: W. Belshaw: Warrington, J. R. Maloney: Liverpool Stanley).

In the first leg, for Bradford, W. Best had played instead of E. Walters, and Barrow's A. Marklew in place of Trevor. For Wigan, Jim Sullivan had played at full back instead of J. Jones.

Amazingly, Trevor's season was not yet over. In the Bradford Northern programme for the Cup semi-final programme on Easter Monday, the following had appeared: "Lift your hats, gentlemen, to the members of the Inter-Services Rugby Football Committee, who by their action of appointing our Captain, Sgt. Inst. Trevor Foster, and Sgt. Inst. W.T.H. Davies as the Army and R.A.F. representatives on the committee who will nominate the League services players for the Inter-Service match to be played at Odsal on April 29th, have shown more than a fine sporting spirit, and by their action every phase of service will get every consideration. On behalf of all connected with the Bradford Northern club we tender to these two great lads, whose play on the field has only been excelled by the way they have 'played the game' off it, our warmest congratulations on receiving such a well-merited honour".

The Inter-Service match referred to, was to be a grander version of the Northern Command Rugby League XV versus Northern Command Rugby Union XV, which had been so popular and so successfully staged at Leeds on 23 January 1943. This time it would not be restricted to personnel from Northern Command. Anyone who was in the nation's fighting forces and available was eligible for selection. The sides were designated as Combined Services Rugby League XV and Combined Services Rugby Union XV. The *Yorkshire Observer's* George T. Thompson, not a journalist prone to hyperbole, recorded on the morning of the match that "today's match must rank as the outstanding match in the history of Rugby football". The teams for this historic engagement were:

Combined Service Rugby League XV: Lance-Corporal E. Ward (Bradford N), Sergeant-Instructor R. L. Francis (Barrow), Leading Aircraftsman J. Lawrenson (Wigan), Corporal J. Stott (St Helens), Corporal A. S. Edwards (Salford), Sergeant S. Brogden (Hull), Bombardier T. H. Royal (Dewsbury), Sergeant-Instructor D. R. Prosser (Leeds), Driver L. L. White (Hunslet), Lance-Corporal C. Brereton (Halifax), Sergeant D. Murphy (Bramley), Flight-Sergeant E. Watkins (Wigan), Sergeant I. Owens (Leeds), Sergeant W. G. Chapman (Warrington), Sergeant-Instructor T. J. F. Foster (Bradford Northern).

Combined Services Rugby Union XV: CSM R. F. Trott (Penarth), Lieutenant G. Hollis (Sale), Corporal T. Sullivan (Swansea), Lieutenant H. Tanner (Swansea), Sub-Lieutenant E. S. Simpson (Bradford), Lieutenant T. Gray (Heriots), Squadron-Leader J. Parsons (Leicester), Sergeant G. T. Dancer (Bedford), Corporal R. J. Longland (Northampton), Captain R. E. Prescott (Harlequins), Lieutenant P. N. Walker (Gloucester), Corporal D. V. Phillips (Swansea), Captain G. D. Shaw (Gala), Captain J. A. Waters (Selkirk), Flight-Lieutenant R. H. G. Weighill (Waterloo).

The referee was Wing Commander Cyril Gadney (RAF), who would become the 55th President of the RFU for 1962-63. His touch-judges were Captain H. A. Haigh-Smith (Barbarians) and Major E. L. Thompson (Harlequins). Captain of the Union XV was Robin Prescott, who became secretary of the RFU in 1963, while another forward, Bob Weighill, succeeded him as secretary from 1971 to 1986. Billy Davies had been selected as captain of the League XV but injury caused him to drop out and that supreme honour fell to Trevor.

The game drew a crowd of between 13,000 and 15,000, who contributed about £1,500 to services charities. It was a memorable occasion but the game did not quite match expectations. George T. Thompson wrote: "As a Rugby Union game, the match at Odsal was good; to regular followers of the Rugby League code it cannot have been too attractive". *The Times* reported: "The football ... was good by fits and starts" and was of the opinion that "the League were a trifle lucky to snatch a [15-10] win" although it acknowledged that "where the League were masters was in quick starting, instantaneous formation and regrouping when the wing's way was blocked".

By the interval the Union XV led 10-0 through tries from Doug Phillips, who became a fellow rugby league Lion with Trevor in 1946, and Tom Gray, who converted both. The League XV had the better of the second half and drew level with tries from Ike Owens and Johnny Lawrenson, both improved by Ernest Ward. Three minutes from time, the crowd got the result they craved, when Bradford-born Stan Brogden scored and Ward converted a try, which the *Yorkshire Post* described as "good enough to win any game". The 34-year-old Brogden had been the star of the show but Trevor had also shone along with Ward, Harry Royal, Ike Owens, Dennis Murphy and Bill Chapman. On the Union side Frank Trott, Gray, Tanner and the 37 year-old Simpson had done well behind a pack whose outstanding performers were Prescott, Phillips and Duncan Shaw.

1944-45

By the summer of 1944 the war had turned in favour of Britain and the Allies. Normandy was invaded in June and in August Paris was liberated. On the Eastern Front the Russians were driving Hitler's armies back toward the Fatherland and in the Far East the Japanese were now fighting a losing series of battles.

There was good news for professional rugby league players as well. The RFL agreed that the 25 shillings for a win and 15 shillings for a defeat flat rates should be abolished and clubs could now set their own rates. Just what difference that would make at Dewsbury, where it was common knowledge that their manager Eddie Waring had been paying his guest stars much more for years, was a moot point, as it assuredly was at some other clubs. For Trevor, it was to be of little import because by January 1945 he had played his last wartime game for Northern and was preparing for service overseas.

Since qualifying as a PTI Trevor had spent the last few years at various locations, mostly in the West Riding. He recalls: "After finishing at Harrogate, I was stationed at Headingley, at the ground, in fact. We were in digs in houses around the stadium and used to take the troops on cross country runs around Headingley. Once I got told off by the Leeds secretary who said we were ruining their grass.

After that I was stationed in Bradford in Manningham Lane at the Ice Rink, which is now Pennington's. It was a recruiting centre and I was put in charge of the incoming recruits. It was towards the end of the war, so we were scraping the barrel for manpower. Some of the recruits came from prison or were men who were trying to dodge service. Each morning we would march some of them along Manningham Lane, some in handcuffs, to appear before the Company Commander for one reason or another. He was often threatened and attempts were sometimes made to injure him as he sat at his desk. Lots of them were sent to us at the Rink to try to instil some normal behaviour into them. It was not easy.

Another aspect of my duties involved working at Pinderfields Hospital in Wakefield. Wounded and injured troops were brought there and sometimes I would watch knee operations and such things. It was part of my job to give these soldiers remedial exercises and get them back to fitness. It was a rewarding and interesting task. I also spent some time at a convalescent home in Nun Monkton, a nice little village near York, doing similar work. I often used to bring the recovering soldiers to watch games at Odsal."

Northern began the 1944-45 campaign on 2 September by losing 2-0 at Hunslet, but quickly made up for that disaster by winning eight games in a row. Trevor was in fine fettle and was soon back in representative action. First on his list was a game for Northern Command against a Rugby League XIII at Fartown on 7 October, where his team went down 27-23 to a side which contained three particularly promising young backs in Bryn Knowelden, Albert Johnson and Willie Horne, all of whom would join Trevor on tour in 1946.

On 21 October he was a leading figure in the Army's 24-8 victory over South Wales at Swansea. One report ran: "Always in the picture were Trevor Foster and E. Jones, the Army's wing forwards. Both played great games, with Foster outstanding. He fitted in perfectly with [half-backs] Tanner and Risman". Trevor scored a try in both halves.

On 4 November at Coventry, Trevor played for the last time in an Army versus RAF fixture. *The Times* described it as "one of the best games of the war". It was played at a furious pace and by the close the Army were relieved to have won 18-15, having led 6-0 at half-time. Trevor claimed a try in the second half. According to *The Times*: "The Army had the advantage in the scrummages and Phillips and Foster were outstanding in the open". Again the Risman-Tanner half-back partnership was in brilliant form.

Three weeks later Trevor appeared at Swansea in his last Services International and his final rugby union match in Wales. Risman captained Wales and was absolutely in a class of his own, as Wales romped home 28-11 before a happy crowd of more than 20,000. Trevor signed off with a trademark try, one report noting: "Trevor Foster again proved his class as a wing-forward. He played a leading part in numerous constructive moves".

While Trevor was busy playing rugby union, Bradford Northern were leading the War Emergency League, not having lost a match since the opening day. They had, however, been knocked out of the Yorkshire Cup in November in the second round by Halifax. Through December Trevor led Northern to five victories, the last of which, a 48-0 home success against Keighley on Boxing Day, brought him his last two tries of wartime rugby league. It was also Northern's 13th straight league win.

New Year's Day, 1945 saw Trevor in recently liberated Paris, where the British Army took on a French XV at the Parc des Princes. The British Army put out a very powerful team. Risman and Tanner were the halves and there were league backs of the calibre of Ernest Ward and Syd Williams, while one of the wingers was Cyril Butler Holmes of Manchester University, a sprinter who had represented Great Britain at the 1936 Berlin Olympics. Apart from Trevor, the pack contained Wales rugby union hooker Bunner Travers, one of Trevor's great friends and former team-mate at Newport, Doug Phillips and Robin Prescott, who captained the side. The

French, who had recently lost 26-6 to the RAF, completely re-jigged their XV. At first sight it seemed that there was not much doubt that the British Army team would win.

There was a slippery surface and by half-time the French were 8-0 ahead, their centre Jean Dauger outshining everyone on the field. Even a wonderful 50 yard try from Risman was of little use as the French eventually won 21-9. The game had been a bit rough and ragged but the Frenchmen fully deserved their unexpected victory. Trevor and his team-mates became aware as the second half progressed that something was affecting the crowd, which had nothing to do with what was happening on the field. Apparently, rumours had begun to circulate that the Germans had launched a determined counterattack and were advancing westwards again. It was certainly true that for a couple of weeks prior to the Paris match the Germans had opened a new offensive through the Ardennes.

Whatever the true situation was, the members of the British Army XV were quickly spirited away after the game to the barracks where they had been billeted, only to discover that they would have to stay overnight, at least, in France, because all flights had been cancelled. Fortunately, the emergency blew over and the Army boys were soon back in England. It was a sharp reminder that the war was not yet over.

Five days after the Parisian jaunt, Trevor was in the Bradford team which finally lost a league game, 6-11 at Huddersfield. It was his 13th game of the season for Bradford and his last of the season. He did, however, make one more appearance at Odsal on 3 February, playing rugby union and leading Northern Command to a 14-11 win over a combined Royal Australian Air Force and South African Services XV.

On 10 February Trevor crossed the Irish Sea for a third time to play for the British Army against the Irish XV at Ravenhill. The 20,000 Belfast crowd witnessed a stern struggle. Risman opened the scoring after 20 minutes with a penalty but by half-time the Irish led 5-3. On the hour Risman kicked a second penalty and the only other score was a late try by the Army winger Knowles. G. Lees of Gala and Trevor were picked out as the best of the Army's forwards. The 9-5 victory effectively ended Trevor's career as a rugby union player in Britain. His next games of rugby would be in far different climes.

Trevor recalls: "Towards the end of my Army service, I was posted overseas. The war looked like ending and they wanted Army Physical Training staff to go out to look after soldiers before they got demobbed. We were required to promote games of all descriptions. I was sent by sea to Port Said, near Cairo in Egypt. We were then sent up to Palestine just to get acclimatised and I was eventually posted to the great barracks in Cairo itself. It's funny because one of the first men I met there was Vincent Dilorenzo, our old hooker at Bradford. We had a wonderful year in the sunshine together organising games – football, swimming, boxing, anything you could think of. Vincent was just a Gunner in the Royal Artillery but he had a lot of influence out there because he had been organising a lot of the rugby for two or three years. He was well known to all the officers. Even Brigadiers would ask him for advice. All the sections wanted him and the rugby that was promoted was really very good. Of course, only rugby union was allowed. I also ran into another Bradford forward there, Frank Mugglestone.

There was a lot of boxing too, which I was involved with because I was in charge of PT in my regiment. We had half-a-dozen young boxers who became champions in their own right. We held a contest between our boys and the Egyptian boys and this was well supported. We had a top class boxing team, who were under my jurisdiction as PT assistant instructors. Once when they needed another contest on the bill, I was asked if I would box. I agreed and fought a Bombardier from the Royal Artillery before a great crowd of servicemen and Egyptians. We went four rounds and I won on points."

Trevor played rugby at locations such as Gezira, Almaza, Cairo and Alexandria. He played for Royal Artillery, Almaza and represented the Cairo Area against the Canal Area. The highlights of his Egyptian days were a series of Middle East international matches for Wales against South Africa (8 December 1945), England (16 December) and New Zealand (23 December), in all of which he captained the side.

Undoubtedly the hardest fixture was the South Africa game at the Alexandria Municipal Stadium. The South Africans were a formidable team and Wales's prospects did not look at all good, when after only 13 minutes they lost their wingman, Walters, who sustained an eye injury falling against a stone kerb near the touchline. Trevor drove his seven-man pack to great heights, a reporter writing: "Foster rallied his men, and the whole side responded nobly". South Africa missed seven penalties in the first 32 minutes, five given against Trevor, whose eagerness to stifle play led him to stray offside. In the 11th minute Trevor won possession at a line-out and created a try for prop forward Evans. A converted try after 33 minutes by centre Williams extended the lead to 8-0 at the break. Williams kicked a magnificent penalty and it was 11-0, against all odds. A try to South Africa followed, but Trevor led a terrific rush into South Africa's quarters and "during a loose maul Foster intercepted a pass and ran through to score while several 'Boks stood still, under the impression that there had been an infringement". At 14-3 the game was won but South Africa did manage to add eight points in the last six minutes against a tiring but heroic band of Welshmen.

On 17 December 1945 Staff Officer for Physical Training, Middle East Forces, A. L. Semmence penned the following testimonial for 4694054 S/SI Foster TJF: "Since his arrival in the Middle East in April 1945 Staff Sergeant Instructor Foster has been employed as a PT Instructor. A rugby player of international standard, he is very modest concerning his achievements. His quiet, effective manner has made him both liked and respected amongst the Officers and men of the Unit with which he served. I have found him a thoroughly reliable, trustworthy and responsible NCO, at all times willing. He has a good capacity for organisation of games and sports. I regard S/SI Foster very highly both as a PT Instructor and as a soldier. He has served the APTC well and I have no hesitation in saying that he will give of the same service in civil life".

A month or so later Trevor was back in England, receiving his release leave from the Military Dispersal Unit at Hereford on 23 January 1946. He was back in Blighty, a great adventure over and another about to unfold.

Wartime rugby:
Top: Trevor meeting the Earl of Harewood before making his debut for the
Wales rugby league team against England at Odsal in December 1939.
Below: 1942: In action for Wales against England at Swansea – playing rugby union.
Haydn Tanner passing, flanked by Trevor on his left, and Ike Owens on his right.
(Photos: Courtesy Trevor Foster)

Top: In action as a PT instructor in the Army
Below: Northern Command versus Scottish Command – 1941 rugby union at Headingley
(Photo: Courtesy Trevor Foster)

Wartime Services Rugby Union: Army versus RAF 1944: Trevor, Ernest Ward, Roy Francis and Jim Stott – all rugby league players in the Army side, before the game at Richmond.
(Photo: Courtesy Trevor Foster)

SOUVENIR PROGRAMME

NORTHERN COMMAND REPRESENTATIVE
RUGBY MATCH

(Under the patronage of Lt. Gen. Sir T. R. EASTWOOD,
K.C.B., D.S.O., M.C., G.O.C. in C. Northern Command)

UNION XV

VERSUS

LEAGUE XV

(Under Union Rules)

at

Leeds R.L. Football Club Ground

Headingley

(By kind permission of the Directors)

on

Saturday, January 23rd, 1943

Kick off 3-30 p.m.

ORGANISED BY THE NORTHERN COMMAND
SPORTS BOARD.

Left: Programme from the 1943 cross-code match
(Courtesy Robert Gate)
Above: 1944 Army rugby union sevens at Headingley: Rugby League VII versus Welsh Command VII. Trevor had to miss the first leg of the Challenge Cup Final to play in this tournament – on orders! (Photo: Courtesy Trevor Foster)

5.   The 1946 Lions tour

Trevor's military service meant that he did not play rugby league for more than a year. After appearing in Northern's 11-6 loss to Huddersfield at Fartown on 6 January 1945, he did not play again until 2 February 1946, when he took his place in the second row alongside Laurie Roberts in an 18-11 win against Workington Town at Odsal. Typically, Trevor celebrated with a try in Northern's first ever encounter with the fledgling Cumberland team.

He had returned to action just in time to stake a claim for a Lions place on the 1946 Australasian tour. The RFL had made an astonishingly quick recovery from the rigours and restrictions of wartime operations and on 24 October 1945 its Council had voted 19-4 in favour of undertaking a tour the following summer. It was a brave decision for there was great concern that a full-strength party might not be available because so many men were still in the services, overseas and at home. The Australian Minister for External Affairs, Dr Herbert Evatt, came to England in September 1945, empowered by the Australian Rugby League to organise a tour and helped to dismiss the idea that such fears should hold sway by pointing out that Australia themselves would not be up to their pre-war standards.

On 30 January 1946 a tour trial took place at Wigan, but no Bradford Northern players were involved. A second tour trial was arranged for Headingley on Wednesday 20 February with Trevor selected as loose-forward for the White XIII against the Colours XIII. None of the England players who were to play France at Swinton three days later were included in the tour trial. It was suggested in the press that men such as Trevor and the Dewsbury full-back Jimmy Ledgard "have only to play well today to make themselves reasonably sure of a tour team place". However, this came true for Trevor, but not for Jimmy, who was reported to have performed well and who had also played in the trial at Wigan. The match was played in four quarters because of a numbingly cold and violent gale. Trevor and Halifax's Chris Brereton were reckoned to be the game's outstanding forwards, both grabbing tries as the Whites won 18-14. Harry Sunderland's pithy report described Trevor "as clever as ever".

The tour party was announced on 11 March and Trevor was thrilled to be included. He would probably have gone in 1940 and would certainly have been selected in 1944. By 1946 he was 31 years old, although the newspapers were under the impression that he was 29, an impression Trevor was happy to maintain. Until recently, most record books gave Trevor's date of birth as 1916, not 1914. Five of his Bradford colleagues were also in the party and a record 11 of the Lions were Welshmen. The party, captained by Gus Risman, comprised:

Full-backs: Martin Ryan (Wigan) and Joe Jones (Barrow).
Wingers: Arthur Bassett (Halifax), Eric Batten (Bradford Northern), Albert Johnson (Warrington) and Jim Lewthwaite (Barrow).
Centres: Jack Kitching (Bradford Northern), Bryn Knowelden (Barrow), Gus Risman (Salford - captain), Ernest Ward (Bradford Northern) and Ted Ward (Wigan).
Stand-offs: Billy Davies (Bradford Northern) and Willie Horne (Barrow).
Scrum-halves: Dai Jenkins (Leeds) and Tommy McCue (Widnes - vice-captain).
Props: Ken Gee (Wigan), Fred Hughes (Workington Town) and Frank Whitcombe (Bradford Northern).
Hookers: George Curran (Salford) and Joe Egan (Wigan).
Second-row: Trevor Foster (Bradford Northern), Bob Nicholson (Huddersfield), Doug Phillips (Oldham) and Les White (York).
Loose-forwards: Harry Murphy (Wakefield Trinity) and Ike Owens (Leeds).

Trevor and his compatriot Doug Phillips were reckoned to be the likely test second-row pairing but would be under severe pressure from White and Nicholson, who were tremendous players in their own right.

Under the squad numbering system Trevor was allotted the number 24 jersey. Unlike modern players, who seem to have access to unlimited amounts of playing equipment, the 1946 Lions were expressly required by their tour agreements, in clause (e) "to be responsible for all jerseys and other football outfit provided by and to be regarded as the property of the <u>Council</u> and under no circumstances to give any jersey away"!

Among the other undertakings specified in the tour documents Trevor and his fellow tourists agreed to:

(a) Complete the tour and return to England;

(b) Obey and fulfil every order given by the managers or either of them;

(c) Act in the capacity of checkers if and when required;

(d). Act as trainers when not required to play and generally to assist the managers in every possible way to the best of their skill and ability; and

(f) Behave themselves in a gentlemanly way both on and off the field and to take every precaution to prevent themselves from losing form and to make every effort by judicious training to retain their form and to make the tour a success from a playing point of view.

As a single man Trevor's weekly tour terms were "30 shillings (British currency - £1.50 today) while at sea and 50 shillings (Colonial currency - £2.50 today) while on land during the continuance of the tour and prior to leaving Australia or New Zealand for England the sum of £20 (British currency)". Married men were given the same but their wives received £3 per week throughout the tour plus seven shillings and sixpence (37.5p today) per child. In addition the players would receive equal shares in one third of any tour profits – invariably a considerable sum.

The RFL instructed the players to be ready to sail on 1 April, but the difficulty in obtaining shipping passages could not be overstressed. Australia House wrote to the RFL saying that getting a rugby league team to Australia was not a high priority because thousands of Australian military personnel had a higher rating. In the event, the tourists were fortunate when they were told on 21 March that they would sail for the Antipodes on 4 April. Even then there was a problem because there were three serving soldiers in the party – Ernest Ward, Les White and Doug Phillips. At first the Minister for War declared that they would be allowed to tour, but on 25 March leave was refused for White and Phillips but nothing was relayed about Ward. Bob Robson (Huddersfield) and Eddie Watkins (Wigan) were selected to replace them, but after representations were made to the War Office by a number of West Riding Members of Parliament the full trio was finally given clearance.

There were a few eyebrows raised in relation to the tour selection, particularly because only 11 forwards were to be taken instead of the usual 12. Taking an extra back was considered by many to be a big risk, when only five front-row forwards – physically probably the most draining of positions – were included. George Curran, who often played prop, was the only alternative hooker to Joe Egan.

On Trevor's departure he received a note signed by Harry Hornby, Bradford Northern's managing director, which read: "A happy journey, a happy time whilst you are away, and the happiest of welcomes awaiting you when you return. From all at Odsal".

The tour managers were Bramley's Walter Popplewell, a market gardener in Churwell, Leeds, who had been a manager on the 1936 tour, and Barrow's Wilf Gabbatt, an engineer and manager of Barrow-in-Furness Corporation Gas and Water Works. Gabbatt was the business manager while Popplewell was more involved with the playing and selection side of the tour. Popplewell had been chairman of the Rugby League Council in 1932-33 and had been succeeded in 1933-34 by Gabbatt. They were men of some gravity, who experienced very little worry from the 26 energetic young men under their charge. Trevor described them as "good organisers, who looked after us very well".

There were four other members of the party too. Walter Crockford went on the expedition as a paying guest. A fish merchant in Hull, he was Hull KR's representative on the Rugby League Council and would become its chairman in 1947-48. And for the first time British journalists accompanied a Lions tour, three venturing where none had been before. Ernest Cawthorne of the *Manchester Evening News* and Alfred Drewry of the *Yorkshire Post* were experienced and respected rugby league men, whose cabled reports back to Lancashire and Yorkshire kept friends, relatives and an eager rugby league public well informed of the great adventure that the 1946 Lions tour became.

The third member of the press was Eddie Waring, who would eventually become more famous than any of the men whose deeds he reported. Eddie, entrepreneurial, full of enthusiasm and affable, was the correspondent for the *Sunday Pictorial*, the *Yorkshire Evening Post* and, under various other guises, for a few other journals. Trevor recalled that "Eddie became a good friend to all the tourists. He was a wonderful character, outstandingly good at organising people. He would get the players together and they would chew the fat with him and Eddie would get his stories, his exclusives, to send back home. He was a players' man, no doubt about that." On returning to England, Eddie conducted a series of lectures on his grand tour and in 1947 produced a 128 page account of the 1946 Lions trip entitled *England to Australia and New Zealand*.

Trevor had experienced a great deal over the preceding six years. His war service had taken him to the Middle East and his rugby exploits had seen him play all over England, Scotland, Ireland, Wales and France but he was now embarking on the experience of a lifetime. The 1946 tour was a genuinely epic journey. There had never been one like it and there never will be again.

Leaving for Australia

The Lions left Devonport on 3 April. The vessel which carried them was the aircraft carrier *HMS Indomitable*. Eddie Waring's first cable from the ship announced: "Two tons of Britain's best Rugby League footballers are now added to the 23,000 tons of the famous aircraft-carrier *Indomitable*. The team had a quiet send-off from Devonport with only the piping of the harbour ships to bid them farewell... History is being made by this mode of travel, and though vastly different to usual methods, the boys are settling down well. Risman, Jenkins, Batten, Owens and Foster are in the Admiral's office, and Davies, Whitcombe, Kitching and Ward are in the air intelligence office, practically on the flight deck. Foster said they had put Whitcombe there because they were frightened his 17 stones would sink the ship."

HMS Indomitable, commanded by Captain Andrews, was built in Barrow, an irony not lost on Wilf Gabbatt and the other local Barrow boys, Jim Lewthwaite, Bryn Knowelden and Willie Horne. Gabbatt was well satisfied with the ship's accommodation and in one of his own cables back to the *North-West Evening Mail* he reported: "The passengers are mostly returning service men. A fair number are leaving us at Malta, and others at Colombo. There is not a woman on board. This type of ship is not at all suitable for female passengers. The whole construction and design do not lend themselves to carrying women". There was also a contingent of six Irish priests on board.

Trevor had no complaints about the arrangements. He remembered: "The accommodation was very good. We were on hammocks or double-decked beds, like we had in the forces. They were quite comfortable. The food was great. We had been used to shortages of almost everything but there were no shortages on this trip. Fresh fruit and vegetables were available in vast quantities and things that you couldn't get hold of at home, like chocolate, were easily had. When we had the first evening meal on board the players ate in the officers' mess. We arrived early and ate everything before the old school-tie chaps arrived. They were not amused and we were quickly given a dining area of our own after that".

Once clear of the Bay of Biscay the weather turned hot and there was more or less wall-to-wall sun all the way to Australia, *HMS Indomitable* keeping up an average of 22 knots in remarkably calm waters. Stops were made at Gibraltar, although no one was let ashore there, Malta, Aden (now Yemen), where the Crown Prince paid a visit to the ship and brought gifts of fruit and coffee in appreciation of the troops' war efforts, and Colombo, the capital of Ceylon, now Sri Lanka. It took the *Indomitable* eight hours to navigate the 100 miles of the Suez Canal.

The journey to Australia enabled the players to relax after a hard season, to recover from nagging injuries, while at the same time providing them with excellent facilities to maintain fitness. Trevor's war-time PTI training came in useful. He says: "I was selected by the managers and Gus Risman to look after the physical training on the boat. It was my job to get the players up at seven in the morning, lead the PE sessions and run the lads around the boat until breakfast time. Getting people like Frank Whitcombe up wasn't much fun sometimes, I can tell you, although they all did take it in good part really. Frank and Ken Gee, our two big props, were quite ill at ease in those hot conditions and they weren't keen on running around. It seemed to affect them badly, probably because of their size. They would try to find a cool, shady corner to hide, where they could sit down and relax, hoping to get their breathing back to normal".

There was a big canvas swimming pool on board which was heavily used by the Lions, who were also able to play basketball in one of the hangars. One of the most energetic and occasionally rough pursuits was seven-a-side deck hockey, several games being played against the ship's crew. A tournament was held in which the Lions fielded several teams but was won by the ship's stokers, who were a pretty tough lot, knocking out one of the Lions VIIs and in the semi-final a team dubbed the Sky Pilots containing the Irish priests, who were also pretty rough, according to Eddie Waring.

After 29 days at sea the *Indomitable* reached Fremantle, the major port of Western Australia, where the Lions were scheduled to change ships for a further six-day voyage to Sydney. Immediately there was a problem. Another aircraft carrier, *HMS Victorious*, was scheduled to take the party, but had suffered severe damage en route through the Great Australian Bight. Five days were lost until the Admiralty back home instructed the *Indomitable* to disembark her passengers, embark the passengers from the *Victorious* and sail back to England. Joe Egan recalls: "We had to stay in Perth, with no accommodation, so we went into a service camp [Leenwin Naval camp] for a week until accommodation was found for us on the railway and that was a five day trip to Sydney."

Captain Andrews had suggested to the tour managers that a match should be played at Fremantle and so, on 30 April, Trevor turned out for a Blues team which lost to the Reds 24-5. Eddie Waring refereed and the ground collection - £44, plus 10 guineas given by the RFL – was donated to Naval charities.

The tourists finally left Leenwin on 7 May. They were assigned to a troop train, which was under Naval control for the 2,600 miles trip to Sydney. Wilf Gabbatt noted in his report to the RFL: "There were no facilities for sleeping on this train. Prior to departure a knife, fork, spoon and military blanket were issued to each person. We were ordered to keep our compartments clean and tidy. There were morning inspections by the Officer in Charge, and it is worthy of note that our party was congratulated by him upon the cleanliness of our quarters. The meals en-route were usually served alongside the railway at various points and eaten whilst sitting on the lines or sand, whilst the presence of flies did not add to the comfort of the situation. The food was served from boilers in front of which we were required to parade. As we approached Adelaide meals were taken in canteens at various points. The food was fairly good in quality, but lacking in quantity, and all found it necessary to make purchases to supplement that provided. An allocation of money was given to meet this extra unavoidable expense."

Eddie Waring declared: "no international touring team has ever travelled as frugally as the 1946 British rugby league team did." Ernest Cawthorne reported that "the five days journey from Perth has been nothing less than a nightmare, and all have been extremely critical of the arrangements made for us. On two nights there was no sleeping accommodation, and one had either to make a bed on the floor or rest as best possible in a sitting posture".

After crossing the seemingly interminable treeless and waterless Nullabar Plain of Western Australia and South Australia, taking in the great cities of Adelaide and Melbourne and myriad tiny, dusty settlements, Trevor and the Lions finally arrived in Sydney at 1.10pm on Sunday 12 May. Interviewed by Raymond Fletcher for the *Yorkshire Post* in 1994, Trevor reflected: "You would have thought we had arrived from heaven the way we were greeted. The media and public were in total awe of us, just as they are with the Aussies over here now. Players like Gus Risman, Ernest Ward, Eric Batten and Ike Owens were idolised wherever they went. Although the Australian public wanted to see us beaten, we were treated with great respect. It was a marvellous feeling. I suppose there was pressure on us because we were expected to win all the time, but I don't remember it being anything we couldn't cope with."

After their horrendous journey all most of the Lions wanted to do was go to bed. While in Sydney their headquarters were the Olympic Hotel in Paddington, which, according to Eddie Waring, was "not a salubrious district by any means, and the accommodation was so cramped that at one time there was talk of moving, as the 1936 tourists did." The advantage, however, as Trevor pointed out was that the hotel practically "overlooked the Sydney Cricket Ground. It was very convenient for us to come out of our little hotel and walk across to the training field. That was a great asset. There was also a Catholic church very near and that was nice for those of us like Joe Egan, Martin Ryan and myself who were Roman Catholics."

If the journey had been wearisome, the Australians soon made up for it with hospitality. Before a match had even been played, Arthur Morley of the *Daily Dispatch* cabled home: "The team is wondering whether they can fulfil all the social engagements arranged by the enthusiastic Australians, and still keep in condition. They have thus far attended four receptions, one ball, and one picnic, and face two official dinners, one ball and a three-day trip to the Blue Mountains in the near future."

On 18 May the Lions were among the 27,866 crowd at the Sydney Cricket Ground to watch New South Wales beat Queensland 24-6. Gus Risman kicked off the match. Portents of what would follow were evident as the Lions party were mystified at Australian versions of the play-the-ball, feeding the scrums and the insistence on awarding penalties for forward passes. Their feet were giving them trouble too, the Lions finding Australian turf harder than in England. They had not yet used aluminium studs, as the Aussies did, but had found that putting cotton wool inside their boots or wearing extra socks helped in training.

On Wednesday, 22 May the Lions played their first match against Southern New South Wales at Junee. Trevor shared the second-row duties with Doug Phillips. The population of Junee was around 5,000 but the attendance was 6,135, with people coming from far and wide. After a 10-hour train trip, it seemed that all the population was at the railway station to greet the Lions, who were soon sitting down with the mayor at dinner which consisted of "three pigs, turkeys, and other meats, with as much vegetables and sweets as they could safely tackle".

The match itself was a triumph. After going behind 2-0, Gus Risman became the first Lions scorer when he equalised with a penalty before half-backs Willie Horne and Tommy McCue brilliantly engineered the first try of the tour for Ernest Ward. The Lions' 36-4 victory gave the watching Australians plenty of food for thought. Full-back Martin Ryan particularly took the eye as he "caught everything on the field except the flies". The *Sydney Herald* writer was particularly impressed with the Bradford right wing pair of Ward and Eric Batten and considered the Lions "would find it hard to improve on the pack fielded at Junee" – Gee, Egan, Nicholson, Foster, Phillips and Owens.

Although it is hard to imagine now, the tour itinerary for the 1946 Lions was not finalised when they arrived in Australia and the New Zealand schedule was extremely vague. The second tour game at Canberra on 29 May had not been scheduled until a few days before it took place and it involved another six-hour train journey. Trevor did not play in a 45-12 success, which was a lot tougher than the scoreline suggested and there was some rough play. The Governor-General of Australia, the Duke of Gloucester was the chief guest. Trevor would meet him again less than a year later when he presented the Challenge Cup to Bradford Northern in their 1947 Wembley victory over Leeds.

The Canberra game was a disaster for loose-forward Harry Murphy who broke his collar bone in the first half and did not play again on tour. Harry had a superb physique and was already being considered "British football's Glamour Boy" by the Australian press. There was another blow when Bob Nicholson contracted pleurisy and became unavailable for the next dozen fixtures. The decision to take only 11 forwards on tour looked as if it might return to haunt the selectors.

On Saturday 1 June the first big game of the tour took place at the SCG where the Lions met New South Wales. It was regarded as a dress rehearsal for the first test and Trevor was paired with Les White in the second row, Doug Phillips having picked up a shoulder injury against Canberra. The British had finally decided to wear shoulder pads as protection against the hard grounds and some had sponge rubber or other padding on their hips. Queues had begun forming before dawn and by 10am there were 20,000 people in the ground for a 3pm kick off, the attendance ultimately reaching 51,364. A hard, gruelling game ensued. Just before half-time Trevor gave away a penalty and NSW stretched their lead to 7-0. A few minutes after the break the Lions trailed 10-0 when Lionel Cooper scored a try. A magnificent rally, however, brought the Lions back from the dead. Tries from Owens and Batten and four goals from Risman fashioned a 14-10 win and gave the Australian selectors much food for thought. This was the first time Trevor encountered Arthur Clues, a second-rower with footballing genius and a short fuse. Clues had scored the first try for NSW but Trevor's main memories of the match are of constantly being battered to the ground by Clues: "Every time I received the ball I was knocked for six by Arthur". Clues joined Leeds early in 1947 and he and Trevor became good friends, even if they were temperamentally completely different on the football field.

The very next day the Lions travelled to Wollongong for the first Sunday fixture Trevor ever experienced and it was a bad one. Britain, fielding seven of the men who had beaten NSW, crashed 15-12 to a South Coast Division XIII and lost another three men injured, in the days when no substitutes were allowed. Joe Jones, Fred Hughes and Trevor were all helped off, only Hughes managing to return. Trevor suffered a severe injury, recalling: "I felt really good that day, extremely fit and ready to take on the world. I was looking forward to playing in the first test match in Sydney. It was a rather innocuous tackle from the side, one of their forwards took me by surprise. I fell at an awkward angle and my left knee buckled under my weight as I hit the ground. I knew immediately that there was some serious damage. I could not straighten the leg and the knee swelled up like a balloon within a few seconds. For the first time in my career I had to be helped off. In the dressing room I was put on the table and was being looked at by the doctor. Then Eddie Waring burst in, carrying a sponge and a bucket of water, and started to try to soothe my knee. He just said: 'Trevor, you can't go back on with that. It's gone.' It was a bad injury all right. The diagnosis was water on the knee. That's what they used to call such injuries. Eddie immediately wired the English press, reporting that I had a bad injury and would be out for the rest of the tour. I was keen to play again soon, though, but I probably should have rested it more rather than trying to train."

That knee injury cost Trevor his place in all the Ashes tests and he did not reappear in a Lions line-up until Saturday, 13 July, when he was in the team which won 34-5 at Toowoomba. Trevor was reported to have "played a solid game, indicating that he has at last recovered from the muscle injuries which have kept him out of the greater part of the programme." The following Tuesday he scored his only try of the tour, one of 13 rattled up in a 53-8 romp against Northern Division at Grafton.

The Lions created history by going through the Ashes series undefeated and are still the only Great Britain team to have achieved that feat in Australia. All three games were marred by a dismissal but overall Australia were clearly inferior. Trevor's verdict was: "Britain were superior all round. We had a good, big pack and clever half-backs with lots of footballing ability. The Aussies were just below-par, good, honest workers. But they would fight to the last before they were beaten."

The first test at the Sydney Cricket Ground drew a massive crowd of 64,527 and ended in an 8-8 draw. However, Australia's limitations were clear for they had the advantage of an extra man for most of the game. Centre Jack Kitching, a Bradford school teacher, tackled the Australian captain Joe Jorgenson in the 28th minute and was sent off. Trevor says of the incident: "Jack was never a dirty player. I remember vividly that they were both on the floor and Jack punched Jorgenson. The referee arrived on the spot and said: 'Kitching, off!' Jack had to walk from the far end of the field. He was called all sorts of names and the Australian crowd booed him all the way. When he got into the dressing room he took off his shirt and pointed at his breast bone. There were bite marks on his chest and that's why he threw the punch. There was controversy in the papers for days on end and Jorgenson said he was going to sue Jack in the civil courts but that never came about."

The second test in Brisbane, at the Exhibition Ground, broke all attendance records for a sporting event in the city. Officially 40,500 paid to attend but another 10,000 or so gained illegal entry. Winger Arthur Bassett destroyed Australia with a hat-trick on his test debut as the Lions won 14-5. Hooker Joe Egan was sent off just before the end after a bout of fisticuffs with Arthur Clues. The victory meant that Britain retained the Ashes, having won them in England in 1937. The third test at back at the Sydney Cricket Ground was played before a crowd of 35,294 and emphasised Britain's dominance. Two tries by Bassett, plus touchdowns from George Curran and Ike Owens, with three goals from Risman and one from Ted Ward saw off Australia 20-7. The dismissal of Arthur Clues after 63 minutes for hitting Willie Horne did nothing to help the Australian cause.

Gus Risman told the press: "It has been a happy tour. I must pay tribute to England's wonderful forwards, who, facing adversity caused by injuries, did not complain of overwork. Some of our players are better now than when the tour started". Gus also caused controversy, telling J. C. Graham of the *Daily Dispatch*: "Compared with the standards revealed in my two previous tours, play in Australia has deteriorated 50 per cent. When the Australians found they couldn't outplay us in the tests they tried rough tactics. These methods were a great mistake, for you cannot produce good play by these means." Trevor confirmed this in 1994, saying:

"There was some nasty business. It was kill or be killed. The Australians would try anything to beat us and you had to stand your corner. If you didn't, they would take full advantage."

The Lions had played 20 fixtures in Australia, winning 16 and drawing one. Trevor had played only five games and scored a solitary try. He was hoping for better things in New Zealand.

The Lions had become used to flying in the latter part of the Australian leg of the trip. More horrendous railway journeys, often without sleeping accommodation, had been endured in Queensland and the tour managers had decided that enough was enough and arranged flights wherever possible, which boosted morale among the sorely-tried Lions. So it was decided that the Lions would fly to New Zealand at a cost of £30 a man. Consequently they flew 1,200 miles across the Tasman Sea to Wellington in three separate parties on 22, 23 and 24 July, their heavy equipment and baggage going by boat – a three-day journey. The flights took just short of seven hours.

From the perfect weather and bone hard grounds of Australia, the tourists experienced extreme amounts of wet weather and mud heaps masquerading as pitches in New Zealand. On 27 July Trevor was in the pack for the opening game against South Island at Christchurch, which was won 24-12. Winger Jim Lewthwaite scored a hat-trick and Eddie Waring's report for the *Yorkshire Evening News* said: "Les White played a fine game at loose-forward and was well supported by Nicholson and Foster." Two days later Trevor was not as happy because he was in the team beaten 17-8 by West Coast at Greymouth on a sodden pitch. The referee was not happy either and dished out 49 penalties, 23 to the Lions.

If he had been frustrated by lack of action in Australia, Trevor found himself busy in New Zealand. On 31 July he turned out in his third game in only five days against the Maoris at Wellington. The Lions were introduced to the Governor-General, Sir Bernard Freyberg, before the game. He must have been impressed by Trevor and his colleagues, who overcame an astonishing 22-0 penalty deficit to win 32-8, playing what spectators described as "easily the most brilliant football seen in Wellington for many years". For Trevor the game probably marked the high point of his form on tour. A New Zealand journalist wrote: "Outstanding English forward was T. Foster... He frequently broke through with the ball to start passing rushes and the ball would then travel through a chain of backs and forwards before the movement was completed. He was well supported by Curran and Egan." He added that the Lions "threw the ball about with reckless abandon, and they were seldom tackled ... Whereas the Maoris were weak on tackling, the English forwards, in particular, were deadly. They simply flattened their opponents and on the subsequent playing of the ball would kick it away from any Maori player."

Prior to their next game against Auckland on 3 August, the Lions were given a state reception. Trevor was not in the team which lost 9-7 under the most atrocious conditions imaginable. This time the penalty count was reduced to 16-6 against the Lions. On 7 August Trevor partnered Bob Nicholson in the second row at Huntley, where Britain hammered South Auckland 42-12. Albert Johnson claimed three of the Lions' 10 tries.

Only one test match was played against New Zealand. It took place at Carlaw Park, Auckland, on 10 August and Trevor at last made his debut in test rugby league – at 31 years of age, one of the oldest men to achieve that status. Unfortunately the playing area was once again a quagmire and heavy rain fell in the second half. The Lions again fell foul of the referee. The New Zealand full-back Warwick Clarke booted three penalty goals to give his side a 6-0 interval lead and added a fourth in the second half. Britain levelled at 8-8 through tries by Ernest Ward and Eric Batten, with Ward converting his own try. The Lions were the more polished side, but the conditions favoured the more rugged approach of the Kiwis, who stole the match when a touchline penalty attempt from Clarke bounced back from the bar and allowed the alert prop Bruce Graham to score a fluke of a try which was converted by Clarke. A 13-8 defeat was not the result Trevor had hoped for, but he had played well. One report ran: "Foster and Nicholson were the pick of the English forwards, with Davies, McCue and Johnson enterprising backs."

Trevor's view of the match is succinct: "It was a very poor type of football match with very little open play. The mud played the biggest part and the referee was tedious, forever blowing his whistle, which made the game a poor spectacle."

A final, unscheduled game was played two days later on the same ground against Auckland, who were defeated 22-9. Trevor did not play and most attention focused on Ernest Ward, who entered the game as the tourists' leading points scorer with 91. Ernest played brilliantly, kicking five goals, the last of which was a touchline conversion of a Jim Lewthwaite try. The referee blew for time after the ball crossed the bar and Ernest had made the century mark by the skin of his teeth.

Shortly before their departure from New Zealand, Trevor and the other Lions signed and submitted a letter to the Rugby League Council, which they handed to Wilf Gabbatt. It read: "The Council is well aware that, during this tour, considerable inconvenience has been caused to the whole party in travel and accommodation which would normally not have been incurred, involving everyone in extra expenses which have had to be met out of their own pockets. Clothes have been ruined and in some cases lost. The success of the tour, both financially and otherwise, was due in no small measure to the way players stood up to the gruelling without complaint and we feel that we are entitled to some measure of compensation." The Lions' plea fell on deaf ears, however, the Rugby League Council decided that the tour bonus of £123 per player was quite sufficient. The players had some grounds for taking their Oliver Twist stance. They had endured hardships and the tour profits had been eroded by the increase in travelling costs as the tour party chose to fly as the tour progressed.

The return home began on 14 August when the Lions left Wellington on *HMS Rangitiki* – "a lovely passenger liner", according to Trevor. This time they were to make a three week crossing of the Pacific Ocean to Panama, largely because the *Rangitiki* was taking about 40 GI brides - girls engaged to American service-men - to New York. They sailed through the Panama Canal but there was consternation, among the brides at least, when because of a dock strike in New York the *Rangitiki* was diverted to Halifax, Nova Scotia, where the girls were disembarked instead. The ship sailed from Halifax on 14 September and, after a sometimes rough crossing, finally docked at Tilbury on 22 September at 10pm.

There to meet the Lions were RFL Secretary Bill Fallowfield, W.H. Hughes, the Chairman of the RL Council and three other Council members Bob Anderton, Richard Lockwood and Bradford's Harry Hornby. A reporter, John B. Hughes, was there too, interviewing Gus Risman. He wrote: "As I spoke to Gus on the dismal dock-side of Tilbury, his 10 Welsh compatriots in the touring team were enchanting English ears by a fully harmonised rendering of the famous Welsh rugger song 'Sospan Fach'. German prisoners working on the quayside looked up and stared. They obviously wondered what weird war-song this was. One member of the touring party told me: 'The 11 Welsh boys sang this song all over Australia. Before long the English joined in. Then the Australians got to know it, and it became our touring anthem everywhere'."

Wales was the next place Trevor headed. Most of the Lions went straight back north but Trevor was keen to see his family again. He caught a train to Newport only to find that his mother had gone out. He recalls: "My sister told me mum was at the pictures at the Odeon. It was about half past six and I dashed to the Odeon. I got the manager to flash up a message on the screen: 'Mrs Foster. You are wanted outside, please. Your son Trevor is here after his trip to Australia'. Out came my mum. It was a great reunion, I can tell you."

Awaiting Trevor at his family home, the Church House pub in Newport, was a letter from the South Sydney club, dated 31 August. It offered him a contract worth £9 a game. South Sydney would also pay his fare as a migrant and give him £50 on arrival. It was signed by Souths' secretary George Ball, one of the great names in Australian rugby league and one of the club's founding fathers. Throughout the tour players had been approached by Sydney clubs and there had been reports of men who had definitely signed for one club or another. This was reflected in South Sydney's letter, which said: "As we have approached a number of the touring side it has been decided that we are prepared to sign on the first who accept the proposition and not necessarily all to whom we have written."

The Lions had certainly been impressed by conditions in Australia, but ultimately none signed. In fact the traffic was all the other way round, a host of Australians coming to England, including four of the Lions' test opponents in Arthur Clues who joined Leeds, Pat Devery and Lionel Cooper who both signed for Huddersfield and George Watt who was recruited by Hull.

So Trevor's great adventure came to a close. He had travelled 33,000 miles by all manner of transport, he had met Prime Ministers, State Premiers and Governor-Generals, and seen different ways of life. He had played some of the hardest rugby of his career and finally become a test player. The 1946 Lions had been a happy and successful group. Adversity had certainly helped to bind them and promoted a priceless team spirit and many playing and financial records had been broken.

Two wonderful appreciations of Trevor's part in the tour were accorded to him in his benefit brochure in 1955. Gus Risman wrote: "It is no exaggeration to say that he was the most popular member of the party. He never said a wrong word, and always offered a helping hand to other members of the party. Coming immediately after the war, it was a trip with plenty of trials and tribulations to tax any man's patience. Trevor would always come up smiling. I also played rugby union with him during the war. He was always the same, right on top of his game all the time, and could be relied upon always."

Lions hooker Joe Egan added: "There is an old saying – and a true one – 'You have to live with a person before you know him'. Living with Trevor for six months puts me in a position to say he was what the rugby league authorities would refer to as a perfect tourist. His character was at all times reflected on the field of play. None played the game as it should be played more than him."

6. A Wembley Cup Final trilogy

One of Trevor's greatest memories of his long involvement in the game is the 1947 Challenge Cup Final. Bradford Northern won the Cup on the club's first visit to Wembley in May, beating local rivals Leeds. Trevor recalls: "We had been considered second favourites, and it was my very happiest moment, walking up to the royal box to receive a winners' medal from the Duke of Gloucester and it was all down to the astute tactics of our team manager Dai Rees."

When Trevor stepped out onto the hallowed turf at the Empire Stadium, Wembley at precisely 2.50pm on Saturday 3 May 1947 to play in his first Wembley final for Bradford Northern against local rivals Leeds, he thought he had gone to heaven. Trevor had always dreamed of playing in a Rugby League final at Wembley. Now at the age of 33, having lifted the Challenge Cup as the captain of Bradford Northern when defeating Wigan over a two-legged final in 1944, he was at Wembley.

Trevor says: "I was up there in heaven, the feelings, the exhilaration was immense, it is difficult to describe the emotion I was feeling at that time. For a second I reflected on my mother and father, sisters and brothers, who would be listening at that very moment on the radio back home at The Church House in Newport. I know my father had a particular keenness to listen to this great event in my life. To cap it all that day, the band of the Welsh Guards greeted us onto the pitch." Bradford versus Leeds in a Challenge Cup Final, they don't come any bigger.

In 1946-47, one of Bradford's all time great teams had been assembled. Apart from Trevor, they had players such as winger Eric Batten, centre Ernest Ward, stand-off Billy Davies and huge Welsh prop Frank Whitcombe.

On the road to Wembley, Northern had defeated Salford 12-5 on aggregate, after losing the first leg 5-2; Huddersfield 8-0 at Fartown; Workington Town 10-3 at Odsal and then Warrington in the semi-final, 11-7 at Swinton. It had been a tough journey to the final.

Leeds, in one of their best ever seasons, had reached Wembley with victories over Barrow, Hunslet and Wigan before they swamped Wakefield Trinity 21-0 in the semi-final. Leeds did not concede a try on their road to Wembley.

The Leeds team

Trevor remembers the Leeds team: "One of my greatest adversaries was the legendary Australian second-row forward Arthur Clues. Arthur was playing in his first Challenge Cup Final, having arrived in England and signed for Leeds in the early New Year of 1947. He was the outstanding Australian forward in the series and a formidable opponent. He was very astute, uncompromising, athletic and had a tremendous will to win. Arthur had been the mainstay of the Leeds pack in the lead up to the final. He had been particularly to the fore in attack and also produced some fierce tackling that had knocked the stuffing and confidence out of opposing teams. Arthur was in his prime at 22 years old.

Playing alongside Arthur in the second row was Alf Watson who had made a remarkable recovery from his six years as a prisoner of war in Germany. Watson's speed and strength made him a power in the loose. I remember the Leeds props that day. One was Chris Brereton, who was one of the cleverest forwards with his hands in the league. He was the focal point of the Leeds short-passing game which had brought so much success. Dai Prosser played at open side prop. Dai was a very determined, strong and a vigorous player who took no prisoners. At hooker was Con Murphy. He was 38 years old, but kept himself extremely fit and his experience as a specialist hooker was invaluable. He could kick and handle with the best and was a Welsh rugby union international.

At loose-forward was the great Ike Owens. He was a powerful, menacing player with the speed of a three-quarter. Along with Arthur, he was considered to be one of the best forwards playing rugby league at that time. Ike was a Welsh league international.

Dai Jenkins was at scrum-half. He varied the tactics to suit the occasion and had an excellent understanding with Ike Owens and the Leeds stand-off Dickie Williams - the trio formed a dangerous midfield triangle. Leeds undoubtedly had one of the finest club packs in the country and boasted 10 international players in their Wembley team."

Northern at that time also had a useful pack. Vic Darlison at hooker was a product of the famous Featherstone Rovers nursery. Barry Tyler, who played in the second-row with Trevor, was from Coventry and had just been demobbed from the British Army. The loose-forward was Hagan Evans, recently recruited from Welsh rugby union. Trevor recalls: "Immediately after the match, having received his winners' medal, Hagan made a dash home by train to Llanelli. He was so proud of his medal and wanted to show it around the town".

Northern's team that day also included right winger Eric Batten, son of the legendary Billy Batten. Eric was a strong and fearless runner. Ernest Ward was the captain that day. He was a most accomplished all-round footballer, great tactical kicker in broken play and supreme goalkicker. The mercurial Billy Davies was at stand-off and at the peak of his form, aged 29. He was a Welsh rugby union fly-half before joining Bradford, and had been the outstanding and most exciting player on the road to Wembley.

Bradford Northern travelled south on the Thursday before the match. Preparation had gone well, the final training session focused on ball handling and defence.

Simple plan

Team manager Dai Rees, a master tactician had a simple plan which he revealed to the players at their Westcliffe-on-Sea training base. Trevor remembers: "As usual for the big games, Dai had carefully thought things through. We had to keep the ball away from the Leeds forwards at all times. When Northern had possession in any phase of play we were to move the ball wide. Scrum-half Donald Ward and stand-off Billy Davies would be acting half-backs and play-makers at all times. The idea was to tire the Leeds six by making them run wide to do their tackling and to keep them moving around. Leeds were keen to play their short-passing game particularly in the forwards. We were not to allow this to happen. The plan was to use the wide open spaces at Wembley to full advantage and counterattack whenever possible. We soon gained control of the match; the big Leeds pack became subdued. We managed to exert control in all areas of the field. I remember the Leeds props tiring significantly in the second half and Frank [Whitcombe] increasingly began to boss the scrums. Dai Rees's tactics had worked to a tee."

As well as being a major player in the Cup Final, big Frank Whitcombe played a significant part in getting the team safely to Wembley in time for the match on the big day.

It would have been easy to understand if Northern had been unnerved before they reached the stadium. For on their way to the game their coach driver became hopelessly lost on the outskirts of London and just could not find his way to Wembley. Northern were running late. It needed a man with nerves of steel to find a solution and Northern had one in giant prop Whitcombe. He held a heavy goods vehicle licence and the coach driver was eased out of his seat to make way for Frank, who had driven heavy lorries during the war. He got the team to Wembley Stadium in time for the match, although they were 30 minutes behind schedule.

Leeds kicked off as 6/4 favourites in front of a then record crowd for the Challenge Cup final of 77,605. The teams were:

Bradford Northern: G. Carmichael, E. Batten, J. Kitching, E. Ward, E. Walters, W. T. H. Davies, D. Ward, F.W. Whitcombe, V. J. Darlison, H. Smith, B. Tyler, T. J. F. Foster, H. Evans.

Leeds: H. E. Cook, A. T. Cornelius, G. M. Price, T. L. Williams, E. C. Whitehead, R. Williams, D. Jenkins, C. Brereton, C. D. Murphy, D. R. Prosser, A. Watson, A. Clues, I. A. Owens.

Referee: P. Cowell (Warrington).

Both sides fenced for an opening in the early minutes of the game and it took a full 27 minutes for the first points to arrive when Bert Cook landed a penalty for Leeds. Northern based much of their early play around keeping the Leeds pack quiet. This was no easy task and Northern had to rely on the counterattack following mistakes by Leeds or from receiving penalties. Fortunately the handling by the Northern side was slick and twice it looked as if winger Emlyn Walters would score but for some desperate Leeds defence.

Centre Jack Kitching threatened to put Northern ahead but was halted by a superb cover tackle from Leeds full-back Bert Cook. The game was poised on a knife-edge with Leeds 2-0 ahead and 40 minutes to decide the destiny of the Challenge Cup. The second half began with Trevor and Frank Whitcombe setting up some good attacking positions for Bradford. However, Leeds hit back and put the Northern line under pressure, but Bradford broke away in classic style with a try scored by Walters. The ball went through seven pairs of hands and featured a superb long pass from Kitching to Ward. Ward, one of the classiest centres around at that time, provided the opening. The conversion failed, but Northern had their noses in front at 3-2.

The next five minutes of the match were even more exciting. Leeds regained their lead from another penalty, this time from 40 yards out. Northern then attacked again and a long pass from Kitching was picked up by Bradford's skipper Ward who coolly dropped a goal from 30 yards, surprising team-mates and opponents alike. All had expected him to try to continue the passing movement, but the drop-goal had put Northern back ahead at 5-4.

The winning try

The last period of the match saw Northern camped in the Leeds quarter and the pressure paid off when Trevor, in acres of space and with the Leeds defence in disarray, strolled over for a try. He remembers: "I was just in the right place at the time – as luck would have it I was able to march over the try line unopposed". Ernest Ward recalled in *Rugby League Gazette*: "Five minutes from time a kicking duel between the respective full-backs saw Bert Cook make his only mistake of the match. He fumbled the ball close to his own line and at the same time he slipped, and Trevor Foster, who was standing up 10 yards away, trotted up, picked up the ball and casually placed it over the line for a try."

That try sealed the cup for Bradford and they were now 8-4 ahead with seconds remaining. At the final whistle the Northern players jumped in the air with delight. As well as the trophy itself the Bradford Northern stand-off Billy Davies picked up the Lance Todd Trophy after a masterful display at number six.

After lifting the cup from the Duke of Gloucester and doing a deserved lap of honour, Trevor recalls returning to the dressing room in jubilation: "Ernest put the cup down on the table in the middle of the dressing room. We were all elated and so very proud for what we had achieved both for the club and the city of Bradford. Harry Hornby, our chairman, was overwhelmed with joy. We stood for a few moments in silence to take in the enormity of the occasion. Dai Rees addressed us briefly with his congratulations on an excellent team performance. He said the super Leeds six had been out-thought and out-played by the superior Northern six. He also happened to mention that nobody had talked about payment. He said that we would be paid for our efforts. Later every player received £30. No one had thought for a second about the monetary reward. Nobody had asked about a fee for the match. It had never entered our heads at any time before, during or after the game. We would all have happily played for nothing to win the Challenge Cup and a winners' medal. There was an overwhelming feeling of togetherness among the team and back-room staff. All we wanted to do now was take the cup back home to our beloved Bradford and show it off to all the proud people there."

The *Yorkshire Observer* reported Northern's return home to Bradford. "An estimated 100,000 people, their faces beaming as brightly as if they themselves had been in the winning side at Wembley, gathered in Bradford Town Hall square and neighbouring streets to welcome the players on Monday evening after the match.

Many were wearing red, amber and black rosettes – some relics of Wembley, others newly bought from vendors on Monday afternoon – and many too, had red and amber streamers which were waved excitedly as the motor coach carrying the victorious team drew near."

The players left Westcliffe-on-Sea at about 9am on their long journey back to Bradford, and it was not until they reached Wakefield that they were recognised as the cup winners. At Gildersome, people waited patiently for the arrival of the coach, but as the party approached Bradford the crowds gradually increased. Wakefield Road was packed with people anxious to catch a glimpse of the victorious team. As cheers were heard from Bridge Street, the word was passed along: "they're here!" and the Bradford City Police Band struck up with: *See the Conquering Heroes Come* almost drowned in the deafening roar of welcome. Sitting on top of the coach, looking rather bewildered by the reception – the team had not anticipated such an enthusiastic welcome from so many people – were the players. In pride of place was the handsome cup, its red and amber ribbons streaming in the breeze. The sight of the cup brought cheer after cheer which continued – without diminishing – as the players left the coach one by one and mounted the steps to the platform where the Lord Mayor and Lady Mayoress of Bradford, Alderman and Mrs T. Clough, were waiting to greet them.

The Lord Mayor, after congratulating the team on its victory said they had shown the team spirit and sportsmanship which belonged to "every good man who plays the great game and above all you won by an excellent display of attacking football".

1948: Return to Wembley

The Challenge Cup win against Leeds had raised expectations at Odsal to a new high. There was an air of excitement which was very evident among the players, the backroom staff and not least the supporters. Trevor recalls: "To have experienced Wembley's twin towers for the first time and returned with the cup, brought home to the players the enormity of what we had achieved. We knew the club was on the brink of something great, there was a feeling of invincibility at that time, particularly in the big cup matches. However, we were soon brought down to earth. At the start of the 1947-48 season, our hopes of a second successive Wembley appearance were made to look pretty sick by our erratic early season form"

Five successive defeats was a disappointing start for Northern in their new role as Challenge Cup holders, but by the time the Cup came round again they were running into form.

So much so, in fact, that there were high hopes of a cup and championship double. Northern started their bid to retain the cup at Fartown and duly lost 6-2 in the first leg. But they made no mistake in the second leg, winning 15-2 at Odsal before a crowd of 33,000.

It was Wakefield away in the second round and the game ended in a 3-3 draw. The replay at Odsal attracted a crowd of 44,132 – then a record for any second-round tie and at the time the largest crowd to watch Northern at Odsal. Northern won despite losing the scrums heavily.

There was no hint of a replay in the third round for Northern ran riot against Oldham winning 30-0 and qualified for a semi-final against Hunslet at Headingley.

Northern beat Hunslet 14-7 in the semi-final watched by a crowd of 38,000. Bradford needed victory in their last seven league games to preserve their double hopes of winning the Championship and the Cup, and they rose to the task magnificently to qualify for a championship semi-final at Central Park against Wigan, who were due to be their Wembley opponents a week later.

Northern won 15-3 to reach the Championship Final, but Wigan were still favourites for Wembley and duly proved the bookmakers right, winning 8-3. The press maintained Northern had become stale and though they played much attractive football in the Final, they paid dearly for defensive lapses and failure to accept chances. Winger Alan Edwards scored for Northern in the first half, after Wigan winger Gordon Ratcliffe dropped a kick, but they trailed 5-3 at half time. A last minute try by Frank Barton confirmed Wigan's win.

No one played better for Northern in the final than the massive prop Frank Whitcombe, who was over 18 stones. While colleagues were floundering and unable to take their passes, he joined in to provide his famous Herculean bursts and put in long kicks to touch in wide open spaces that others seemed to ignore. The final was the first attended by a reigning monarch, King George VI enjoying the spectacle. The teams were:

Bradford Northern: W. Leake, E. Batten, D. Case, E. Ward, A. S. Edwards, W. T. H. Davies, D. Ward, F. W. Whitcombe, V. J. Darlison, H. Smith, B. Tyler, T. J. F. Foster, K. Traill.
Wigan: M. Ryan, G. W. Ratcliffe, E. H. Ward, E. J. Ashcroft, J. Hilton, C. R. Mountford, T. Bradshaw, K. Gee, J. Egan, F. Barton, L. White, W. Blan, W. Hudson.
Referee: G. S. Phillips (Widnes).

The attendance was a world record 91,465, paying £21,121. The cup was lost, but Northern still had the chance to lift the championship and a week later they met Warrington at Maine Road in the final. But the Lancastrians won the day 15-5 and Northern, so close to the game's two major trophies, had to be content with one – the Yorkshire League Trophy.

Trevor comments: "While the Championship Final defeat was a great disappointment, we had never really recovered mentally from the Cup Final loss against mighty Wigan. All our efforts that season had been geared towards another Wembley win.

Wigan had been the masters at Wembley; their hooker and my great pal [from the 1946 Lions Tour], Joe Egan led them magnificently, his rugby brain dictated their positional play and he used their prop Ken Gee to maximum effect. Ken and our own prop Frank Whitcombe were locked in a titanic battle, like rhinos they charged and counter charged. Frank was a deserved winner of the Lance Todd Trophy.

I recall Wigan taking the lead early in the game when a harmless kick through was unusually fumbled by Eric [Batten], Jack Hilton pounced on it and was over in a flash. We were on the back foot from that point.

Constant rain for two days before the final made the turf very slippery, we made too many unforced errors on the day.

There was a quite remarkable try from Wigan which reminds me now of the Leeds versus Wakefield Trinity Watersplash final in 1968. Wigan's second-row forwards Len White and Billy Blan dribbled the ball between them, soccer style right up the field and Frank Barton dropped on the ball over the line."

When the 1948-49 season opened, centre Jack Kitching, who had missed the 1948 final because of injury, had left the club to join newly-formed Whitehaven, but George Carmichael, who had twice announced his retirement, was back in training.

A newcomer to the club was Welshman Bill Jenkins, signed after appearing in trials the previous season as 'Jenkinson'. Another Welshman, forward Brian Radford arrived at Odsal in the December and Kitching returned to the club after his brief spell at Whitehaven in time for another tilt at Wembley.

Despite having won the Yorkshire Cup, Northern's form had not been all that impressive, but the smell of Wembley again brought the best out of the side and by the time the first round arrived they were also challenging again for a top four place.

True to form they lost in the first leg of the first round 4-3 against St Helens – but a 5-0 away win in the second leg set them heading for the unique record of three successive Wembley finals.

Castleford were beaten 11-5 in the second round at Odsal in a match remembered more for the conditions than the play. A snowstorm raged throughout and obliterated the line-markings; two players – Northern's Ron Greaves and Castleford captain Storey – were sent off and at one point a Castleford player simply found the conditions too much and collapsed.

Belle Vue Rangers, who had the tag of giant-killers that season after beating Warrington, were the third round opponents and went near to slaying the giants, but Northern scraped home 8-7 and then had no trouble accounting for Barrow 10-0 in the semi-final at Swinton. Trevor comments: "Before the semi-final Ernest Ward took some time out to watch Barrow. He took special note of the clever touch-kicking, mainly the rolling grubber kicks of Willie Horne, Barrow's test half back. When the semi-final arrived Ward had one of our wingers standing close up to intercept the kicks and Ernest, with majestic, high, bouncing kicks to the open side corner flag, repeatedly drove back Barrow's most promising attacks." Bradford Northern were at Wembley again – despite being written off earlier in the season as a team of 'old men'.

A third final

And so the record was set and the last final in the trilogy was the game against Halifax. In it, Trevor was to score a try, skipper Ernest Ward to earn the Lance Todd Trophy and Frank Whitcombe was to be hugely influential once again.

But the question pundits and supporters were asking before the game was: 'Would Northern, whose average age was 31, be able to maintain the pace? Would Halifax, a team in their 20s show more endurance?'

Bradford Northern made history by appearing in the Challenge Cup Final for the third successive year. The attendance of 95,050, with receipts of £22,000, was a new world record for a rugby league game.

The victory was also a personal triumph for team manager Dai Rees, who made his fourth visit to Wembley – one as captain of the victorious Halifax side in 1931, and three times with Northern. His team-building policy over a period of 12 years with Northern had produced some of the best talent in the game. Amazingly, the team personnel for the Halifax final would be almost the same as that of the previous cup finals. Dai's involvement with both clubs brought added spice to the eagerly anticipated West Yorkshire derby.

Dai played his master card in the 1949 final, although he would later admit it was a gamble. It involved that genial forward, Frank Whitcombe, now a huge 18 stone 6 pounds, and the heaviest man ever to appear at Wembley. Frank had not played a game since January; indeed he was close to calling it a day as a player. He had, since his last match, become licensee of the King's Head in Westgate, Bradford. Before that he had been at the Hallfields Hotel in Trafalgar Street. Later he would move to the Airedale Heifer at Sandbeds near Keighley. His untimely death at the age of 42, in 1958, shocked the rugby world.

After Frank's death, Trevor spent several years supporting his widow Doris and her sons Brian and Frankie on busy Saturday nights at the family pub near Keighley. Trevor was a natural at pulling pints and exchanging rugby stories with the regulars, having grown up as the son of a licensee in Newport.

So it was Whitcombe, self-appointed minder to the frail-looking stand-off and fellow Welshman Billy Davies, to whom Rees turned to give him the weight in the pack and hold the opposition at Wembley in 1949.

Halifax had managed to unsettle themselves, without any help from Rees, by mixing up meal arrangements on their train and arriving in London without having had dinner. They were to spend the Friday at a hotel in Weybridge and to announce their team during the day. Northern, experienced Wembley campaigners by now, unveiled their side earlier. The Duke of Edinburgh was to be the chief guest. Royalty had attended all three Bradford finals. The teams for the big match were:

Bradford Northern: W. Leake, E. Batten, J. Kitching, E. Ward, A. S. Edwards, W. T. H Davies, D. Ward, F. W. Whitcombe, V. J. Darlison, R. Greaves, T. J. F. Foster B. Tyler, K. Traill.

Halifax: D. Chalkley, A. H. Daniels, P. J. Reid, G. M. Price, E. McDonald, G. Kenny, S. Kielty, M. J. Condon, A. Ackerley, J. W. Rothwell, D. Healy, J.S. Pansegrouw, F. Mawson.

Referee: G. S. Phillips (Widnes)

With the exception of prop Ron Greaves, every member of Bradford's side had played in a Wembley final before. Nerves were not much in evidence as the players left their Guildford hotel on the Friday for a day at the seaside. The players who travelled but were not picked – Gwylfa Jones, Brian Radford, George Carmichael, Emlyn Walters, Herbert Smith and Bill Jenkins – hid their disappointment, congratulated their pals and remembered that not only a team effort, but a club effort, was needed.

Meanwhile a large slice of the West Riding was mobilising itself, while in the capital the transport operators were preparing to receive them. On Saturday morning 35 special trains left Yorkshire for Kings Cross. The regular services were also booked solid. Hardier and thriftier souls caught the dozens of coaches to make the long journey. In those pre-motorway days London could be up to eight hours away, even more in bad weather.

Some, armed with thermos flasks and sandwiches wrapped in waxed paper which had once contained a sliced loaf, caught coaches running non-stop to Wembley without a meal break. Those set on merriment gave the thermos flasks a miss and loaded up with beer bottles, many labelled with long-gone, but fondly remembered names: Hey's, Hammond's, Melbourne and Bentley's for the Bradford contingent; Ramsden's and Whitaker's for the Halifax travellers.

In London the Bakerloo and Metropolitan lines put on a joint service which aimed to despatch a tube train to Wembley every one-and-a-half minutes. London trolleys were even more ambitious – a 45-second wait between buses was the hope. London Transport did its level best, and by a combination of goodwill and makeshift plans, Wembley Stadium welcomed 95,050 spectators – on a dampish day.

Northern were favourites to win. The form book and experience were on their side. To reach Wembley, Halifax had beaten Hull, after losing the first leg in the first round 4-0, dispatched Swinton 5-0 and Oldham 7-2, and then scraped past Huddersfield 11-10 in the semi-final, in front of 64,250 fans at Odsal. But tragedy had overshadowed their trip to Wembley – the week before they beat Swinton, winger David Craven had died following a collision in a match at Workington.

And win Northern did, though Halifax made it difficult. The points feast which Northern followers had been expecting and hoping for was not served up.

Dai Rees's Whitcombe gamble paid off. The giant prop dominated the Halifax forwards in the scrums. The Northern pack never looked like being beaten and much of the game was played in Halifax territory. But the backs, led by captain Ernest Ward, looked a little listless. Passes were fumbled and sometimes the centres tried to take a closed route though the opposition when a more original approach might have been more fruitful.

The dropped passes were part of a small controversy which had been going on for a few weeks. Brand new rugby balls were harder to handle than those which had been through a couple of matches. And indeed the ball which was placed on the centre spot at the start was less than pristine, having been kicked around a little, with the blessing of the Rugby Football League, before the game to roughen it slightly and get rid of some of the shine. But still Ernest Ward and others from both sides said they had found handling difficult and even suggested that future finals might be better if played with a ball which had been used in a couple of previous games.

Ward had helped put Northern into the lead early on. His kick into space allowed winger Eric Batten to time a run perfectly, gather the ball without breaking stride and cross for a try. Ward converted from the touchline.

Things went fairly quietly until 20 minutes into the second half when Ward added a penalty goal to give Northern a 7-0 lead and a slight safety margin. The last score came 12 minutes later when Trevor found a gap opening for him in front of the posts. He walked through for the try, Ward converted and that was that. Trevor played against Halifax 13 times in the first team, and only scored two tries against them.

A rather uninspiring final was not without its drama. Winger Eric Batten, famous for his ability to jump over an opposing player like an Olympic hurdler, had broken his shoulder in the 20th minute. No substitutes were allowed, so Batten, strapped with bandages, played for the rest of the game in considerable pain. He almost collapsed at the finish and had to be taken to hospital. It was a courageous performance, but it failed to win him the Lance Todd Trophy as man-of-the-match.

That went to Ernest Ward who said afterwards: "With all due respect to Halifax, I think it was the easiest final in which I have played. We should have had many more points, but our finishing was not too good [centre Jack Kitching had crossed the line but dropped the ball on one occasion]. Our forwards excelled themselves, and they made our task in the backs much easier by obtaining such an abundance of possession."

So it wasn't a feast – though a win, looking back, was as good as one – but it sent the crowds away happy, preparing for the long journey home before greeting their heroes in the sooty streets of Bradford for the third year on the trot. Twice they had returned as conquerors.

And the man on whom Dai Rees had pinned so many hopes, Frank Whitcombe, played his last Challenge Cup final on the Wembley turf that day, leaving the field with a handshake from his captain. It was a mark of Whitcombe's spirit that, a year earlier, he had become not only the first forward to win the Lance Todd trophy, but also the first to win it as a member of the losing side. Northern's average age may have been high but so was their team spirit.

Trevor's memories of the match are still vivid: "Frank, though semi-retired, was persuaded by Dai Rees to play and he made sure we got plenty of possession from the scrum. He was like a cat with a mouse, chasing the Halifax forwards. Another factor in our victory was the mental strength of Eric Batten. He scored a typical try from the wing-threequarter position but then felt his shoulder stiffening up. Our sponge-man came on to treat him and immediately diagnosed a badly damaged shoulder. However, Eric insisted he would stay on. He made several important tackles and never once complained.

It was loose-forward Ken Traill who made the try for me. At a scrum just inside the Halifax half the ball was fed out to our threequarters and then quickly back inside to the forwards. Ken drew three men towards him and put me into a gap with a divine pass and I was able to score comfortably under the posts. Ken celebrated by jumping on top of me and giving me a kiss. Scrum-half Stan Kielty, hooker Alvin Ackerley and full-back Dennis Chalkley, with his deep kicking game, were the pick of the Halifax team."

Four days after the 1949 final against Halifax, Frank Whitcombe played his last game and Northern's incomparable side was starting to break up.

There was another Yorkshire Cup triumph early in the 1949-50 campaign, but the results generally were slipping. Nonetheless, the magic touch was still evident in the cup and for the fourth successive year Northern reached the Challenge Cup semi-finals. Ten players who had been to Wembley were in the line-up against Widnes at Wigan, but this time experience wasn't enough. The unfancied Chemics won comfortably 8-0 and Northern's season went to an inglorious finish with a run of 11 successive defeats. They slumped to 21st in the league table and the golden era was passing.

Army service in the Middle East: Trevor, Vincent Dilorenzo and Frank Mugglestone – all Bradford Northern players (Photo: courtesy Trevor Foster)

Wartime rugby union: Wales versus England in Cairo March 1945. Vincent Dilorenzo is in the foreground of the picture. (Photo: courtesy Trevor Foster)

The 1946 Lions tour
Top: HMS Indomitable
Bottom: The train journey from Perth to Sydney:
Joe Egan, Albert Johnson, Trevor, Ken Gee, Martin Ryan, George Curran and Billy Davies
(Photos: Courtesy Trevor Foster)

Action from the first tour match against Southern New South Wales at Junee.
(Photo: Courtesy Trevor Foster)

Great Britain versus Combined North Coast XIII at Grafton on 16 July 1946. Great Britain won 53-8.
(Photo: Courtesy Trevor Foster)

Wembley 1947
Top: Trevor shaking hands with the Duke of Gloucester
Below: Trevor scoring. (Photos: courtesy Trevor Foster)

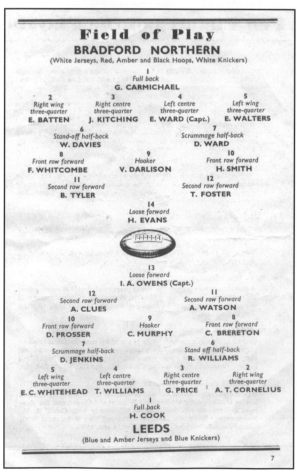

Top: Bringing the cup back to Bradford
(Photo: courtesy Trevor Foster)

Left: The teams from the match programme.
(Courtesy Rugby Football League)

7.   Captain of Wales, winning the Ashes

Despite being an honorary Yorkshireman, qualifying for that title through his 67 years of residence in 'God's own county', Trevor's sense of his Welshness has not been eroded. He would dearly have liked to have won a Wales rugby union cap before decamping for Bradford, but no-one, of course, can have everything.

When Trevor was posted to the Middle East in 1945, he had already represented Wales in five rugby league internationals and in seven rugby union Services Internationals. All 12 had been against England. That posting cost him an eighth rugby union Service International at Gloucester on 7 April 1945 and two rugby league caps for games at Wigan on 10 March and Swansea on 24 November. He also missed out on appearing in the last two great rugby union representative matches of the war, for which he would certainly have been selected if available – Great Britain versus The Dominions, at Leicester on 31 March, and The British Empire versus France, at Richmond on 28 April. Domestically, in rugby league, Trevor was also deprived of appearing for Bradford Northern in their Challenge Cup and Championship Finals in April and May 1945 and he was still basking in the heat of Cairo when Northern won the following season's Yorkshire Cup on 3 November, beating Wakefield Trinity 5-2 in the cooler climes of Thrum Hall, Halifax.

On returning from Egypt in 1946, Trevor was soon back in the swing of things, almost immediately playing himself into the touring squad for Australia and New Zealand. His international career with Wales was also re-ignited. In his absence Wales had beaten England 11-3 at Swansea in their first post-war international, when Gus Risman made his last appearance for his native country. Trevor came in as captain for the game against France in Bordeaux on Sunday 24 March 1946, leading a weakened team (six of the forthcoming Lions tourists were missing), which contained four debutants in Barrow's Roy Francis, Wigan's Ted Ward, Salford's Reg Jones and Glyn Jones of Broughton Rangers. Trevor had originally been selected at second-row but was moved to loose-forward when Ike Owens withdrew. Things went swimmingly in the opening stages. Ted Ward kicked a penalty in the first minute and four minutes later Trevor crossed for a try straight from a scrum, touching down near the posts. Moreover, he kicked the conversion, the second and last goal of his career in first-class rugby league. His only other goal had come in a 15-0 win against Dewsbury at Odsal back on 15 April 1939. Trevor recalls, "I remember getting the ball straight from a scrum about 25 yards out and this big gap suddenly appeared. I went through more or less unopposed. I was never a great kicker of the ball and only occasionally had a dab when playing for Northern. I think that Ted Ward must have taken a knock and was not ready to take the conversion. So I kicked it. Mind you, it was an easy kick, although it definitely was unusual."

Unhappily, that was as good as it got for Wales. Their instant 7-0 lead had been wiped out by half-time. Full-back Puig Aubert, the most famous of all French players, had kicked a penalty and converted a try by front-rower Martin Martin, to level the scores. Just before the break Puig started a passing bout which ended in centre Paul Dejean scoring and France led 10-7. The French really had their tails up and Puig added a 45-yard penalty after 54 minutes, followed by a drop goal. France were unstoppable and veteran loose-forward Maurice Brunetaud grabbed a final try, converted by centre Gaston Combes. A 19-7 defeat was not the result Trevor was seeking on his return but his personal efforts were appreciated, one report declaring: "Foster and Ward were the most notable players for Wales". Had Wales avoided defeat they would have taken the European Championship but their loss meant a three-way tie, the Welsh, English and French all having won one match and lost one. Points difference was not used to decide the title.

67

Trevor's next game for Wales was altogether more satisfying. It was against England on 12 October 1946 at Station Road, Swinton, where a crowd of 20,213 gathered. It was the first international match since the 1946 tourists had returned home and England fielded ten Lions to Wales's six. Trevor's Northern colleagues Frank Whitcombe and Billy (W. T. H.) Davies were in the Welsh side, while Ernest Ward was England's full-back and Jack Kitching had curiously been drafted on to the wing when the injured Eric Batten pulled out. Trevor was back in the second-row with his old Army and Lions partner, Doug Phillips.

The game was brilliant in patches and there were some sparkling movements, particularly from the Welsh backs. At other times it was a dour struggle. Wales led 5-3 at the interval, Huddersfield centre Bill (W. T.) Davies having scored in splendid style and then landed the conversion. Les White had scored a try for England following a mesmerising passing movement over three-quarters of the length of the field. In the second half Johnny Lawrenson tied the scores at 5-5 with a penalty before wingers Reg Lloyd, on his debut, and Roy Francis claimed tries for Wales, one of which Davies converted for Wales to lead 13-5. During the last ten minutes England strove might and main to pull back the deficit and loose-forward Alec Dockar put the game on a knife edge at 13-10 with a try, converted by Lawrenson.

E. G. Blackwell, alias 'Observer' of the *Daily Dispatch*, wrote of those last 10 minutes: "In this hectic period it was thrilling to see how Trevor Foster, Ike Owens and Doug Phillips covered up and trebled, whilst in the very last minute Gareth Price enabled his side to draw winning money by bringing down Ernie Ashcroft close to the line". Winning pay for Trevor and his Welshmen, incidentally, was £8. Blackwell commented: "There was not a lot between the forwards. If England had an advantage in securing possession, the Welshmen, brilliantly led by Trevor Foster, were the more mobile and enterprising".

The 1946-47 season had seen the expansion of the European Championship into home and away fixtures for all three countries. Consequently, it was only just over a month before Wales met England again on 16 November. The venue was the St Helen's Ground, Swansea and 25,000 fans turned up in the hope and expectation of seeing another victory for Wales. Wales had beaten England six times running in peacetime and England had not won in Wales since 1928, when they had crushed the home team 39-15 at Sloper Road, Cardiff. There were several changes to the English XIII, but only two to the Welsh team, Joe Jones returning for Tuss Griffiths at full-back and Arthur Bassett coming in for Roy Francis on the wing. Theoretically, with the addition of these two Lions, Wales were now even stronger.

Most unusually, Bradford supplied both captains for this game, Trevor retaining his position and Ernest Ward taking the England captaincy for the first time. Ernest had already taken over the Bradford captaincy from Trevor and would retain it for the best part of a decade. The two men were firm friends and genuinely delighted for each other, although they differed as to what was going to happen at Swansea. Ernest told a local reporter that the England team was a strong one and predicted: "I think we will give Wales a better match than we did at Swinton". Trevor declared England would need a five-point start, adding: "The Welshmen will get all the encouragement they want when they hear their national anthem being played before the commencement of the game".

The unpredictability of form which afflicts and enhances sport was certainly at work in Swansea and at the end of 80 minutes Ernest Ward was a lot happier than Trevor. Wales were nonplussed as England took a 14-point lead before Dai Jenkins finally scored a try, goaled by Bill Davies, just before half-time. England eventually won 19-5, thanks to Joe Egan's overwhelming scrum supremacy in the first half and the brilliance of an all-Yorkshire back-row comprising Les White, Bill Hudson and Alec Dockar. All England's points came from the left-wing pairing of Albert Johnson, with three tries, and Johnny Lawrenson with two tries and two goals. Ward's great leadership and skill was also a major talking point.

There was more disappointment for Trevor and Wales at the Stade Municipal, Marseilles on 18 January, 1947. Frank Whitcombe accompanied his captain to France but Billy Davies was out through injury. There was much head scratching when Davies was replaced by fellow Bradford player Des Case at stand-off. Case was, of course, a good winger but had hardly played stand-off. Eddie Waring, writing in the *Sunday Pictorial,* strongly disagreed with the selectors, insisting that Leeds's Dickie Williams was obviously the man who should wear the Wales number six jersey. In the event Wales lost 14-5 in glorious weather before a crowd of 24,500. Frank McDermott reported: "It was a sporting match, a good deal more exciting than the score suggests and gave immense pleasure to the crowd". Trevor kept his side competing to the end and his pack out-scrummaged the French. Their only reward, however, was a 75th minute try by debutant second-rower Elwyn Gwyther and a conversion by Bill Davies.

Injury kept Trevor out of the return fixture at Swansea on 12 April when, ironically, France were beaten 17-15. Northern's only representative, Emlyn Walters, was one of the Welsh try-scorers.

The New Zealanders visited Britain in the 1947-48 season and Trevor must have hoped to figure in the three tests and the international at Swansea. He played in none, however, appearing against the Kiwis only for Bradford, who lost 17-7 to the tourists on 11 October before a crowd of 17,519. The selectors caused a great surprise by choosing only five of the 1946 Lions for the first test at Headingley, which was won 11-10. They plumped for Oldham's Les Thomas and St Helens' Len Aston as the second-rowers, with Wigan's Les White replacing Thomas for the second test which was lost 10-7 at Swinton and third, which was won 25-9 at Odsal. Trevor was the reserve forward for the second and third tests.

Wales had a poor campaign in 1947-48. Trevor missed their only success of the season, a 10-8 win over England at Wigan on 20 September, and their 20-28 loss to New Zealand on 18 October, in a wonderfully entertaining game. He returned at loose-forward for the trip to Bordeaux on 23 November, where 26,000 witnessed another points extravaganza. Wales played beautifully in the first half to lead 13-7 but were gradually overrun and lost 29-21. Puig Aubert made the difference by landing seven goals to Ted Ward's three, both teams scoring five tries. Ted Ward had taken over the Wales captaincy from Trevor and held it throughout the season.

For Wales's next fixture, against England at Swansea on 6 December, Trevor moved up to second-row to partner Les Thomas. Extraordinarily, he was the only Bradford player in either side. It was not a good day for the Welsh. They scrummaged well with hooker Mel Meek matching Joe Egan for possession but England were much the sounder combination. Wales trailed 10-2 at the break and, although they tightened their defence in the second period, their 18-7 defeat was perhaps flattering to the losers. Trevor crossed for Wales's solitary try, Ted Ward kicking two goals. A national petrol shortage and torrential rain conspired to restrict the attendance to 10,000. Perhaps the one scant consolation was the RFL's decision before the game to pay all the players £8, win, lose or draw. It was remarked, however, that the decision clearly did not affect the competitiveness of the play.

Wales's final match was also at Swansea on 20 March 1948, against France. Besides Trevor, there were three other Bradford players in the Welsh XIII – Alan Edwards, Billy Davies and Frank Whitcombe. Things did not go at all well for Wales. Skipper Ted Ward was up all night with neuralgia and had to have teeth extracted at 5.30 in the morning. Harry Sunderland in the *Sunday Dispatch* reported: "He played, nevertheless, but he and some of the other Welshmen found the pace too fast in the last 20 minutes. The match was controlled by a Frenchman for the first time in Wales. Monsieur Pascal, of Toulouse, frequently penalised the Welshmen, and constantly had the crowd in uproar". In fact Pascal's penalty count went against Wales 18-1 and he appeared to have a strange concept of how the ball should be played. Wales trailed 8-7 at half-time but scored a fabulous try through centre Gareth Price, after a sublime passing movement involving Joe Jones, Ike Owens, Ward, Billy Davies and Trevor, whose pass put Price through. In the 46th minute Trevor burst clear near halfway, dodged two French tacklers and went on for a terrific try, converted by Ward, for Wales to lead 12-8. It was to no avail, however, as France finished strongly, scoring two converted tries and a penalty to win 20-12, leaving Wales with the Championship wooden spoon.

By the start of the 1948-49 season Trevor was approaching 34 years-of-age but was playing as well as ever. He had never played a test against Australia and the Kangaroos were in Britain that season. Realistically, he would never get another chance to play in Ashes tests. The representative season started inauspiciously for Trevor. He and Ernest Ward had been selected as captains of the Wales and England teams for the opening international at Wigan on 22 September. Neither was fit to play and Wales lost 11-5. Trevor was also selected to lead Wales against France at Swansea on 23 October but again withdrew, Wales losing 12-9.

He had better luck in the test arena, however. On 9 October Trevor packed down alongside Bob Nicholson in Great Britain's pack for the first Ashes test at Headingley. Trevor's long-held ambition to face the Australians in test match rugby had finally been realised and what an experience it was. The 36,529 inside the ground were about to witness one of the most spectacularly open tests in history. In terms of sheer good football the Headingley test of 1948 was a glorious freak. Ashes tests were not supposed to be like this. Twelve tries were scored, despite the fact that there were 58 scrums, which Britain bossed 40-18, but referee Albert Dobson only awarded nine penalties, seven to the Aussies, most of which were for scrum offences. The teams were:

Great Britain: J. Ledgard (Leigh), J. Lawrenson (Wigan), A. Pimblett (Warrington), E. Ward (Bradford N) (captain), S. McCormick (Belle Vue Rangers), W. Horne (Barrow), G. Helme (Warrington), K. Gee (Wigan), J. Egan (Wigan), G. Curran (Salford), R. Nicholson (Huddersfield), T. J. F. Foster (Bradford N), D. D. Valentine (Huddersfield).

Australia: C. Churchill (Souths), P. McMahon (Toowoomba), D. McRitchie (St George), N. Hawke (Canberra), J. Graves (Souths), W. O'Connell (Easts) (captain), K. Froome (Newtown), A. Gibbs (South Newcastle), K. Schubert (Wollongong), D. Hall (Valleys, Brisbane), J. Holland (St George), J. Rayner (Souths), N. Mulligan (Newtown).

This was a game that was so breathtaking that Alfred Drewry of the *Yorkshire Post* famously declared: "Fifty years hence the recital of its story will be a sore trial to bored grandchildren". Good old Alf was spot on. More prosaically, he added: "The playing of the ball was, I think, the best I have ever seen". It was not the play-the-balls which took the spectators' eyes, however, in the first 15 minutes but the power and directness of the Kangaroo forwards. In that period Hall and McMahon scored unconverted tries before Britain really knew what was happening. Then the tide turned and Trevor played some of the most inspired football of his entire career.

Ernest Ward touched down after following up a kick from Stan McCormick but the try was disallowed. "Then", after about 20 minutes, Arthur Haddock wrote in the *Yorkshire Evening News*: "Britain struck again, this time successfully. Pimblett and Nicholson paved the way for Lawrenson to dart ahead. He came inside, got the defence on the wrong foot, and, after making about 40 yards, passed to Foster, who, though sandwiched between two defenders, crashed over the line for a try to which Ward added the goal". Ten minutes later there was another British score "and what a beauty it was", according to Haddock, "Ledgard was the architect. Joining in an attack, he baffled the defence, put the ball inside to Horne who, when overtaken, lobbed a pass to Foster for that forward to run in for his second try". 'Veteran' in *Yorkshire Sports* was much taken by Trevor's "smart side-step" in this movement and remarked that "Britain were well on top now, doing all the attacking and supplying thrilling moves. Foster repeatedly excelled, beating man after man".

Trevor's tries had given Britain an 8-6 lead but he was not finished. Haddock wrote: "Britain continued to dictate matters, and Foster, a towering figure, made another glorious midfield run, showing great artistry in the way he served out a dummy. Britain's third try was again one to remember and how the crowd rose to McCormick, who scored. Gee and Foster – the latter was outstanding amongst the 12 forwards in loose play – sent the winger pounding up his wing. He side-stepped Churchill, and, although Froome chased him to the corner, McCormick dived the last two yards. The corner flag lay broken after his effort". Britain now led 11-6, 'Veteran' noting with fine understatement: "It had been a pleasant first half".

McCormick was over again in spectacular style at the corner five minutes after the restart and the lead extended to 14-6. Then after 56 minutes Valentine, on the end of a well-worked overlap, added a further try. It was 17-6, but the game was far from over. Trevor was still making life difficult for the Australians, Haddock continuing: "Foster, playing brilliantly, was handling and running like a centre. Once he turned inside magnificently, found Egan, and Lawrenson came within an ace of getting away".

Australia hit back with a try from Froome, who snapped up a loose ball to score near the flag. Graves piloted a lovely conversion and it was 17-11. Pimblett was next to score, bluffing his way through with a classic piece of centre play, using Lawrenson as a foil. Britain were now 20-11 ahead and the last 11 points had come within four minutes – the Ashes tradition of low scores was in tatters. Australian winger Graves brought the crowd to its feet as he streaked 50 yards for the next try, which he converted himself. The last 10 minutes were frenetic. Pimblett seemed to have settled the issue when he beat man after man to score a sizzling try to give Britain daylight at 23-16 but, five minutes from time, with Lawrenson off the field receiving attention to an injured arm, McMahon crashed over for Australia's fifth try. Graves hit another touch-line conversion and, at 23-21, no-one was leaving the ground. The drama continued to the very end when Churchill was collared just short of the line after a desperate dash to pull the game out of the fire.

Trevor's Ashes debut could hardly have been better – a magnificent, free-flowing game, played in the best of spirit, and he had been the shining star. Almost six decades later he says: "That was one of my greatest games and one of my greatest memories. I scored both my tries at the dressing-room end [the St Michael's Lane end]. I don't think anyone laid a hand on me for the second one but I didn't have far to go for it. I knew then what great feeling it was to score in a test match. I also remember that evening Harry Hornby took me to the speedway at Odsal. They used to get crowds of about 20,000 for meetings. I went down to the track with him and all of a sudden the announcer was telling the crowd all about the Headingley test and I got a really wonderful reception. That made it even more special for me".

There was not much doubt that Trevor would be selected for the second test at Swinton on 6 November and there were only two changes, Jimmy Ledgard and Willie Horne being replaced by Martin Ryan of Wigan and Leeds's Dickie Williams. Australia reshaped their team considerably more. Their centres were replaced by Jack Horrigan and Col Maxwell, the tour captain. Thompson took over at scrum-half and Hand and Tyquin came into the pack for Hall and Holland.

Trevor was having a fruitful period. The Saturday prior to the second test he had been a try-scorer in Bradford Northern's 18-9 victory over Castleford at Headingley in the Yorkshire Cup Final. An Ashes-winning triumph at Station Road would round the past month off nicely.

71

The immediate post-war period was a boom time for rugby league and there was another big crowd, 36,354, at Swinton. The weather and ground conditions were ideal and, like the first test, the game was contested in a good spirit. Australia had far more possession this time, Schubert losing the scrums only 23-27 to Egan. Surprisingly they could do little with the ball, becoming obsessed with passing for its own sake and generally getting nowhere. Britain were just too good all round for the Kangaroos. Ward gave them the lead after only three minutes, kicking a penalty after Churchill fouled Helme as the latter broke from a scrum. In the 19th and 30th minutes Albert Pimblett, the man-of-the-match, scored tries, the second a stunning effort. Ward converted the latter and Britain led 10-0. Graves replied with a fine penalty goal in the 39th minute but Britain had already established a superiority, which Australia clearly could not break.

Australia botched a succession of chances in the first 20 minutes of the second half and could have been further in arrears had Trevor not failed to pass to Dickie Williams at the crucial moment. The killer blow was delivered, however, when Williams broke down the left before the ball was switched to the right and Johnny Lawrenson swept over for a cracking try. Australia finally crossed Britain's line six minutes before the whistle, when debutant winger Horrigan scored. Graves's conversion made the score 13-7 but in the 78th minute Lawrenson gained his second try and Britain won 16-7 to take the Ashes for a 10th consecutive series.

Eddie Waring, writing in *Rugby League Review*, was certainly impressed by the British performance, writing: "They were as nigh the perfect side as it is possible to be with any football team. Each player was a star in his own right." Of the forwards, he said: "The English (sic) pack had no holes in its defence as at Headingley. Gee, Egan and Curran were strong, dour forwards. Their tackling was grim, with Ken Gee in great form... Nicholson and Foster roamed and covered effectively to some purpose while Valentine rewarded the criticised selectors with a display of some standing".

The Swinton test proved to be Trevor's last. The third test at Odsal was scheduled for 18 December but Trevor damaged a nerve in his back and, with the Ashes won, the selectors chose not to risk him and brought in Warrington's Jimmy Featherstone. Ironically, the Odsal test was called off when fog engulfed the stadium 40 minutes before kick-off, yet half an hour after the scheduled kick-off time Odsal was bathed in sunshine. The Kangaroos left England for a 10 match tour of France and returned for the rescheduled test on 29 January 1949, when a record British Ashes test crowd of 42,000 attended. Britain completed a clean sweep of the series with a 23-9 win.

Trevor's luck had temporarily taken a dive after the Ashes-clinching test at Swinton. The following Wednesday, 10 November, he had played for Bradford Northern against the Kangaroos, who gave one of the best performances of their tour in winning 21-7. His back problem kept him out of action until 27 December, when he returned in an 11-6 win at Bramley. The injury had cost him a place in the Wales team which met Australia at Swansea on 20 November. Wales lost 12-5, their sixth straight defeat, the last three of which Trevor had missed through injury.

Fate had decreed that Trevor would never play in a winning Wales team again. He was absent once more when Wales finally succeeded again on 5 February 1949 with a tremendous 14-10 victory over England at Wigan. Trevor returned for the final game of the European Championship on Sunday, 10 April, when France clinched the title with an 11-0 win before 30,000 happy spectators at Marseilles. The Welsh pack held its own but could not prevent the French wingers, Vincent Cantoni, with two, and Ode Lespes from scoring the three tries which settled the issue.

The 1949-50 European Championship saw the introduction of the celebrated Other Nationalities side. Anyone who did not qualify for England, Wales or France was eligible for selection for this new force but its prime sources of players were the New Zealanders and Australians, who had taken up contracts with English clubs. A few South Africans, Scots and Irish also won Other Nationalities caps, which were much prized. Trevor was restored to the captaincy of Wales for their first game against Other Nationalities at Abertillery on 22 October 1949. Unfortunately, torrential rain fell throughout the match and conditions were so vile that Trevor and his opposing captain Pat Devery of Huddersfield asked referee Charlie Appleton to abandon the match after an hour's play. The game was played to its conclusion, however, ending in a 6-5 victory for Other Nationalities. Unsurprisingly, the game was attended by only 2,000 people at a ground almost bereft of covered accommodation.

On 12 November Wales gained a 16-8 victory over France at Swansea but again Trevor had had to withdraw through injury, Swinton full-back Ralph Morgan replacing him as captain, while Elwyn Gwyther of Belle Vue Rangers, normally a prop, took his place in the second-row. He returned to lead Wales on Wednesday 1 March 1950 against England at Wigan. The game drew a crowd of 27,500 and was in effect a tour trial. It was also the last time that Trevor would captain Wales. It was a fitting occasion, for his friend Ernest Ward was again captain of England, and the game lived up to expectations. Wales lost 11-6 but undoubtedly deserved to have won. Seven minutes from time, with the scores locked at 6-6, Wigan's Jack Hilton, England's left winger, intercepted Welsh passing to streak away for the winning try, converted by Ward. It was his third try of the match, Wales responding with touchdowns from Halifax's Arthur Daniels and Leeds's Dickie Williams.

Tom Longworth wrote in the *News Chronicle*: "The performance of the Welshmen, admirably led by Trevor Foster, was one of the best I have seen for a while. In fact the match was of rich quality throughout and excellent entertainment". Tom Reynolds baldly stated in the *Daily Herald*: "Foster was the best Welsh forward" and Alfred Drewry in the *Yorkshire Post* thought that England's "Fred Higgins and Foster were the most impressive second-row men".

Trevor was several months past his 35th birthday when the 1950 Australasian tour party was selected. It was remarkable that pundits were still putting him in the frame for a tour spot. The selectors decided that Fred Higgins (Widnes), Harry Murphy (Wakefield), Doug Phillips (Belle Vue Rangers) and Bob Ryan (Warrington) would be the second-rowers in the party, so there was no second Lions tour for Trevor.

Eddie Waring in the *Rugby League Review* was one critic who did not concur. He remarked: "The second row was the real problem with a large number of players banging at the door. Bob Ryan was something of a surprise but he should do well and be a good tourist. Trevor Foster was the real surprise omission and I understand it was his age which ruled him out. His football against England was sound enough". Ernest Ward achieved the supreme accolade of being chosen as tour captain, while there was also a Lions place for Northern's skilful loose-forward Ken Traill.

Eddie Waring was right about Trevor's age counting against him. In fact, if he had been selected, Trevor would probably have been the oldest Lion ever selected. Gus Risman had been 35 when he toured in 1946 but Trevor would have been three months older. Trevor recalled: "I would have gone on tour if they had picked me. I was the official Rugby League Coach then [he had been appointed early in 1949] but that would not have affected the decision. After the Wales versus England game, the selectors went to a hotel in Southport to pick the tourists and there was an argument about my age between Harry Hornby, who proposed that I should be picked, and George Oldroyd of Dewsbury, who was one of the tour managers. Mr. Oldroyd said: 'We don't want to take old men.' As he was the manager, I suppose he was bound to get his way. Bill Fallowfield told me about it the next morning in confidence". On the bus on the way to work at the RFL the day after the England match, Trevor had seen a headline in the *Yorkshire Post* with his name and 'tour' visible. His hopes were raised, but at the office, when RFL secretary Bill Fallowfield arrived at 9.30 am, he told Trevor the bad news.

In the 1950-51 season Trevor did not play a game until 9 December. He remembers: "I seemed to be getting a few injuries in that period. Actually, for a while I was really worried that my playing days might be coming to an end. I had a bad knee injury. It was the same knee I hurt in Australia. It was something to do with the cartilages and it constantly swelled up. It was never operated on though and I returned to fitness".

The injury caused him to miss Wales's opening European Championship match against England at Abertillery on 14 October and he was also injured when they met Other Nationalities at Swansea on 31 March 1951. He was not picked for the final game of the season against France at Marseilles on 15 April. Wales lost all three internationals. It was beginning to look as if his career with Wales was over, especially when he was ruled out again from the start of the 1951-52 season until 1 October, missing the England game at St. Helens on 19 September. He was then overlooked for Wales's fixture against Other Nationalities at Abertillery on 1 December, when Ted Ward filled one of the second-row spots.

Trevor was recalled, however, six days later, appropriately enough, for Wales's game against New Zealand at Odsal. It was a historic occasion because it was the first international or test to be played under floodlights. Trevor had played for Bradford against the New Zealanders on Wednesday, 31 October, when Odsal's floodlights (modified from those used for the speedway) had been inaugurated. Northern had won a famous 13-8 victory. A crowd of 29,072, a figure only beaten on the tour by the first test, which was also staged at Odsal, prompted the Kiwis to request another game under floodlights at the stadium. Consequently, the game against Wales, originally scheduled to be played at Penarth Road Stadium in Cardiff on 12 December, was re-arranged at relatively short notice.

Obviously Trevor was not expecting another international cap, although he was still hoping. "It came right out of the blue", he says, "But it was a great occasion. I remember those early floodlit games. We went onto the field in the dark and took up our kick-off positions. Then they turned on the lights. It was really electrifying and the game was pretty close, I think". Unfortunately, the evening was awful and the attendance was only 8,568. John North of the *Daily Express* wrote that the game "was spoiled by bad weather. The ground was heavy, with pools in the middle, and rain became more severe as the match proceeded. Until half-time the players overcame the handicap of the mud by quick handling, fast running and good backing up. After the interval... play deteriorated."

Trevor, partnering his old tour colleague Doug Phillips, could have hoped for a better result to his last game for Wales, a 15-3 defeat. It had been his 16th international for Wales, a figure which he would no doubt have doubled had circumstances been different. His test career had yielded a mere three Great Britain caps, when he could reasonably have expected five times that figure, if peace had persisted through his playing career.

Over half a century from his last appearance for Wales his joy in his achievements is undimmed. He says: "Wales are a proud nation with a particular regard for sporting prowess, especially in rugby. I always found there was a special atmosphere in the Welsh dressing room when I played. It was never quite the same for Great Britain. I think we always felt we owed something to the Good Lord for allowing us to wear the three feathers. I always wanted to wear that scarlet jersey".

8.   Playing for Bradford Northern 1945 to 1955

The second half of the 1940s was a boom time both for rugby league and for Bradford Northern. The end of the war and the gradual return of the troops from overseas saw huge crowds attracted to all forms of entertainment, as people put the bleak period of the war behind them.

Bradford's three Challenge Cup Finals in this period are covered elsewhere in this book. However, the five years up to 1950 also included three Yorkshire Cup wins, the runners-up spot in the Championship in 1947-48, and a Yorkshire League win in the same season.

Trevor was on military service until January 1946, and thus missed Bradford's first post-war Yorkshire Cup Final win, a 5-2 victory over Wakefield Trinity at Halifax on 3 November 1945. He returned to the Bradford team on 2 February 1946, in an 18-11 league win over Workington Town, and celebrated his return with a try. Four weeks later, Trevor "led the Bradford pack splendidly" at Barrow in the second round of the Challenge Cup, but could not prevent the home side winning 5-0 in front of a 16,549 crowd.

But his stay in the Bradford team was a brief one. His selection for the Great Britain touring party to Australia meant he departed on the long voyage by ship on 4 April. He missed Bradford's last 11 matches, and ended the season with only seven appearances for his club, and one try. Despite losing Trevor and five other players to the touring party, Bradford finished fourth in the league. This gave them a Championship semi-final place, but they lost 18-4 to Wigan at Central Park.

The Lions tour finished on 12 August in Auckland, but the party finally returned to Tilbury on 22 September, so Trevor and his colleagues had missed the first four weeks of the season, including a 40-8 aggregate defeat for Bradford over two legs in the Yorkshire Cup against Huddersfield.

Bradford hit a good run of form up to Christmas, with only two defeats in the league, at Barrow and Dewsbury. This good form continued in January, with four wins and a draw at York. But then freezing weather severely disrupted the season. Bradford lost 10-0 at Wigan on 15 February, and then did not play in the league again until 4 April, with an 11-8 defeat at Huddersfield. However, in the meantime they had managed to reach the Challenge Cup semi-final, and went on to win the Cup against Leeds at Wembley on 3 May.

The weather, combined with government restrictions on playing midweek matches in the afternoon because of concerns about absenteeism from the factories, meant that the season ran on until the middle of June. Northern could not recapture their form from earlier in the season in the league, and eventually finished sixth, with 51 points from 36 matches. Only the top four contested the championship, so Bradford missed out. Trevor finished the season with seven tries from 24 appearances.

The next season, 1947-48, was one of the most memorable in Trevor's time at Odsal. He played in 41 out of 48 Bradford first team matches, and the team reached – and lost – both the major rugby league finals, the Challenge Cup and the Championship. And he set a club record for a forward by scoring six tries against Wakefield at Odsal on 10 April, in a 28-16 win.

A notable recruit that summer was Ken Traill. Trevor played with him for the rest of his playing career, and believes he was one of the outstanding players at Bradford Northern at this time. He remembers: "He came to us from Hunslet in the summer of 1947, just after we had won the Cup at Wembley. The astute Dai Rees had followed up information about the Hunslet youngster and signed him, and what a great capture he was: a most dedicated and natural ball player – rugby league football was his delight. He was a very competitive loose-forward, and proved to have very high standards on the field of play, always probing, looking to put players into try scoring opportunities. He was a master craftsman around the ruck area. I always think of our victory at Wembley against Halifax in 1949 when he put me in for a try after he cut out three or four players near the Halifax goal line and passed for me to stroll in to score.

Ken could never accept second best in any game. He was a source of inspiration and the mainspring of many attacks. He was a footballer to his fingertips. After great service to Bradford Northern he went on to become a winner with Halifax and Wakefield Trinity as a player and coach. He reached the pinnacle of rugby league honours with two Great Britain tours down under. He was a most wonderful team comrade to me — we had a special relationship on the field of play, winning games was our great desire whatever or whenever we played. He was an outstanding player around the rucks, both on attack and defence, with an excellent left-foot kick.

He played rugby the way it was meant to be played, with his spectacular ball skills creating openings with both short and wide passes. He also had a fine kicking game when he would relieve pressure from his own line to gain vital yards during tense moments.

He could read the game well, his long passes were always effective, he constantly backed up the play and seldom missed a tackle. Ken Traill was a rugby league giant."

The season started with wins at Wakefield and Leeds. But then a run of seven defeats in 11 games did not hint at the glory to come. This spell included being knocked out of the Yorkshire Cup by Leeds, two league defeats against Castleford, and a 19-7 defeat against the touring New Zealand side. But from the beginning of November, Bradford's form improved, and only three more matches were lost to the end of January, when the Challenge Cup started.

Despite the pressure of extra fixtures because of their Challenge Cup run, Bradford only lost one more league game before the end of the season, 21-5 at Warrington in March. But their patchy early-season form meant a final league place of fourth, with 52 points from 36 matches.

Trevor scored 22 tries during the season for Bradford, with only wingers Alan Edwards and Eric Batten, with 36 and 33 respectively, finishing ahead of him at Odsal.

The match against Wakefield was when Bill Jenkins made his Odsal debut. He played under the name of 'Jenkinson' and went on to become a solid performer for Northern.

Trevor recalls his six-try feat: "This was a day that dreams are made of when nothing went wrong for me on the field of play. We were in a rich vein of form and Wakefield were there for the taking. I did not have to run any great distance for any of the tries. My plan was to support any of my team mates near the opponents' line. My fifth try was laid on a plate by our great winger Alan Edwards. He was about to score himself and then turned waiting for me to arrive before giving me the ball literally on the line to score. Low and behold, I crossed the line on a seventh occasion, but referee Mr Dobson ruled out a try, saying I had not taken the ball from the spot where he had given the penalty kick... I had taken advantage of the situation, you cannot win them all".

His performance had journalists scouring the record books. Harry Sunderland's report said that it was the most impressive try-scoring performance by a forward since Frank Burge scored five for Australia against Lancashire in 1921. Sunderland outlined that Trevor "beat several men" to score his first try, and then "was alert" to score when Edwards made a run to the corner, only to be tackled. Sunderland wrote that his sixth try "followed brilliant passing in which Edwards, Traill, Davies and Foster backed up each other in successive transfers."

Bill Bowes, in his 'Sportsman of the Moment' column said that Fred Webster, a Leeds forward, had scored eight tries against Coventry in 1913. However, he pointed out that the result of that game was 102-0. He said that Trevor's was "a magnificent performance" and said that Webster's achievement, which was against a struggling team, was not comparable with

Trevor's, "which gives Foster the honour, among the forwards, of being the League's leading try scorer of the season".

Tom Reynolds pointed out that Trevor should have been credited with seven tries. He wrote: "Only six tries were allowed. 'The one that got away', however, was the most remarkable of all; it beat the Wakefield Trinity defence, and the referee as well. Edwards had been obstructed while following up a kick about 15 yards from the Wakefield line and the referee (Mr A. S. Dobson) awarded a penalty to Bradford Northern. Scarcely had he signalled this before Foster seized the ball, tapped it forward into an open space and followed up to touch down for a try. Astonishment was written broadly across the Wakefield players' faces, but they made no appeal and raised no objection; they had been caught off guard by a very slick tactician and they knew it. Their astonishment, however, was transferred to Bradford faces when the referee paused for a moment and finally decided not to allow the score. Foster was unlucky. Many poorer tries, scored the same way, although far less quickly, stand in rugby league records".

Reynolds went on to say that he had never seen a forward score six tries in first-class football against first-class opposition. He said that he had met Jack Waring before the game, a Lancashire County centre who was playing for Featherstone. Waring had told him that "Foster is playing now as he has never played in his life before. I doubt if there's a better forward in the country".

Writing in October 1949, Eden Reynolds recalled the match, and said that Trevor's disallowed try "was all done in a flash, but as the referee hadn't seen it he brought Foster back and told him to do it again. No referee may allow a try unless he has actually seen it touched down". Reynolds said that Trevor was "still the craftiest scheming forward in the country".

A few years later, the referee was more sympathetic to a Bradford try from a penalty against Dewsbury in the early 1950s. Trevor recalls: "We were awarded a penalty and Joe Philips placed the ball near the touchline as if to kick a goal. Surprisingly he then tapped the ball forward, picked it up and passed it to me. All the Dewsbury players were on the goal line waiting for the penalty kick to be taken and I went over to score a try in the corner through a most unusual occurrence. The Dewsbury players were very upset and complained bitterly to the referee. We practised this at Odsal a couple of times but it was eventually banned by the Rugby Football League".

Trevor's contribution to the team also came in defence. Alfred Drewry's report of Bradford's 7-2 win at Huddersfield on 30 March said that he "did the work of four in a solid Northern pack and did it brilliantly".

Bradford's league programme finished at York on 21 April, with a 23-12 win. This result saw Bradford finish top of the Yorkshire League, with 42 points from their 26 matches against Yorkshire opposition. Three days later, they travelled to Central Park to face Wigan in the Championship semi-final. Their hosts had finished top of the league table, with only four defeats in 36 matches. But Bradford restricted Wigan to just one try, winning 15-3. Unfortunately for them, they could not repeat this result the following week, losing the Challenge Cup Final 8-3 to Wigan.

Warrington, who had finished second in the league table, were Bradford's opponents in the Championship Final at Manchester City FC's Maine Road ground. A crowd of 69,143 saw a poor performance from Bradford. The team had played eight matches in 28 days to finish the season, including the Wembley final. Warrington were 5-0 up at the break and, although Bradford played better in the opening period of the second half, they could not score. A further try and conversion from Warrington put the game beyond Bradford, and although Des Case scored for Bradford, with Ernest Ward converting, a further Warrington try, converted again by

Palin, made the final score 15-5. So Bradford had to be content with the runners-up spot once more.

Bradford Northern: G. Carmichael, E. Batten, D. Case, E. Ward, A. S. Edwards, W. T. H. Davies, D. Ward, F. W. Whitcombe, V. J. Darlison, H. Smith, T. J. F. Foster, B. Tyler, K. Traill.

Scorers: Try: Case. Goal: E. Ward

Warrington: L. Jones, B. Bevan, B. Knowelden, A. J. Pimblett, S. Powell, J. Fleming, G. J. Helme, W. Derbyshire, D. Cotton, W. Riley, J. Featherstone, R. Ryan, H. Palin.

Scorers: Tries: Knowelden, Pimblett, Powell. Goals: Palin (3).

The season finished with a short tour of France. It was the first time that Bradford had played abroad. They won both the games, beating Toulouse Olympique 21-17, and Carcassonne 16-10.

1948-49: Two trophies

The Challenge Cup and the Yorkshire Cup were the two highlights of the 1948-49 season, with both trophies ending up at Odsal. Trevor played 29 matches, a good total for a man who became 34 years old during the season, but only scored three tries. Bradford's form in the league was less consistent than in the cup competitions, and they fell to 10th place, with 44 points from 36 matches. In the Yorkshire League, Bradford were runners-up to Huddersfield.

The Yorkshire Cup campaign did not start well, with a 5-3 defeat at Dewsbury. But Bradford won the second leg of the tie 20-5 at Odsal, and then beat Huddersfield 19-12. This produced a semi-final with Hunslet, and a 7-7 draw at Odsal was followed by a 12-5 win at Parkside in the replay.

In the final, on 30 October, Bradford faced Castleford at Headingley. Bradford were relying on the players who had provided so much success for them since the war, and the press often commented about their – in rugby league terms – advancing ages. Castleford's team – younger than Bradford's – started the match well, and were 2-0 ahead after three minutes from a penalty. At half-time, Castleford were winning 4-2. They had been well on top, and their narrow lead was mainly due to hard-working defence from Trevor, Ron Greaves and Frank Whitcombe. Castleford could not maintain their pace of the first half, and Bradford dominated the game in the second. Ernest Ward played a key role, creating two tries for Alan Edwards. After an hour, Bradford were 10-9 ahead, and Trevor's try after 70 minutes made it 13-9. In the closing minutes, Bill Leake scored Bradford's fourth try to seal the win, Edwards' conversion making the final score 18-9. A crowd of 31,393 had enjoyed Bradford's sixth Yorkshire Cup win.

Bradford Northern: G. Carmichael, E. Batten, W. Leake, E. Ward, A. S. Edwards, W. T. H. Davies, D. Ward, F. W. Whitcombe, V. J. Darlison, R. Greaves, T. J. F. Foster, B. Tyler, K. Traill.

Scorers: Tries: Edwards (2), Leake, Foster. Goals: Edwards (3).

Castleford: R. Lewis, A. Bastow, L. Skidmore, N. Guest, W. R. Lloyd, A. Fisher, G. Langfield, D. L. Harris, J. Jones, J. Crossley, D. Foreman, C. Staines, F. Mugglestone.

Scorers: Try: Foreman. Goals: Langfield, Foreman, Staines.

In January, Trevor was appointed as the first national Rugby League coach by the Rugby Football League. However, he still continued to play for Bradford, and their Challenge Cup campaign was the highlight of the second half of the season. As so often happened with a successful team in those pre-floodlights days, Bradford faced fixture congestion towards the end of the season, playing 10 games in April including the Challenge Cup semi-final, and did not finish their league fixtures until 11 May, when Dewsbury were beaten 10-9 at Odsal. Four days earlier, Bradford had won the Challenge Cup at Wembley, beating Halifax 12-0.

The season again ended with French opposition. Roanne won 13-5 at Odsal on 18 May, as part of a tour that included matches against Wigan and Leigh.

The 1949-50 season saw Trevor again play consistently, making 37 appearances and being second top try scorer with 11, only winger Emlyn Walters finishing ahead of him with 17. But the years were catching up with Bradford. Des Case and Len Higson had retired in 1948. Frank Whitcombe had finished playing at the end of the 1948-49 season and Alan Edwards only made a handful of appearances in this campaign. The club recognised at the start of the season that they were in a state of transition. The match programme for the game against Swinton on 22 August said that: "We should all feel much happier if we had been able to recruit a few ready-made stars during the close season to fill the places of one or two of our older star players, but so far our efforts in that direction have not produced the desired results; we could, of course, bring in plenty of new players of good club standard, not, however, up to the standard of our requirements."

The season started with three defeats in the first five games, including a 30-7 crash at Warrington on 7 September. But manager Dai Rees got the best out of his players in the Yorkshire Cup. York were comfortably beaten over two legs in the first round. A report of the second leg, which Bradford won 25-11 at Odsal, said that "Trevor Foster was the man of the match... Foster, who recently expressed a wish to retire, was one of the fastest men on view, and played cleverly too." The next round produced a repeat of the previous season's final. Castleford came to Odsal, and were beaten 13-6. In the semi-final, Bradford avoided Dewsbury and Huddersfield, and travelled to lowly Bramley, winning 8-6.

The final was again at Headingley, on 29 October. Huddersfield were, on paper, tougher opponents than Castleford, with Australian winger Lionel Cooper and loose-forward Dave Valentine among their stars. A Yorkshire Cup Final record crowd of 36,000 crammed into Headingley. Dai Rees used a defensive system of man-to-man marking for the match to restrict Huddersfield's potent attack. While this produced a dull game, it paid off. However, Bradford's attack was unable to penetrate the Huddersfield defence to any great extent.

At half time, Bradford were 4-2 up, with a drop goal and a penalty from Ernest Ward. The second half was not much more lively. The only try came after a run by Walters, who passed to Trevor just inside the Huddersfield 25-yard line. He put Davies in to score out wide. Ward missed the conversion, but as Huddersfield became frustrated with being unable to break Bradford down, scored two more penalties. Bawden notched his second goal for Huddersfield, and Bradford hung on to win 11-4. The record crowd had not seen much good rugby, but it was a triumph for Bradford's manager, whose tactics had frustrated the Huddersfield team.

Bradford Northern: W. Leake, E. Batten, E. Ward, J. Kitching, E. Walters, W. T. H. Davies, D. Ward, E. Day, V. J. Darlison, R. Greaves, B. Tyler, T. J. F. Foster, K. Traill.
Scorers: Try: Davies. Goals: E. Ward (4).
Huddersfield: E. Swallow, G. Wilson, J. Bawden, P. C. Devery, L. W. Cooper, G. R. Pepperell, W. M. Banks, J. Maiden, A. M. Meek, J. C. Daly, I. A. Owens, R. Nicholson, D. D. Valentine.
Scorer: Goals: Bawden (2).

Bradford's form continued to be erratic. A 13-7 win over Wakefield Trinity at Odsal the week after the Yorkshire Cup win was followed by four consecutive defeats. The Christmas and the New Year period were more positive, with four wins and a draw, including a 7-3 victory at Fartown.

In the New Year, the Challenge Cup was the main highlight. Oldham were beaten in the first round, a 16-8 win at the Watersheddings in the first leg being followed by an 8-6 defeat at Odsal. But although Keighley and St Helens (after a 0-0 draw at Knowsley Road) were beaten, there was not to be a fourth consecutive Wembley final. Widnes beat Bradford 8-0 at Central Park in the semi-final.

The Challenge Cup replay win over St Helens on 15 March was Bradford's last win of the campaign. A run of 10 consecutive defeats saw a final league place of 21st out of the 29 teams, and showed the need for some urgent rebuilding.

Trevor was now 35 years old — at the veteran stage by rugby league standards. But the respect for him in the game was shown by a letter he received from Mr W. Jones, a Salford supporter, in January 1950. Mr Jones wrote: "I must write to you to say how much I appreciated the wonderful display of classic forward play as given by you particularly against the team I support. It was a delight to watch... All around where I stood during the match appreciated your glorious display and also the brave fight of all your team." The letter concluded: "You and players of your type, clean, clever and sporting do a great deal to raise the standard of rugby league. The best I can say is you brought back memories of Salford's glorious days. Good luck to you and may you coach some more forwards into a likeness of your own classic mould."

The decline over two seasons from fourth in the table to the relative ignominy of 21st finally made the club's management realise that urgent action was necessary. Club chairman Harry Hornby visited New Zealand when he was accompanying the Lions tour, and recruited five players from rugby union. He had been in contact with former Bradford players Mike Gilbert and George Harrison for advice on local talent. His recruits included full-back Joe Phillips, winger Bob Hawes, backs Norman Hastings and Bill Dickson, and All Black winger Jack McLean.

Trevor's own position with the club had been uncertain. In April 1950, Barrow had written to Trevor asking for advice about appointing a new coach or player coach. Trevor was interested in the position, and had correspondence and a series of meetings with Barrow. However, he wished to continue playing and this would have meant Barrow paying a transfer fee for his services to Bradford. A report by 'Sentinel' in the *North Western Evening Mail* on 4 July said that Trevor had turned down Barrow's offer. It was said to have been a 'handsome' one. Another issue was that Trevor was due a testimonial from Bradford, which he would have lost had he moved to Barrow. The latter had offered compensation for this, but Trevor decided to stay at Odsal. The report commented: "Foster is regarded as one of the best forwards the code has ever known, and Barrow certainly put everything into their effort to persuade him to join them... Bradford thought they had lost his services at the beginning of last season when he told the directors he intended to retire, but he was persuaded to see the club through a difficult period — they had just lost Whitcombe from the pack and wanted Foster to give the benefit of his experience to the younger players."

A further change early on in the 1950-51 season was the retirement of Billy Davies to take up a teaching post in Somerset. Also, Vic Darlison, the team's hooker in the post-war period, only made one appearance.

Billy Davies had signed for Bradford in August 1939. Although much of his career with Bradford was during the war years, he was one of the key figures in the great post-war period. Trevor recalls his Welsh colleague: "'Great', 'legend' and 'genius' are the words which are written to describe this sportsman. Many of the things Billy did on the pitch were marvellous. He was rugby in motion, with his great skill of carrying the ball in both hands. He would go though gaps with a movement of the hips to draw the opposition and make space for the next receiver. This resulted in numerous tries being scored. He was a Lance Todd Trophy winner at Wembley in 1947 when he gave a tremendous exhibition of the beauty of rugby football. A great team man who really loved his rugby, his handling was outstanding. He was a target for many opposition players who tried to put him off his game, but his outstanding genius and love of rugby league were so much in evidence in whatever situation he found himself.

His quiet and outstanding personality both on and off the field was good for rugby league. He commanded great respect in the world of rugby football of both codes."

Billy's star quality would ensure an extra 400 to 500 on the gate whenever it was announced he would definitely play. Jack Kitching once saying about Billy: 'If he gave you a pass, you knew you were heading for a gap'. Billy used to carry the ball in front of him. There were no elaborate dummies, but he was a brilliant all-round footballer. A little shimmy here and he was through, putting Eric Batten or Alan Edwards in the clear. Signing Davies was no easy matter; though. Negotiations lasted for three months and, among other things, involved trips down to Swansea and walks on the Yorkshire Moors."

Charlie Ebbage is an honorary vice-president of the Bradford Bulls, and has worked tirelessly for the club and the Supporters Club for many years. He recalls: "First-team coach Dai Rees used to have more spies than Churchill, and he got a whiff that Davies was interested in turning professional. Billy's wife Dorothy once told me that they paid him £1,000 to sign, which was quite a substantial amount at the time."

Davies had his nose broken in the 1947 Cup final and, typical of the man, he talked about that afterwards rather than being named man-of-the-match. Ebbage said that Davies would have enjoyed playing league under the modern laws. "I have spoken to Trevor about this, and he said Billy would have loved the 10-metre rule."

Billy Davies died on 26 September 2002. In the obituary in *League Express*, Trevor commented: "Along with Ernest Ward and Jack Kitching he was a key figure in the Northern team and was held in great esteem. Billy was always cool and calm and was the most unselfish player. I scored many tries he could have scored himself. He was a wonderful player and had a wonderful habit of veering towards a man then moving away and creating a gap."

The first half of the season was not a happy period for Trevor or Bradford. He missed much of it with a groin injury, and during the season only made 19 appearances, scoring four tries. However, the quality of his play was as high as ever. Writing in *Rugby League Gazette* at the start of the season, Tom Longworth said that the "absence of tactics" appalled him. He said that "most successful players have been quick thinkers. As a present day instance take TREVOR FOSTER. Observe his methods even without the ball. Note his positioning and then, when in possession, how he attempts to avoid his opponent and how he gives a pass."

Bradford's campaign started with four defeats and, although there was a slight improvement in September with a victory over two legs in the Yorkshire Cup over Halifax, and a league win against Liverpool Stanley at Odsal, only four more games were won up to 9 December, when cold weather forced a mid-season break until 13 January 1951. On 5 January, 'Pilgrim' looked at Bradford's position in *Rugby League Review*. He said that "Trevor Foster has been missed this season more than we have perhaps realised. Once Trevor gets down on that Odsal pitch, he sheds his quiet, unassuming off-field manner and takes over the role of a dominant personality. The Bradford forwards have very definitely been lost without his inspiring leadership. Trevor's return, after a slow recovery from a troublesome groin injury, and his subsequent appointment as trainer-coach at Odsal can be accounted bright spots in what has been a dark period."

The New Zealand contingent gradually adapted to British rugby league. Phillips and McLean both made massive contributions at Odsal for the rest of Trevor's career. They both left Bradford in April 1956. Hawes was also a consistent scorer until returning home in 1954.

Although the New Year did not start well for Bradford, with a 5-4 defeat at Whitehaven, the second half of the season showed considerable improvement. In the Challenge Cup, Bradford scraped through the first round 11-10 on aggregate against St Helens. A 14-4 victory over Swinton at Odsal was followed by a third round 5-4 defeat at Barrow. But after a 22-0 defeat at Workington the next week, Bradford won eight of the next nine matches to achieve a mid-table position of 14th, with 38 points from 36 matches. Their involuntary mid-season break caught up with them, because again 10 matches were played in April.

1951-52: Top of the table

The improvement in form over the last couple of months of the 1950-51 season was not enough to give Bradford's supporters hopes of a top four finish in the 1951-52 season. But, remarkably, the team managed to finish top of the table, only to lose the Championship Final to Wigan. In the close season, Huddersfield had been interested in Trevor becoming their player-coach, but again he decided to stay at Odsal.

The season started with two wins in the first five league games. In the Yorkshire Cup, Featherstone were knocked out after three matches. Bradford lost the first leg at Post Office Road 4-2, but then won 11-9 at Odsal. There should have been extra time, but confusion at the end of the match meant that some players were in the bath by the time the rules were clarified. Two days later the teams met again at Wakefield and Bradford won 17-9. However, Leeds won 14-13 at Odsal in the next round to end hopes of another Yorkshire Cup triumph.

Leeds repeated their victory in the league three days later, winning 18-9 on 29 September. But then Bradford suddenly embarked on a run of 18 consecutive victories until a 12-8 defeat by Hull at The Boulevard on 2 February 1952. This run included a 13-8 win over the New Zealand tourists, and a 38-5 win over Cardiff at Odsal on 12 January, notable for being a rare match against Welsh opposition, and for being the first league match played under floodlights in the north.

On 10 January, *Rugby League Review* said that "It's like old times at Odsal. Sixteen wins in a row, and with power to add! Trevor Foster's return to the Bradford pack has made quite a difference to its effectiveness. And when you look at Jack McLean's growing total of tries, don't forget that the master-hand of Ernest Ward has been behind quite a lot of them."

When the run came to an end, with Bradford third in the table, a point behind leaders Wigan, Trevor, who was Bradford's captain at Hull, magnanimously commented: "We are naturally disappointed to lose, but at the same time we give Hull credit for a really grand game. It was a pleasure to play in."

Naturally, Bradford's tremendous streak raised hopes of a good Challenge Cup run. However, after a narrow victory over league newcomers Doncaster, with a 6-5 win at Odsal, and 7-4 victory in the second leg, Bradford lost 28-12 at Wigan. The Lancashire side's win was controversial – Bradford's supporters believed that Northern's Bob Hawes had touched the ball down behind his own line, but the referee ruled that he had bounced it, and gave a try by Brian Nordgren for the home side. Bradford's supporters also claimed that the ball had hit the straw behind the goal and the dead ball line before Nordgren scored, so it was not a happy trip back to Yorkshire.

The battle for top spot continued until the last week of the season. On 22 March, Bradford travelled to Headingley, and drew 16-16. The lead changed hands eight times. But Bradford then won their last eight matches to claim the league leadership by one point, with 57 points from 36 matches. A review of their league season in the *Rugby Leaguer* on 3 May highlighted Trevor's important role as the "leader of the pack", and wondered how he could be replaced "if and when [he] retires".

In the Championship semi-final, Bradford faced Huddersfield at Odsal. They reached the final with a narrow 18-15 win. Allan Cave's report was headlined: "Panic passed as Foster took charge", and said that the Bradford forwards were "immense" and "the Foster-Traill twin-cylinder pressure ripped many a hole in the Huddersfield defence". Trevor was "the grandest forward on the field" and was captaining the side in the absence of Ernest Ward. A massive crowd of 56,478 enjoyed the match.

The next week, on 10 May, 48,684 fans saw Bradford's title hopes frustrated again, as Wigan won the Final 13-6. Wigan played better on the day, and the *Rugby Leaguer's* report said "it was simply amazing how Northern stood up to that early barrage". Silcock put Wigan ahead with a try in the first half, and although two penalties from Joe Phillips made the half time score 5-4, Wigan continued to control the game, and the final result was 13-6, Bradford's points coming from a further Phillips goal. The report said that "Foster had too much work thrown on to his shoulders, but never flinched." It was Wigan's fourth championship win since the war.

Bradford Northern: J. Phillips, R. Hawes, J. Mageen, N. A. Hastings, J. McLean, L. Haley, G. Jones, W. Shreeve, N. Haley, B. Radford, B. Tyler, T. J. F. Foster, K. Traill.
Scorer: Goals: Phillips (3).
Wigan: M. Ryan, J. Hilton, J. Broome, G. Roughley, B. C. Nordgren, J. Cunliffe, J. J. Alty, K. Gee, R. Mather, G. Woosey, N. Silcock, J. Large, H. Street.
Scorers: Tries: Silcock, Cunliffe, Ryan. Goals: Gee (2).

1952-53

At the start of the season, Trevor, now with coaching responsibilities at the club under manager Dai Rees, was 37. But he played 34 games, scoring four tries, and retirement from playing was still three seasons away.

Bradford finished third, with 56 points from 36 matches, 10 points behind league leaders St Helens. An early disappointment was defeat by Doncaster in the Yorkshire Cup. Bradford lost the first match in Doncaster 12-11, and must have expected to go through easily at Odsal. But at half time, Bradford were 8-0 down. Although Trevor scored a try in the second half, and Joe Phillips kicked three goals, Doncaster also scored a try; Bradford lost 11-9, and on aggregate 23-20. The crowd blamed the referee, who they considered made some bad decisions against Bradford, and he was attacked by angry supporters on his way back to the dressing room. Among the Rugby Football League's recommendations after the match was that changing facilities should be provided at pitch level, so the players and officials would not have to walk off through the crowd. The Odsal dressing rooms were at the top of the terracing at this time. This was implemented – in 1985.

Bradford's form improved after this debacle, and only three more league games were lost before the New Year. In November, the *Rugby League Gazette* said that Northern had made an "excellent start... the best effort for several seasons, blemished only by the Doncaster cup-tie debacle." Among the league successes was a 35-8 win at Doncaster, revenge for the cup disaster. Another highlight was the match against the Australian tourists. A crowd of 29,287 saw a floodlit 20-6 victory for the tourists. And this season saw a first for the club with a live appearance on television, their 34-5 victory over Leeds on 10 January being shown by the BBC.

In the New Year, Bradford beat Batley and Salford in the Challenge Cup before a 17-7 defeat against Huddersfield at Odsal ended their cup run. Their league form remained fairly consistent, and third place produced a Championship semi-final against local rivals Halifax at Thrum Hall. But in a close match, Bradford lost 18-16.

In the summer, Ernest Ward left Bradford. He had coaching ambitions, and there was no opening for him at Odsal, with Dai Rees and Trevor already running the team. He accepted a coaching position at Castleford, but Bradford retained his playing registration, which led to obvious dispute between the clubs. The matter was not resolved until the end of November, when a transfer fee was agreed, and his 17 years with Bradford ended. It meant the departure of another of the greats from the immediate post-war period, with only Trevor, Ken Traill, Barry Tyler and Ron Greaves still playing.

Trevor had great respect for Ernest Ward and regarded him very highly: "Dai Rees signed Ernest Ward for Bradford Northern on 30 July 1936, his 16th birthday. What a capture he turned out to be. For loyalty and commitment to our great club he shone out as an inspiration to others. As a player, he had the ability to turn a match in an instant, either with a fast solo break or a brilliant sidestep and pass out to an unmarked team mate. His football knowledge and quick thinking in tight situations made him an outstanding and feared player. His timing of the pass was near perfect and a great boon to his wing partner giving them great space to cross the line. His goal kicking from almost impossible angles was a revelation.

He was a players' player who commanded respect from his team mates and opposition alike. Playing mainly in the centre he built up a reputation of being an outstanding and gifted player. He went on to represent Great Britain 20 times in test matches during his playing career. He was our captain in the three Wembley finals after the war. Ernest made two trips to Australia with the British Lions, in 1946 and 1950, and was captain of the 1950 tourists.

Ernest was a true gentleman, and a quiet, unassuming man. I remember him receiving a standing ovation at Twickenham during the war when playing full-back for the British Army. Another indication of what a great player he was. He was the centre supreme, but as Eric Batten said, if you played Ernest at scrum-half, he would have a good game – he was so good."

Trevor's last cup triumph

Trevor was now 38-years-old, and the *Rugby League Gazette* said in August that he "cannot be expected to go on much longer, but he can certainly pass on a lot of experience to the younger lads". In fact, Trevor had two seasons left as a player.

The Yorkshire Cup was the highlight of Bradford's 1953-54 season. In the first round, Bradford managed to lose 18-15 at Odsal against lowly Batley. But because they had won the first leg at Mount Pleasant 34-10, the result was of little consequence. Leeds were more serious opposition in the next round, but Bradford won comfortably, 27-9, and then won 11-10 at Huddersfield in the semi-final.

The final was at Headingley on 31 October, with Hull providing the opposition. Inevitably, much of the coverage leading up to the final focused on Trevor. The *Yorkshire Evening Post* pointed out that he was Bradford's only survivor from the 1941 Final when they had beaten Dewsbury. He had played in five Yorkshire Cup Finals, and scored in four of them. And Trevor, with fellow forwards Barry Tyler and Ken Traill, were the only players who had played in the 1949 Final and were still at the club.

George M. Thompson's report said that Bradford expected Hull to come at them strongly in the second half of the game, and prepared for this. He said that Trevor had "coolly led" the team in their plan. Joe Phillips put Bradford ahead with a penalty on seven minutes. Bob Hawes then scored the game's only try and, although Phillips missed the conversion, he scored another penalty before half time to give Bradford a 7-0 lead. The second half was indeed a tough encounter, as Bradford expected, but Hull only managed a penalty, to give Bradford victory 7-2, and the Cup.

'Airedale' in the *Rugby Leaguer* said that the "drizzle, murky light, greasy ball and wet turf all militated against the spectacular." He commented on the close spotting and marking by both sides, in particular Bradford. The scrums went 25-19 to Bradford, but he felt that Hull should have done more with their early possession, and there was little variety in their play. In the same paper, the Bradford Northern correspondent, 'Odsal' argued that the cup win was a triumph of tactics and teamwork, and gave credit to the victory to Dai Rees. One supporter commented afterwards that it was Bradford's fault it had not been a good match – they had knocked out all the best teams in the earlier rounds.

Bradford Northern: J. Phillips, R. Hawes, J. Mageen, W. Seddon, J. McLean, W. Jenkins, R. Goddard, B. Tyler, N. Haley, W. Jones, T. J. F. Foster, A. Storey, K. Traill.
Scorers: Try: Hawes. Goals: Phillips (2).
Hull: C. Hutton, K. Bowman, W. Riches, C. R. Turner, I. J. Watts, B. Conway, A. Tripp, M. Scott, P. T. Harris, R. Coverdale, H. Markham, A. Bedford, J. W. Whiteley.
Scorer: Goal: Hutton.

In the league, Bradford finished ninth, with 44 points from 36 matches, a decline of six places from the previous season, and a warning of a gradual decline through the 1950s that would end in the club's collapse in 1963. The Challenge Cup did not lighten Bradford's hearts – a first round win over Rochdale being followed by a 15-10 defeat at Wigan. In the *Rugby League Gazette* in March, Dai Rees pointed out that the club had been hard hit by the loss of Ernest Ward, Norman Hastings (who had returned to New Zealand) and Len Haley through injury. He also pointed out that Bradford's wingers had scored almost 70 tries between them, and the team's performance was "not bad at all" given the problems they had faced.

Trevor had been as consistent as ever, playing 35 matches, and scoring five tries. Phil King's report of the last home match of the season, against Barrow, was headlined "Tattered Barrow torn apart by brilliant Foster". The report said he "raced through the Barrow defence as nimbly as a fox terrier dodges bulldogs, and was the mainspring of Northern's attack in the absence of tourist Traill." He made three of Bradford's tries in six minutes in the second half. Team manager Dai Rees joked afterwards that he would sign "that trialist second-row forward".

Finale – and a testimonial

At the start of the 1954-55 season, Trevor was approaching 40, but as George M. Thompson pointed out, despite being an age that was "some five or six years after many forwards have had to quit, is still the Odsal leader".

Thompson said that he was "maybe slower, slightly slimmer, yet fitter than most, [and] he starred in Northern's first match". He also commended Trevor's "agility and inspiration". But a few weeks into the season, Trevor announced that it would be his last as a player. 'The Oracle' wrote that "Trevor has started this season with some brilliant performances and there is still no sign of his work deteriorating." Harry Hornby, the club's managing director, said: "We are losing a grand player, but he will continue as a coach." Dai Rees commented that he did not know any player in the game who had given more loyal service. He continued: "He has never given me any trouble and he will always be one for whom I shall have the greatest respect. The Northern pack has been developed around him and they could not have wished for a better leader." It was also the 20th anniversary of the club's move to Odsal. Harry East, writing in the *Rugby League Gazette*, outlined the progress the club had made since those days, when they were "destitute and almost deserted... penniless and practically friendless."

Trevor was typically consistent in his final playing season, making 29 appearances and scoring three tries, despite fracturing a collar-bone mid season. But Bradford's decline on the pitch continued. In the Yorkshire Cup, Castleford and Hunslet were beaten before Bradford lost 10-5 at Hull in the semi-final.

In the Challenge Cup, memories were still strong of the massive crowd that had seen Warrington win the Odsal Final Replay the previous May. It was one of those ironies that cup draws produce which saw them return to Odsal in the first round as holders, and being beaten 9-4. Derek Marshall's report said that "Trevor Foster… was the man behind the biggest of the rugby league cup shocks this weekend. It was his splendid leadership that inspired Northern to beat Warrington… and it earned for him the privilege of being chaired off the field by his team-mates." Allan Cave wrote about Trevor's performance: "Where play was there always was this great Welshman. He showed his men what to do by doing it himself – and they followed suit most successfully." But in the second round, Featherstone Rovers won 7-2 at Odsal.

Trevor's last appearance at Odsal was a 30-25 win over Hunslet on 16 April. He entered the pitch alone to a terrific ovation. At half time there were tributes to Trevor, and the crowd sang *For He's A Jolly Good Fellow*. And he marked the occasion by scoring Bradford's final try, three minutes from time. Bill Seddon offered him the chance to kick the goal, but Trevor declined, and Seddon converted. At the end of the game, Arthur Clues and Ken Traill carried Trevor off on their shoulders.

Trevor first played against Arthur Clues on the 1946 Lions tour. Clues then came to England to join Leeds, and finished his career with two seasons at Hunslet. They were great opponents on the pitch and friends off it. Trevor remembers his great colleague and adversary: "Without a doubt Arthur Clues was one of the most outstanding forwards from my era. I first met him on the 1946 tour. A former policeman in Sydney, he came to Leeds after the 1946 British Lions tour. He was outstanding against the Lions. In the first big game at the Sydney Cricket Ground against New South Wales before a packed house, Arthur with his powerful physique was in the second row. He was the most prominent of a tough pack of hardy Aussies. From the kick off, Arthur made his mark on me with a robust tackle when I was trying to make headway. As the game progressed I seemed to be spending my time knocked to the ground with or without the ball and it was always Arthur who was putting the pressure on me.

At Leeds, he became an idol with his outstanding talents. I remember seeing his picture in the *Yorkshire Post* arriving at Leeds City station with heavy snow falling. It shocked Arthur, who had come from sunny Sydney.

Arthur was a very outgoing character. He was always the joker and he became one of the most popular overseas players at the great Leeds rugby league club. We had some big battles on the pitch, including the 1947 Challenge Cup Final, but were great pals off it. He was a real terror, but had some great skills, including a deft chip over the defence.

I remember an incident that took place at Odsal when we played Leeds in a midweek fixture. At the halfway line, near the old stand, the ball had gone loose, and Gwylfa Jones, our scrum-half bent down to pick it up. At that moment Arthur came rushing in with all guns blazing. He knocked Gwylfa breathless. Nearby was Frank Whitcombe, who with all his great strength and 18 stone knocked Arthur back many yards. Arthur was semi-conscious, laid out by the touchline with the sponge man endeavouring to bring him to his feet. This took a few minutes, and meanwhile the referee sent Frank Whitcombe off. He had to walk up the walkway through the terraces to the dressing room – the famous Odsal walk for a sent-off player. When Arthur was back on his feet, partly recovered, he started to walk to his place on the field, when the referee pointed at him and sent him off.

As time went by, they became great friends and visited each other very often for the odd pint or two. They would spend time at Frank's pub, the King's Head at Westgate, and after closing time would sit in the cellar for a great part of the night sampling all that was good.

Arthur was one of the greatest forwards that I faced – a true Aussie who wore the green and gold jersey with great pride."

In 1988, Arthur Clues was invited to a dinner to celebrate Trevor's 50 years in rugby league. He was unable to attend, but replied: "Please convey to Trevor my sincere congratulations. Not only was he one of the greatest forwards I have ever had the privilege of playing against, he is the nicest bloke I have ever had the pleasure of meeting. Nature's gentleman. This celebration could not happen to a nicer feller."

Arthur Clues died in November 1998. He stayed in Leeds after he retired from rugby league, and his funeral was attended by many great players from the game.

Trevor's testimonial, granted in recognition of his long service to Bradford Northern, took place during the season. An appeal letter from his testimonial fund's committee said that Trevor "has gradually built up for himself a reputation as an 'Ideal Sportsman' who at all times is scrupulously fair and courteous, with a keenness to play rugby football as it should be played. Many great men have adorned the rugby league game, both from a playing and administrative sense, but few have equalled, and none excelled, the services which Trevor has rendered to his club in particular and the game in general."

In the booklet issued for the testimonial, Harry Hornby recalled how it had taken him 12 months to persuade Trevor to come to Bradford. He concluded: "Trevor's name will go down in history as one of rugby's greatest and cleanest players." The booklet included many tributes from press reports, and from playing colleagues, opponents and other people in the game. Warrington manager, and former Wigan star Ces Mountford said that Trevor was "one of the greatest forwards it has been my pleasure to watch." Rugby League secretary Bill Fallowfield commended Trevor's "superb handling ability and his sportsmanlike style of play", while his predecessor, John Wilson, believed that young forwards should model their style on Trevor. Joe Egan recalled their time together on the 1946 tour, and said that he was the most popular member of the touring party. Gus Risman added that Trevor was "a model for any budding player".

'Veteran' in *Yorkshire Sports*, reproduced in the *Rugby League Gazette*, said that he was glad to hear that Trevor had been granted a testimonial, as he was a 'gentleman of rugby'. He continued: "For two decades, Trevor Foster has set an example, not only in fine forward play, but in clean play as well. He has shown that success needs no rough stuff." Harry East, in the same magazine, also spoke about Trevor's "uncanny ball sense, his superb positional play, his strong running, his brilliant defence, his wise captaincy." But above all, East recalled Trevor's "fairness, his sportsmanship, his complete unselfishness, his kindliness and courteousness..."

Part of the testimonial was a benefit match at Odsal. Yorkshire and England cricketer Johnny Wardle kicked off the match, and Bradford beat local rivals Keighley 23-22, in front of 5,727 fans. There were many examples of the respect for Trevor that was present among Bradford's supporters. One newspaper reported that before his last game, "scores of people whom he had never met before were thanking him for the many hours of pleasure he had provided for them. Someone gave him an envelope containing £11. It was a gift from the Spenborough Supporters Club, asking him to use the money to buy a bookcase."

Charlie Ebbage, a life vice-president of Bradford Bulls, described for this book Trevor's playing career as follows: "Trevor was 30 years ahead of his time. He was the complete athlete. Big and strong with tremendous pace, he would have excelled in today's game. He was like a centre playing in the pack and he is without doubt Bradford's greatest ever player."

Return to action

Trevor's rugby league activity continued on the coaching front, which is covered elsewhere in this book. In 1957, in an injury crisis at Odsal, he turned out for the 'A' team and "proved as fit as the rest" according to Ray Oddy's report, which also said that "those in command at Odsal... would give anything to turn the clock back to the time when Foster was in his prime." For the record, the 'A' team won 30-16 against Dewsbury at Odsal.

In 1966, the Rugby Football League organised two charity matches at Headingley on Sunday 6 November in aid of the St John's Ambulance Brigade. The main match was between the 1966 British Lions tourists and the Rest of the League. But as a curtain-raiser, a match featuring retired players was arranged. The teams were a West side, representing players who had played for Lancashire or Cumberland clubs, captained by Gus Risman, and an East side with players from Yorkshire clubs, captained by Trevor.

A letter from Bill Fallowfield said that the public were looking forward to seeing the former players in action, and "Trevor Foster and Ken Traill will have a chance of showing us once again the forward combination which played such a large part in Bradford Northern's post-war success." The match was played over four 12-minute periods, with three three-minute intervals. Plenty of substitutions were allowed to give everyone a game. Bill Fallowfield wrote to Trevor before the game, suggesting that a rota of players be drawn up beforehand because the public announcer may not recognise all the players, as "loss of hair and alteration of shape is at times a very effective disguise."

Trevor was pictured before the game with Gus Risman, and looked little changed from his playing days. Another photo of the match showed him scoring a try. Arthur Haddock's report said that "the spectators seemed to enjoy the turn-out of former players as much as the main attraction... the stars of yesteryear provided entertaining fare." His report concluded that "The veterans obviously enjoyed their moment in the limelight again". Almost as a footnote, he said that the Rest of the League won the main match 38-31.

Trevor with his MBE at Odsal.
(Photo: *Telegraph & Argus*)

Trevor receiving the Papal Medal from Father Lawrence Lister, Parish Priest of St Cuthbert's, in St Cuthbert's Church (Photo: Courtesy Trevor Foster)

Trevor with his Honorary Doctorate, presented by the University of Bradford in 2002.
(Photo: Ede & Ravenscroft)

Trevor introducing guest of honour Neil Kinnock to Robbie Paul before the 2003 Challenge Cup Final.
Brian Noble is watching the formalities. (Photograph: *Telegraph & Argus*)

Festival of rugby league at Rugby School prior to the 2000 World Cup.
Trevor, Billy Boston, Neil Fox and Sir Rodney Walker join officials from Rugby Council.
(Photo: Courtesy Trevor Foster)

Trevor with Henry and Robbie Paul holding a piece of Wembley turf.
(Photo: *Telegraph & Argus*)

Trevor with Billy Watts – the Leeds timekeeper.
(Photo: David Williams)

Diamond Jubilee Dinner at the Norfolk Gardens Hotel to celebrate
the 60th Anniversary of Trevor joining Bradford Northern.
Top: The Display stand (Photo: David Williams)
Left: Trevor with Bullman. Right: Trevor with Ray French
(Both photos: Courtesy Trevor Foster)

2003: Bradford Bulls return to Odsal.
Top: Trevor with the past players who played an exhibition game
to celebrate the return to the club's spiritual home.
Bottom: Trevor kissing the ground to mark the great day.
(Photos: Courtesy Trevor Foster)

Trevor celebrated his 90th birthday with a party for family and friends on 4 December 2004
at the Bradford Police Club for Young People. Here he is surrounded by members of his family.
(Photograph: *Telegraph & Argus*)

Trevor at the opening of Trevor Foster Way in 2002.
(Photograph: *Telegraph & Argus*)

9.   Coaching: Inspiring young talent

Trevor's wartime experience as a Physical Training Instructor (PTI) pointed to a future in coaching rugby league. He must have anticipated moving in that direction at the end of his playing career, but in fact the opportunity came much earlier.

Towards the end of 1948, the Rugby Football League decided to appoint an official national coach for the first time, and Trevor was offered the job. Bill Fallowfield sent him a telegram to Newport on 18 January 1949 saying that Bradford Northern had agreed he could do the job, and he could 'start when he liked'. His first work was to be to prepare a camp for young players in the summer. One newspaper report by 'The Oracle' said of Trevor's appointment that the Rugby league was attempting to develop the junior side of the game, and that "there are few people more fitted for this job".

The first course was held that summer at Otley, over four weeks, with 52 young players attending each week. Trevor remembers "one part of the coaching courses was an outstanding success. A party of youngsters from all parts of the rugby league area would assemble at Otley on a Monday morning, and stay until the Friday evening for coaching classes under staff like former Huddersfield star Alec Fiddes, Tom Sale, Ginger Crossley and myself to put the pupils through the various coaching lessons. We were bedded down in the Otley Church Hall... Towards the end of the week a competition took place with the teams being awarded points for skills at the game — a truly fascinating way of improving individual ability. We would organise play-offs towards the weekend when senior members of the RFL would visit and watch the games. Many players on those courses became professional club players and I was often informed how beneficial those courses were." It was reported that the courses were oversubscribed. The pioneering element was shown with one newspaper featuring a photo of a 15-year-old player being given his bedding on his arrival in Otley. Trevor remembers these courses as the "outstanding memory of my coaching career... we were made most welcome by the kind people and officials of Otley, with free access to cinemas and such like, and most importantly, improving the great comradeship which the game of rugby league produces."

The course also included films and lectures, as well as practical demonstrations from the organisers involved.

Another initiative saw Trevor and Ernest Ward encouraging coaching and involvement in the game through a stage show, *Focus on Rugby*. The first was in St Helens, and included Wigan's Martin Ryan and local Saints star Jim Stott. The Central Council for Physical Recreation (CCPR) were supporting the initiative, which also included a three-day course for teachers in the Wigan area. In January 1950, Trevor reported in the *Rugby League Gazette* that over 10,000 schoolboys and adults had seen the show in all the main rugby league areas, including South Wales. He also said that three coaching courses for schoolmasters had been held, and junior club coaching was being held in seven towns.

A document headed 'A basis for a development plan for Rugby League Football' produced by the RFL in 1949 recognised that it was necessary to build a coaching structure throughout the game. The RFL had recognised the importance of paying attention to coaching in schools and junior clubs. The document outlined: "If the services of the chief coach are to be used to achieve the most effective results in the minimum amount of time, it is essential that they should not be dissipated by his making an undue number of personal visits to clubs and groups in every part of the Rugby League area." It proposed developing, with the help of the CCPR, a network of part-time assistant coaches, with one for each district, holding a residential course for potential coaches, and outlined a syllabus for the week. It suggested that trainee coaches would be tested for the RFL coaching award, and put forward that a Class II award for voluntary club coaches should start in 1950. It then outlined a more detailed plan for publicity and events in different areas, and how the effectiveness of the scheme could be monitored through advisory visits to clubs with volunteer coaches.

Many of these ideas will seem very familiar to those involved with rugby league development work today. But in 1949 they were groundbreaking.

The first course for regional coaches was held at Headingley in July 1949 and the theoretical exam for them is fascinating reading. The exam paper said that the aim of the course had been twofold: to examine and appoint regional coaches, and to improve coaching by individuals. The prospective coaches were asked which parts of the course had been most useful for regional coaches, and which aspects of coaching had not been covered. Candidates were invited to "briefly criticise the course".

Other questions asked that if a regional coach was conducting evening classes, what steps could he take to ensure constant attendance; to describe with diagrams three games for encouraging teamwork in passing and handling the ball; the duties of forwards and threequarters in the game, and to discuss the statement: 'Without class control the greatest player in the world cannot hope to become a great coach'.

By October 1949, of the 40 coaches who had attended the course at Headingley, it was reported by the RFL that four had attained Grade 1, and seven reached Grade 2. The four Grade 1 coaches were Gus Risman, Alex Fiddes, Emlyn Jenkins and Tommy Sale. More courses for school teachers, junior club coaches and visits to schools were being organised. Teachers were offered the chance to qualify for a Schools Coaching Certificate from a three-day course, usually held during the school holidays. The course combined lectures and films with practical demonstrations and practice of skills. Each day ended with a practice game. The courses for voluntary club coaches concentrated more on positional play and team training. Successful candidates were also given a certificate.

In November 1949, writing in the *Rugby League Gazette*, Trevor said that on his visits to junior clubs, he found "players neglecting the fundamentals" of the game. He felt that "the talent is certainly there but it needs encouragement and the right type of coaching".

In 1950, a further course for schoolboy players was held at Otley. The RFL also held a course for 34 players aged under-21 at Bisham Abbey. As well as rugby league, the course included other sports such as cricket, swimming and canoeing. A course was also held for senior coaches at Lowther College in North Wales. Among the players present were Ces Mountford, who went on to have a distinguished coaching career, first with Warrington and then in New Zealand, including a period as coach of the New Zealand national team.

Trevor worked for the RFL as chief coach until November 1950. Cliff Worthington's report on his departure said that "Trevor's ability has never been in question, but the job is obviously far too onerous for anybody who still has obligations to a club. Such a strenuous and important post, which entails, among other things, a lot of travelling, positively shouted for a man whose playing days were behind him." He also said that the £400 a year salary that Trevor had been paid was far too low. Another report said that Trevor's departure was a big blow to the League's coaching projects.

Trevor explains that it was his playing commitments that made him give up the post: "Bill Fallowfield, the secretary of the RFL was very keen to keep me. We had made some real strides in developing a structure for rugby league coaching across the North of England. The courses we organised had become extremely popular and were influencing the development of the game at grass roots level and improving coaching methods in the well established amateur and professional clubs. However, the job was too much for one person and with my involvement at Odsal (I was still playing for the first team) it was not possible to sustain my rugby league coaching duties to the level required at headquarters. The job and the coaching structure needed a rethink. Bert Cook, the former Leeds full-back, took over the reins and became RL coach on a temporary basis."

Trevor still continued to develop his coaching, soon starting work with Dai Rees at Bradford as assistant coach. Even before being officially appointed to his coaching role at Odsal, he had taken charge of the side that season when team manager Rees was ill. Trevor also continued his work with young players. In 1955, he coached 40 of them for the RFL at Bisham Abbey in Berkshire over a week, working with Alec Fiddes. He also ran a two-day course in Rochdale for teachers. The topics included 'fundamental skills, handling, passing and receiving', a lecture on positional play and tactics, and 'application of rugby league coaching to schoolboys'. The course ended with a lecture on the laws of the game, and a one-hour written and practical examination for the Schoolmasters' Rugby League Coaching Certificate. In 1956, Trevor repeated the course for Halifax's schoolmasters, although the letter he received from the RFL's amateur rugby league organiser said that "I understand that one or two [of the teachers] are in the older age group and will not wish to be very energetic."

At Odsal, Trevor continued to work as coach with Dai Rees. His fellow Welshman had been the team manager when Trevor came to Bradford in 1938 and Trevor had a great deal of respect for him, remembering him as: "The man behind all our great success at Odsal, a tourist to Australia and New Zealand in his day as a Halifax player. He was a most far-sighted coach and manager and a most outstanding man manager, he could deal with most events on or off the field in his years at Odsal. A very shrewd tactician, he could pinpoint the rights and wrongs of a player's performance during the game, and pass on advice to any individual at half time with excellent talks. He guided the team with his plans to suit all occasions, and was a person who never sought the limelight, but had the respect of all players who would seek his advice on or off the field. He had an outstanding relationship with his chairman, Harry Hornby."

The team's fortunes fluctuated between mid-table respectability and the lower depths of the league. In March 1960, with Bradford towards the bottom of the league – they eventually finished 26th out of 30 teams and only won four games after Christmas – Dai Rees was sacked as team manager and Trevor was given sole control over playing matters.

Dai Rees had taken over as team manager in 1936, and had been responsible for the great Bradford teams of the post-war era. But the supporters felt it was time for a change, and he was offered the position of stadium manager.

Trevor was in the unusual position of being both coach and a club director at this time. There was not much he could do to improve the side's performances that season. There was little money for new players at Odsal at this time, and it was a financial crisis that ended Trevor's association with the club in December 1960. He resigned both as director and coach. The club's bank had asked for the directors to be guarantors against the club's overdraft. However, Trevor had only joined the board on condition that he did not have to make a financial commitment, and – probably wisely – refused to be a guarantor. (These events are covered more fully in the chapter on the 1963 to 1964 'resurrection' period).

Trevor began helping out Keighley for a period in an advisory capacity, mainly looking for young players for the club. There was speculation that he would move to coach Wigan when Joe Egan was sacked, but this did not materialise. Then on 4 December 1961, Trevor became first team coach at Leeds. He took over from Dai Prosser, and fellow Welshman Jack Evans became 'A' team coach.

Arthur Haddock's report in the *Yorkshire Evening News* said that Leeds had been working for a month on a new structure to improve their performance, and that Trevor had been chosen from a shortlist of two. He wrote: "With sole responsibility for coaching, training and selecting of the first team Foster has powers which are rarely given in rugby league." Noel Stockdale, the Leeds chairman, commented: "When making all these appointments the committee's first consideration has been to choose men who in their opinion have the ability to bring the best out of each individual, foster team spirit and accept responsibility for their players". The *Rugby Leaguer* reported that moves behind the Headingley scenes took first priority last week. "On the grounds of experience alone the new mentors could not be bettered and with coaching, team selection and scouting (both in near and far territory) all overhauled and modernised there should now be nothing to stop Leeds going places – providing the necessary degree of ACTION and consistency of performance on the field is attained."

In May 1961, Leeds had beaten Warrington in the Championship Final, and finally brought the league title to Headingley, after more than 60 long years of trying. But the team's early season form in 1961-62 had been erratic, with only seven wins from the first 12 matches. There was the compensation of a Yorkshire Cup Final, but that was lost 19-9 to Wakefield Trinity at Odsal. The *Rugby Leaguer* wrote on 29 December, three weeks after Trevor's arrival: "Frankly only on a few occasions have Leeds looked like worthy champions... The coaching, selection and scouting changes earlier this month were made with but one end in view – to make the very best use of the available talent; to ensure no likely acquisitions are missed and to put Leeds back where a club of its reputation should be – well up amongst the leaders."

Trevor soon found that coaching could be a hazardous business. He was taking a training session on the snow-bound Headingley cricket outfield on Boxing Day morning when he was injured. The Leeds players included Lewis Jones, Ken Thornett, Louis Neumann, Derek Hallas and loose-forward Brian Shaw. Trevor recalls "Brian had been signed for a record fee from the Hunslet club and was keen to impress in the touch-and-pass session at the end of training. He was in a somewhat boisterous mood and decided to tackle me full on to show he had the beating of the coach. Suddenly it was as if I was back in Wollongong [where Trevor first injured his knee on the 1946 Lions tour]. I fell down in the same awkward way and immediately felt an intense stabbing pain through my left knee. I was carried off by the players and keen to save face made not a murmur, though the knee was the size of a football. I had travelled to training from Bradford in a pair of hefty Wellington boots, since the weather was so inclement. When I got home I was not able to remove my left Wellington due to the swelling and had to sleep in the boot for three nights. Brian Shaw had a lot to answer for."

Leeds's form improved after Trevor's arrival. After a 10-5 defeat at Hull KR on 23 December, only four more league matches were lost, and there was a run of seven consecutive league wins from 6 January to 10 March, the last being a 20-10 triumph over Bradford Northern at Headingley. After a 17-10 win at The Boulevard in January, the *Rugby Leaguer* commented: "the Leeds form of the last two months has been a very different thing to some we saw earlier in the season." However, in the Challenge Cup a 34-6 win over Bramley was followed by a 7-7 draw at Leigh, with a 17-16 defeat in the replay at Headingley ending Leeds's Wembley hopes.

The sort of pressure a coach comes under is shown by a letter to Trevor dated 26 February 1962, probably from the Leeds chairman. Despite the team's success, and being written after a 34-8 win over Doncaster, he said: "...there is some cause for concern in the pack, that as individuals, they are undoubtedly a match for any in the game, but there is a tendency to play as individuals and not together as a unit." He went on to say that referees had said to him that there was too much 'chuntering' from the Leeds pack, and only Brian Shaw (the pack leader) should speak to the referee. He also said that the ball should be cleared quickly from acting half, "preferably with a long pass" and that the acting half should not try to break through on his own. He also said the forwards should work more as a unit at the opposition's play-the-ball and not as individuals, and there should be a tightening up in the tackle.

Leeds finished the season in seventh place, mainly due to their inconsistent start, although their form after the defeat against Leigh in the Challenge Cup had raised concerns for supporters. On 30 March, the *Rugby Leaguer* reported that "recent form has not been impressive" (after a 24-7 victory against York), and continued: "As it is management cannot be satisfied with the present situation either and it was announced on Saturday that the Leeds scouts were out in force with two senior Rugby Union games and a number of junior League and Union matches engaging their attention."

The next week, after a 25-9 defeat at Featherstone, their correspondent said: "Once again the weaknesses in the middle back play and the old forward deficiencies were only too apparent... Young players of great promise have been 'blooded' into the senior side but up to date that has not been a complete solution." A week later, despite a 24-2 win at Dewsbury, he continued in the same vein: "Ever since the cup-tie debacle against Leigh the local fans have been voicing their concern at the lack-lustre brand of football that has come from Leeds."

Despite two further victories over Castleford and Warrington, there was still criticism the next week: "...it must be remarked that the way that Leeds have let some of the recent opposition slam away down the centre of the field and an inability to do more than mount the odd retaliatory attack in reply has been disconcerting to say the least. But all has not been gloom. The obvious enthusiasm of such men as Thornett, Simms, Fairbank (and when he has played) Lou Neumann augur well for the recovery campaign – especially if Thornett is to return to the No.1 berth. Don Robinson has been a tower of strength in the pack – I think he has been one of our most consistent forwards this term and his discontent at being moved from his favourite no.8 spot is regrettable. Over and above all has been of the contribution of the maestro Lewis Jones. He has produced some copy-book performances and without him at times the team has appeared as a ship without a rudder."

On 4 May, he concluded: "In my own view the Championship crown really slipped in the games at Castleford and Featherstone before Easter and it must be generally admitted that (though some good football has been played) the old Headingley bogy of inconsistency has been a decisive factor in the 1961-62 Headingley story."

Trevor did introduce a number of young players during the season, including Mick Shoebottom, who was one of the club's key players in the 1960s, until injury ended his career prematurely in 1971. The *Rugby Leaguer* reported on 2 March: "Our man at Headingley spoke eloquently of the blooding of teenagers Michael Shoebottom and Robin Dewhurst." Eighteen-year-old Geoff Wriglesworth ended as top try scorer with 34. Thirty-five players had been used in the first team: 17 backs and 18 forwards.

Trevor's second season in charge was marred by the worst winter since 1947. Once again, expectations were high. The *Rugby Leaguer's* comment at the start of the season was: "Even apart from the ideas of strengthening the side (which may crystallise quite quickly now) the talent on the Leeds books is not inconsiderable. The aims of the Football Committee were aptly summed up by a recent comment – a team to compare with the very best – one that will bear comparison with any of the great Leeds teams of the past."

The Rugby League operated in two divisions this season, and it opened with a separate competition to provide additional fixtures. The clubs were divided into Eastern and Western Divisional Championships, with Leeds in the Eastern competition. Each team played eight matches, and Leeds finished fifth, with six wins and a draw, but not high enough for the semi-finals which involved the top four clubs. A couple of weeks break between the end of this competition and the start of the league fixtures gave Trevor the chance to address some of the team's problems. The *Rugby Leaguer* reported: "[The] Loiners have been without a match for a fortnight during which time intensified coaching has been in progress with the aim of ironing out some of the difficulties so apparent in the Regional matches and of attaining greater cohesion between pack and backs."

Life in the First Division was tougher. The main problems seemed to be in the pack, although against Oldham on 20 October, despite Alan Rees receiving a double broken nose, Leeds won 23-5, and the pack played well. But three weeks later, a 27-0 defeat at Swinton was the first time Leeds had failed to score since 3 December 1960. Leeds got revenge for this embarrassment on 1 December, winning the return 30-3, with six tries.

Up to 15 December, Leeds played 10 matches, and won five. Their next match was a 10-8 win at Castleford in the Challenge Cup on 9 February. Five weeks later, they lost 20-11 at Wigan, who went on to reach Wembley. Although Leeds's form improved in April and this continued until the season eventually finished on 24 May, they still finished seventh, with 16 wins from 30 matches. The *Rugby Leaguer* said on 17 May: "Much of the Loiners' football, even in victory, has not been of the quality so long traditional with the Leeds club." A week later, their correspondent wrote about constant changes in line ups, and said that only on five occasions has the same pack of forwards played consecutive matches. The end of season report on Leeds said that the first team had used four hookers and five full backs.

Trevor's hopes of a higher finish were hit by Ken Thornett returning to Australia and Robin Dewhurst breaking his leg. However, he had introduced some young players to first team action, including Barry Seabourne, who formed a crucial half-back combination for Leeds with Mick Shoebottom.

After only one-and-a-half seasons, and his only full season disrupted by the Arctic winter, the powers that be at Headingley decided on a change in management, and Roy Francis arrived from Hull to take charge of the first team. Ironically, Hull had just finished 14th, only three points above relegated Oldham. But Trevor continued at Headingley until October 1966, coaching the 'A' team.

It is often forgotten that during the time he was working to relaunch Bradford Northern after the club's collapse in December 1963, he was a coach at Leeds. In June 1964, Leeds wrote to Trevor asking whether "in view of your possible commitments with Northern at present and during the forthcoming football season you will be able to continue as our 'A' team coach. Please do not misunderstand this letter! We would of course like you to continue but it is just that if you are asked to remain on Northern's Committee it may be difficult for you to run the 'A' team too!"

Trevor replied to confirm that he wanted to continue as assistant coach, and Noel Stockdale wrote to say that this was unanimously endorsed by the Leeds committee, and praised his work with the club's younger players. When Trevor left Headingley, the Leeds Supporters' Club wrote to say "how much we have appreciated your work, always giving of your best, especially to the Supporters' Club. Your kindness and help to us during your stay at Headingley has been wonderful. Nothing was too much, whatever we asked, you were always ready to help. I can assure you there will always be a warm welcome whenever you care to visit us at Headingley."

Phil Hodgson's recent book on Leeds in the 1960s and 1970s, *Headingley Heroes*, recognises that in the period after 1961: "Leeds signed and blooded a number of fine youngsters in the early 1960s, with two of the Loiners' brightest stars emerging in half-backs Mick Shoebottom and Barry Seabourne." Trevor had given both players their first team debuts.

Reflecting on his time as first team coach, Trevor remembers a very different relationship between directors and coaches compared to nowadays. He says: "Coaches were 10-a-penny as far as the directors were concerned. Their attitude was that they could hire and fire a coach at any time, the coach was totally under the supervision of the football manager, unlike today."

After leaving Headingley, Trevor continued his coaching work with young players back at Odsal, running an under-17 (colts) team. When the new Bradford Northern had been set up, Joe Phillips had asked Trevor to be the first team coach, but he declined, preferring to continue his work with Leeds's young players for a couple of years before returning to a similar role at Odsal. In June 1970, club chairman Harry Womersley wrote to Trevor to congratulate him on his team's "fine performance in winning the League Championship of the Leeds League. We would also like to convey to you our sincere thanks for your dedication to the job of coaching these youngsters. It is felt in the Board Room that in two or three years' time we will be in the same position as Castleford with a wealth of junior talent on our doorstep."

Les Priestley was a young player at Bradford Northern at this time. He has fond memories of Trevor's coaching: "In the mid-1960s, the rebirth of Northern kindled a new enthusiasm for the game in Bradford. When the club advertised for new players to form under-17 and under-19 teams, many local teenagers enrolled and could be seen muddying each others' shirts twice a week on the pitches (more aptly called the Rec) behind the stadium. There were talented players, average players and downright poor players. Understandably, most of the coaches were ruthless – it was a professional club after all – and spent their time with the talented.

Trevor Foster was different. While he probably had the best 'eye' for talent, he never ceased encouraging all – of whatever ability. As long as you tried, you received praise. His enthusiasm for the game was obvious and infectious, and I'm sure that the vast majority of those he coached retain not only affection and tremendous respect for Trevor the man, but were inspired by him to love the game. I was never very talented, but I don't think I was downright poor – I played in the team that first season, but was never good enough to play professionally. Trevor encouraged me, and always coached good habits, organisation and techniques; skills which stood me in good stead and helped me overcome that lack of special talent."

Trevor's commitment to young players continued and in 1975 he was involved in setting up a new under-16 league to play on Sundays. Trevor had written to the RFL to try to secure some financial support, but they referred him to BARLA, although they did suggest he contact Albert Fearnley about help with coaching. The formation of the league followed coaching courses in Bradford and Keighley. In the late 1960s, he had been involved in the Bradford Sunday Youth Rugby League through his work with the Bradford Police Boys' Club.

In 1974, Trevor applied to work for the Rugby League in another capacity, as public relations officer. In August, he wrote to the RFL, following an advert in the *Telegraph & Argus*. However, he did not get the job – a young David Howes was appointed.

Left: The match programme from the 1948 Final
(Courtesy Rugby Football League)
Above: Trevor being tackled in the 1948 Final.
(Photo: Courtesy Trevor Foster)
Below: The 1949 Challenge Cup Final; Frank
Whitcombe with the ball, watched by Paddy Reid.
(Photo: Courtesy Robert Gate)

Above:
Bill Leake, watched by Trevor, runs at the Halifax pack.
(Photo: Courtesy Robert Gate)

Left: The match programme
(Courtesy Rugby Football League)

Above: Trevor introduces the Lord Mayor of Swansea to Billy Davies before
the 1946 Wales versus England match.
Below: Wales team versus England at Wigan March 1950.
(Photos: Courtesy Trevor Foster)

10. The fall and rise of Bradford Northern 1963-64

Trevor's retirement in 1955 meant the last link with the great post-war team was gone. Harry Hornby's injection of New Zealanders in 1950, in particular Jack McLean and Joe Phillips, had helped the team greatly. However, as the 1950s wore on, it was apparent that the club were becoming increasingly dependent on McLean's try-scoring and Phillips's play at full-back and his goalkicking. When those players were absent Northern distinctly lacked star quality.

In his six years at the club Phillips kicked 661 goals from every conceivable angle and proved to be one of the club's greatest ever players. He was a magnificent attacking full-back, immaculate ball handler and tactician. His compatriot Jack McLean also had a great impact with an amazing 261 tries in 221 games and is regarded as the best winger ever to play for Bradford, with an ability to score from anywhere on the field. Had he enjoyed more longevity at the top of the game he would have certainly rivalled great wingers like Brian Bevan and Billy Boston for the number of tries scored.

Although both men have secured their positions as playing legends at Bradford Northern, it was Joe Phillips who would leave the more lasting legacy. His role in helping the club back from the dark days of 1963 would guarantee him a special place in the history of Bradford Northern.

Start of the decline

When Phillips and McLean left in 1956, fortunes at Northern began to take a clear downturn. Good players need to be replaced with similar quality ones if a club is to stay at the top and unfortunately this wasn't the practice at Bradford at the time. Once they'd gone the team was bereft of any true stars and wins became increasingly rare. With increasingly poor form, the crowds dropped and less money was coming into the club. Gates had already declined from an average of 17,791 in 1951-52 to a mere 4,645 by 1956. This partly reflected the general decline in attendances at live sports events, due to the end of the post-war boom in spectator sport and the growth of television. But it also reflected poor performances on the pitch.

The club had recently lost its driving force in the boardroom with the retirement of the great chairman Harry Hornby. He was widely regarded as the visionary who helped lead Northern into the great period of success in the 1940s. His work in recruiting players and coaching staff along with the development of Odsal Stadium had made Northern the top club in the game. Indeed, without the work of Harry Hornby, Trevor may never have even joined Bradford Northern.

Hornby officially resigned from the board on 5 December 1957 and commented at the time: "No man knows better than himself when he has done enough. My doctor long ago told me to cut out most of the worrying activities. I have done so gradually and he is satisfied with my health as I am now, so why should I undo all the good he has done? I don't go out at nights and therefore cannot attend the directors' meetings or take an active part in Odsal's administration. It's a wrench in leaving."

His retirement from the board of directors left a vacuum that the club found hard to fill. His directorship was the most notable in the club's history. In any era, a team relies on its board of directors to provide sound leadership and judgement. With Hornby's departure things at Northern took a turn for the worse.

Falling gates had been having a knock-on effect on the club's finances, so the club's directors had looked to other sports to help share the financial burden, with speedway and baseball being staged at Odsal Stadium. However, speedway finished in 1960, meaning another loss of income. They also ran a fairly successful pools competition on whose proceeds they relied heavily. Despite the extra income, it seemed the club was locked into a downward spiral. Supporters' and shareholders' meetings became heated with fans becoming frustrated at the club's policy of selling its better players. Ken Traill, Jack Scroby and Milan Kosanovic were all sold for the sole purpose of raising finance and less talented players were bought in their places. This of course had a detrimental effect on the club's long-term fortunes.

Although Trevor had retired from playing, he neither severed his connections with Northern, nor with the game. On 8 February 1958 he was invited to join the board of directors at Northern by director Cyril Bunney. Trevor's appointment was welcomed by all those connected with the club. He became a director with the team seriously struggling and attendances having slipped to an average of 3,747 for the 1958-59 season. Trevor's appointment to the board prompted many to send their best wishes, G. E. French of Low Moor and Wyke Juniors wrote: "We wish you every success in your new venture, knowing full well that that the appointment is a fitting tribute to your many long years of service to your club and our rugby league game. Best wishes for a successful future."

Congratulations also came from the Bradford business community. John Illingworth wrote from the Widex Works in Brighouse: "As a supporter and a shareholder I was very pleased to read you have become a director of Bradford Northern. I hope this gives you a great deal of pleasure for a long time and very few disappointments."

The sale of star players didn't mean directors didn't try to have the best interests of the team at heart. On the day Trevor was appointed as director, the Cyril Bunney announced that after training "the players would enjoy a thick underdone steak and chip supper". Who needs modern day dieticians?

Unfortunately the players' steak dinners didn't have the desired effect on performances and as gate receipts decreased the club had to twice turn to the council for reductions in rent for Odsal Stadium. The negotiations enabled the club to save some money, but it was unlikely to be a long-term solution to the club's problems.

Against a backdrop of poor performances, supporters and shareholders understandably became more frustrated. In 1957, the club announced the transfer of Malcolm Davies to Leeds for £3,000. Davies had been an important signing from Leigh in 1956, where he had scored 79 tries in 84 appearances, including a record 34 tries in a season. However, he was sold to Leeds for £3,000. Crowds dropped following his departure, just when the club needed to build on such players. He returned from Leeds at the start of the 1957-58 season, before leaving again in 1959.

The directors unfortunately seemed to have no way of stopping the spiralling debts and needed to sell players in order to keep the club afloat. Promising players understandably did not want to join Northern, so the club's fortunes on the field deteriorated with every sale of one of their better players, and with every departure the attendances declined further. Nobody seemed to be able to provide a fresh injection of finance needed to stop the decline that was gathering pace.

As the club lurched into the 1960s there was little to cheer about at Odsal. On 22 March 1960 Dai Rees was relieved of coaching duties and Trevor was appointed as his replacement. Rees had been Bradford Northern's most successful coach and had been in the job for 24 years, coaching Northern for more than 1,000 games. As the team's fortunes faded in the late 1950s some argued that it was down to Rees's dated tactics. They argued his ideas may have been successful in the 1940s, but had little relevance in the 1960s. Rees was given the job as stadium manager and asked to join the board of directors.

Northern director Cyril Bunney handed full control of the team to Trevor who said: "I am expecting 100 per cent effort and will not accept anything else. I always played in that manner. We can forgive if the ability is not there but I will never stand for half-heartedness."

Like many clubs of the time, team selection was done through a committee of directors. It is hard to believe now, but teams really were picked by people who had little, if any, experience of playing and coaching. The directors had hoped that a change in coaching personnel would provide the much-needed impetus to drive the team back in the right direction. This was asking rather a lot given the paucity of Northern's playing talent and the lack of money available for new signings. It is testament to Trevor's determination and passion for the club that he was prepared to try.

However it would not be long before the club found itself minus a director and a coach. Strange dealings behind the scenes were to lead to Bradford Northern's most tragic episode and one of Trevor's saddest moments.

Looking back on this time, Trevor's view is that: "Bradford Northern had a weak board of directors by this time. They were poor administrators with no real vision for the future and this made them collectively very weak. Too often they were very indecisive and had lost the plot over many months and presided over the decline of the club."

Things came to a head when on 7 December 1960 Trevor resigned as coach and director. His decision to quit Northern was not made lightly and the events that precipitated his departure began at a meeting of the directors on 28 November. The meeting was held in Trevor's absence and its business was to have far reaching effects.

A copy of the minutes of the meeting reveal that a motion for the directors to guarantee the club financially was made in the knowledge that both Trevor Foster and Dai Rees would resign because they had not agreed to act as financial guarantors. The minutes even went on to state that "The shares held by Mr Rees and Mr Foster in trust for the club would have to be shared between Mr Barritt, Mr Bunney and Mr Hornby." That the directors were prepared to make such major decisions without consulting Trevor made his position very difficult.

Trevor later revealed his thoughts: "I wasn't able to attend the meeting on 28 November but during the week Dai Rees told me the question had arisen about both of us becoming guarantors with the other directors at the bank. When originally approached to become football director I was told there would be no call made upon me on the financial side. I did however sign straight away and without hesitation as a part guarantor for the loan received from the Rugby Football League.

When I later received the minutes from the meeting I couldn't attend I found out what course had been decided in my absence. That was when I became intensely annoyed. I could have done my part financially and had been inclined to do so, but the minutes of the meeting indicated that they had already decided about me in my absence. This changed my whole attitude and brought about my decision to quit."

Trevor's decision to sever his connections with Northern was widely reported in the press. At the time of his resignation the full story had yet to be made public and Trevor's comments were guarded so he didn't cause the club any bad publicity. He said: "There is no chance of reconciliation. I sent in my resignation on Tuesday and I expect the club has received it today, I do not want to say a lot but at the meeting of directors on Monday night certain matters were discussed and I did not like what was being discussed – I told them I did not agree with what happened. There was no falling out or bad feelings, but there is no hope of reconciliation."

The *Yorkshire Sports* reported that an unnamed Northern official had said "Northern is Trevor Foster's life. There is nothing he wouldn't do for the club." It went on to report that "Since he took over control of the teams almost nine months ago he has shown the same zest as a coach as he did as a player. Trevor Foster kept his word. He has not had the best ability to work on but as he told me of his decision last Thursday he added – 'The club has a few good players and I think improvements are on the way'."

The full reasons for the resignation became public at a special shareholders' meeting in January when it emerged that the bank had asked that all directors become guarantors against the club's overdraft. Trevor resigned because he had only agreed to join the board if there were no financial strings attached. Through Trevor's actions the meeting had to be called to discuss the situation regarding the overdraft, which many knew nothing about.

The meeting was a stormy one with shareholders angry at the club's rapid decline and many looked for a scapegoat. Dai Rees was voted off the board and he later departed for a post on the board at Halifax, resigning from his position as stadium manager. Trevor meanwhile began work in an advisory capacity at Keighley RLFC on a temporary basis. All official connections with Bradford Northern were now over and despite efforts by director Cyril Bunney to persuade him to return, Trevor did not rejoin the board.

To leave Bradford Northern after 22 years as a player and coach was a major decision for Trevor and not one that was made lightly. To leave the club in such hard times was extremely difficult, but he was not prepared to be party to the poor decision-making in the boardroom nor to sacrifice his principles. The club was in freefall financially and desperately needed strong leadership; unfortunately this quality wasn't in abundance in the Northern board of directors. Their ill-considered course of action had alienated the one man they had earmarked to lead the team to success. By now it was obvious that the board was unable to lead the club in a coherent manner.

Trevor had not envisaged any of these problems when he joined the board: "When I was a director I was not one for controversy or confrontation. As things got worse, alarm bells were ringing, especially when the bank asked for personal financial security against the club from all directors. This was not for me. I was prepared to put my thoughts and points across with conviction and emotion. I wanted to support the development of the footballing side and not become involved in finance where I had no experience or expertise. I was praying the club would come through this torrid time."

Trevor received formal acceptance of his resignation on 8 December 1960 from the club secretary that read: "We would like to thank you, on behalf of all at Odsal, for the valuable work and time that you have spent with everyone concerned at this stadium. No person can have been more sincere in his job than you have been since your playing career ended. This must be a very severe break for you to make this decision. You will at all times be very welcome whenever you care to visit Odsal."

The uncertainty off the field did nothing to help matters on it and results did not pick up. In turn, crowds decreased further with the average attendance at Odsal in 1959-60 dropping to 2,960. It was increasingly apparent that if the rot was not stopped then the club was in real danger. The next season saw a marginal improvement, to 24th place, with 10 league victories, but also first-round exits in both cup competitions.

As 1961-62 got underway things got even worse for Northern on the field when they suffered their worst defeat in 30 years. They succumbed 73-5 at Wakefield in the Yorkshire Cup. The *Telegraph & Argus* summed up the performance with the headline "Feeble, Pathetic – Northern just gave it up!" This result was made worse by the fact that Northern had fielded their strongest team. Fans were left with the prospect of little if any winning football.

While Northern were struggling Trevor moved from Keighley RLFC to be given the head coach job at Leeds on December 4 1961.

Meanwhile at Odsal poor performances meant low crowds with the 1962-63 season seeing nine games attracting fewer than 1,000 fans. This in turn caused Northern's debts to grow. By December 1963 the bank would not lend any further money, directors were either unwilling or unable to put their own money in and no new investment was coming into the club. The team finished bottom of the second division in 1962-63 after finishing last in the one division competition the previous year. They were rooted to the foot of the table. That, coupled with the lack of finance, meant the end was nigh.

From the start of the 1961-62 season until withdrawing halfway through 1963-64, Northern played 90 matches and won only nine. It was a woeful record and each of those nine wins had been achieved at home. The last away win had been at Doncaster on 11 March 1961.

When the 1963-64 season got underway the lack of new signings meant it was likely to be another difficult time for Northern. Repeated calls for more support appeared in the local press but a poor start to the season ensured crowds continued to fall. Rather suddenly, on 14 November, the first team coach Harry Beverley resigned without making his reasons public. However, when Northern's fate became known it was thought he had seen the iceberg coming and jumped ship.

On 23 November 1963, Northern entertained Barrow who ran out 29-0 winners in front of a 'crowd' of just 324. Clearly, attendances of this size were not going to sustain the club for much longer and time was fast running out. The club was losing £400 a week, the pools contributed only £50 and the team had won only one match that season. It was feared that the city of Bradford, which then possessed two association football clubs, City and Park Avenue, would lose its professional rugby league club. The result of the financial decline was that Northern could only afford to fulfil one more fixture against Leigh at Odsal on 7 December 1963. The team lost 33-5 and the few fans who attended the game must have been in low spirits. The attendance was recorded as 841, but it was estimated that between 500 and 600 fans were from Leigh.

Northern fans were soon to find out how serious things had got off the field when on 10 December the *Telegraph & Argus* headline read "End of road for Northern! Money difficulties! 'Can't go on!' – Chairman".

The whole of the rugby league world was shocked to hear the news. Northern had made the decision to give up playing completely and the League authorities were told that the club would not be finishing the 1963-64 season.

The *Daily Express* on 12 December had the headline: "Northern's Lights Flicker and Die – A Far Cry from 1954". Its reporter, Jack Bentley, went on to state: "Bradford Northern, a second division club born in 1895 as a founder member of the old Northern Union lay down to die last night – a sobering, shocking warning to the rest of the League".

Northern had not been alone in suffering financial difficulties at this time. Both the Oldham and Bramley clubs were in the situation of having to sell their better players to survive and the media was full of discussion about the plight of failing rugby league clubs. The last published accounts of Bradford Northern for the period ended June 1963 show a loss of £4,143 with several large outstanding loans awaiting repayment.

Halifax chairman Ted Horsfall, who was also the RFL's finance and general purposes committee said at the time: "The whole position has got to be examined. We could put in a caretaker board [into Northern] as was done to help Leigh in the old days. But times are vastly different and directors of most clubs are finding it difficult. Do the people of Bradford want rugby league?" RFL council chairman Harry Roebuck said, following news of Northern's demise, that "It is up to every official connected with the game to try to sort this out and keep Bradford Northern!"

The decline in support for the club is shown by the decline in average attendances from the early 1950s:

1951-52: 17,791	1954-55: 8,577	1957-58: 4,645	1960-61: 1,858
1952-53: 16,862	1955-56: 6,911	1958-59: 3,747	1961-62: 1,522
1953-54: 12,134	1956-57: 4,791	1959-60: 2,960	1962-63: 1,209

For the last two seasons, only perennial strugglers Liverpool City had a lower average than Bradford Northern.

Rise from the ashes

The apparent demise of Bradford Northern stirred many people into action – not least Trevor who was coaching the 'A' team at Leeds. Within days of the shock announcement the *Telegraph and Argus* ran the headline "Everything ready – if and when Northern dies".

It emerged that a group of businessmen and fans had allied themselves with Trevor and had announced they were prepared to take over if the present board of directors would put the existing club into liquidation. Trevor had been keeping a watching brief on events at Odsal since he left the club and now saw his chance to help.

He said at the time: "I am in it as an enthusiast. I can't just stand by see such a great club go down." Another member of the new consortium said: "We know what we are doing, and how we can do it, but there must be a fresh start. We would only go in if the present board left the club."

While these momentous events were taking place Trevor was in regular contact with the former chairman Harry Hornby. Trevor received many telegrams and letters from Mr Hornby pledging all his support and many ideas to help save the club. He wrote on 14 December 1963 with ideas to aid the 'resuscitation fund' by requesting a payment from various media for the use of photos of the players and club under copyright guidelines. He went on to suggest: "Tell anyone interested in Odsal's future that I am on call to answer any reasonable question – keep the publicity going with the newspapers, remembering that if they keep Odsal's name before the public that's all to the good, feed the reporters with worthwhile news."

This was to start a dramatic process that intended to save the club and prevent it suffering the ignominy of celebrating its demise in the year of its centenary. Over the Christmas and New Year period of 1963-64 discussions were ongoing between the club, shareholders, creditors, Bradford Council, the RFL and Trevor's consortium to try to find a solution that would prevent the club from dying.

On 2 January 1964, the club wrote to all its shareholders urging them to resist the resolution to wind up the old company that had been proposed at the last AGM. However, as time ticked away it became apparent that the likelihood of the club being saved was slim and so it proved.

The end came on 19 January 1964, when the RFL announced that Northern's membership had been terminated as the club had not fulfilled its fixtures, and nor was it likely to do so. Northern's players were given free agent status and were allowed to join other clubs. The club contested the decision until 18 March 1964 when Bradford Northern RLFC became extinct.

During the time these difficult discussions were taking place Trevor had been hard at work, meeting with other interested parties with the aim of forming a new club that would take the place of the old Northern. On 12 February 1964 Trevor convened a working committee at the Bay Horse Hotel on Wakefield Road with the aim of forming a new club. That committee included Mr R. Coultous, Mr A. Baxter, Mr L. Brooks, Mr D. Dobson, Mr M. Lambert, Mr W. Cooper, Mr J. Phillips, Mr G. Brown, Mr R. Betts, Mr A. Sykes, Mr W. Smith and Mr J. Mylrea.

Trevor explained that: "This working committee of 13 met on a regular basis and gradually got support from all over the country."

Trevor and the committee were hopeful that the game of rugby league could be revived in Bradford. He hoped that if the local council, RFL and local businessmen could see that they were "working in a correct manner and that an atmosphere of mutual trust and respect existed then they would come forward and help."

Trevor had been fortunate to be joined in his efforts by none other than Joe Phillips who had starred for the club 10 years before. The new committee ensured that when the club died there was an organised and highly motivated group ready to keep the issue in the public eye. Trevor recalls: "Lots of our meetings were held at the Bay Horse Inn at Dudley Hill. The landlord, Phil Lloyd, was a very dedicated supporter and became a member of the committee. I had asked Joe Phillips to join us as he was a very eloquent speaker and had a great passion for the club."

At this time Trevor was still receiving lengthy correspondence from former chairman Harry Hornby and on 18 February he received another letter, this time from Morocco where he was enjoying a holiday in Marrakesh, no doubt worrying over the future of his old club.

He wrote: "You will know of course, without any confirmation from me, that I should stand four square with you and all our Odsal friends, who are prepared to WORK for the establishment of our old team. Lip service means nothing – what is wanted is the development of the enthusiasm of 1936 and everything else will fall into line. A certain amount of money will of course be required and the equity which Bradford Northern have in Odsal Stadium which the club has paid for in hard cash should go a long way towards promoting this."

The words of Harry Hornby are particularly inspiring and must have proved to be excellent motivation for Trevor and his committee in their aim to set up a new club.

The committee quickly gained the permission of Bradford Council to use Odsal Stadium if they were successful in forming a new Bradford Northern. This at least ensured they had a ground to play at and would not have to leave the club's natural home nor seek to share with another team.

By now the charismatic Joe Phillips was elected chairman of the Bradford Northern Development Committee and efforts were made far and wide to raise enough money to help make the intentions of the committee and the rugby league public in Bradford reality. The formation of a new club would not be cheap, but it was not going to founder on lack of effort.

On 23 March 1964 a formal application for membership of the Rugby Football League was made and letters appealing for financial help were sent to parties far and wide in the hope of raising much needed cash. The RFL had stipulated that the new club must have at least £1,000 in the bank before its application would be approved.

The letter, signed by Joe Phillips, made an impassioned plea: "It will be very easy to place this appeal on one side and forget about it, but if you did, then you would be very wrong, in our judgment. We are confident that you will help us by giving generously, either by way of shares or donations. There is so much to be done in such a short time, that we would very much appreciate your prompt response. Please help the sporting life of Bradford."

The appeal proved to be very successful and Trevor remembers especially a contribution from an unusual source and a trip to City Hall: "The committee received a gift of 30 US dollars posted from Iceland by a man who had been a Northern supporter long ago and who had since found himself in the United States Army. I also led a deputation to the full council meeting at City Hall. Lord Mayor Tom Wood and senior Councillor Eddie Newby gave me permission to speak for 10 minutes to put our case for Bradford Northern and were very supportive of our application to rejoin the Rugby League. They promised to help the new Northern in any way they could, which was a real tonic."

Despite all this hard work, what Trevor and the rest of the committee still needed was a full show of support from the people of Bradford. The last years of the old Northern had seen crowds plummet and interest in rugby league in Bradford dwindle. Public reaction to a new club needed to be gauged if the new venture was to be a success. A leading member of the committee said: "If the public of Bradford show they want rugby league played in the city then I can assure them that it will be. But they must show they want it and be prepared to support any new club which is launched."

Resurrection

19 March 1964 will go down as one of the most momentous days in the history of rugby league in Bradford. The much-awaited public meeting at the imposing Victorian grandeur of St George's Hall was to be the acid test as to whether the new Bradford Northern was a viable concern. The meeting was also to be attended by the secretary, chairman and officials of the RFL who were to assess the support for the new club. If the attendance at the meeting turned out to be poor then the hopes for starting the new club would be in tatters.

As Trevor remembers the hour leading up to the meeting was a tense and worrying time: "About half an hour before we were due to start the meeting only a few people had arrived. I was really concerned that our efforts had been for nothing. As it happened, I needn't have worried because in the final minutes before the meeting began a large crowd assembled."

In fact more than 1,500 people attended the meeting that night to hear the committee's ideas and proposals for the new club. Great former players such as Ernest Ward, Donald Ward, Eric Batten and Vic Darlison all made their support clear and addressed the crowd from the podium. Ernest Ward said: "It is gratifying to see so many people here tonight, and it is up to us to back those men on the platform." Dai Rees, Northern's coach from their most successful era added his support via a telegram that read: "It's a long way from Birch Lane to Wembley, it can be done again!"

The meeting proved to be rousing and enthusiastic and as the *Telegraph & Argus* reported: "Not since the Wembley days has the city seen such concerted zeal from its rugby league minded profession."

Joe Phillips opened the meeting and announced that Bradford Council had virtually promised to lease Odsal Stadium to the new Northern on very favourable terms and that the RFL had moved to allow them to re-sign players who had been on the books before the old club went out of business. He added: "We know this team would not be strong enough to maintain support and it would be our first job to strengthen as much as possible."

The target was to raise £5,000 before July, which was to be the absolute minimum with which a new club could be started. It was proposed to raise this money through the sale of shares at £1 each and the new club had already received some donations and offers of financial assistance. Joe Phillips said: "We have several promising people who have promised us financial help – quite exciting help – but they want to see there is support and concrete plans first."

When Trevor took the podium he announced: "Whoever the officials of the new club may be, you will have people who love the game and people who are prepared to work for the club night and day. It is a tremendous task. We think it can be done and you have shown tonight that you want it done. In recent months I have met with nothing but goodwill, enthusiasm and courtesy from within the game."

The speeches and appeal for help made by the speakers had the desired effect. A great enthusiasm had been rekindled and members of the audience purchased close on £1,000-worth of shares that night.

The observers from the RFL were also impressed and Dr Harry Roebuck, the RFL chairman told the meeting: "The League are behind you in this venture and I know most of the clubs are willing to take up shares in the company as a token of the goodwill which everyone in the Rugby League world feels towards you. You are the people who are capable and enthusiastic and who have the backing of the League, and I sincerely hope there will be a new rugby league club in Bradford next season."

A further promise came from Jack Edden of Swinton RLFC, the chairman of the League's Management Committee who said the RFL was prepared to match £1 up to a maximum of £500 for every £10 the Bradford public donated.

Joe Phillips said about the meeting: "I was thrilled and delighted. I had visions of anything between 50 to 500 for the meeting, but 1,500 showed they really wanted to revive rugby league in the city. The terrific enthusiasm was wonderful."

Of the 1,500 people who attended the public meeting at St George's Hall many were fans of Bradford Northern who had seen their club go from the top of the game to extinction. It was an emotional night for all. A member of the audience was Ron Oldfield, then a 16-year-old apprentice wool sorter from West Bowling. He recalls: "I had been supporting Northern throughout my school life and I was devastated to hear they were about to fold. I went along to the meeting to see if there was anything I could do to help. The atmosphere in St George's Hall was electric. It was like a call to arms, to fight a war. I remember Joe Phillips and Trevor Foster addressed us with great emotion: 'We will not allow this club to die', said Trevor. As we left the meeting a very elderly lady handed some loose change to Trevor. She was in tears."

The meeting at St George's Hall proved to be the defining moment in the effort to raise a 'new' Bradford Northern. It showed to all that there was sufficient support for rugby league in Bradford. Trevor's efforts and those of the consortium had not been in vain.

It later emerged that Widnes had promised £50 to the appeal and that many other clubs in the Rugby League were prepared to take shares in the new company. And it was not only in a financial sense that other clubs were prepared to help. Trevor said in the days following the meeting: "Clubs have offered to help with donating players. And I don't mean players who have been cast to one side."

In the weeks after the meeting shares continued to be sold and this enabled the consortium to officially form their company on 20 April 1964 with Joe Phillips as chairman. The committee from which the new company was drawn included Trevor, A. Baxter, R. Betts, L. Brooks, M. Lambert, W. Cooper, G. Brown, A. Sykes, J. Mylrea, P. Lloyd, J. Cameron, R. Johnson, R. Coultous, J. Pell, G. Turton, J. Fricker, H. Womersley, E. Orford and Frank Hillam. These dedicated men worked to ensure that rugby league and Northern remained alive in the city of Bradford and without their collective contribution there would probably be no rugby league team in the city today.

By mid-May Bradford Northern (1964) Ltd had raised the £5,000 necessary to reform the club and on 22 May their request for membership to the RFL was accepted. The worst period in the club's history was over. A new dawn had broken at Odsal and better times were ahead.

Trevor remembers receiving the news that the RFL had given the club the green light: "I was working as a barman at Frank Whitcombe's pub, the Airedale Heifer at Sandbeds, when I received a phone call from Joe Phillips. He told me that the club's application had been approved and he immediately offered me the job as first team coach. I was overjoyed at the news and it was a wonderful gesture by Joe to offer me the job as coach because I had brought him onto the committee originally to revive the club. I had felt in my heart of hearts, after playing all those years, the club could not die because it had all that tradition. I felt it was only a matter of time that given the right lead we would get a new club together.

I still have the letter from the Rugby Football League that accepted our application. I have been offered quite a lot of money for it but will treasure it always. Nowadays scarcely a day goes past without people stopping me in the street to remind me how we helped save Bradford Northern. And each time I thank God for giving me the strength and confidence to have had a go. It's the proudest thing I ever did."

The club now had the go ahead to prepare for the 1964-65 season and the new board of directors set about recruiting a team. Only six players that had been on the books before the collapse were re-signed. The board needed to ensure a better quality team was recruited and started well by signing Jack Wilkinson as player-coach from Wakefield Trinity, after Trevor had refused the coaching role. Players such as Fijian Joe Levula from Rochdale, Brian Lord from Oldham, Gilbert Ashton from Leeds, Johnny Rae and Ian Brooke were also recruited and gave the team a much stronger look than in previous years. This was to be proved on the field too when the club swept to victory in the pre-season Headingley Sevens competition. Northern took the trophy beating many stronger teams; it was just the boost the new club needed prior to the season's start.

While this was going on Trevor was still coaching the 'A' team at Leeds. Despite his hard work in launching the new Bradford Northern, he stayed at Headingley. It is testimony to his enormous energy, generosity and diligence that he did both tasks to his usual high standard. He recalls: "I could not leave Leeds in the lurch. I was happy there and saw my job there as my first loyalty. They had treated me fairly so it was only right I did the same for them." He stayed at Leeds until 1966.

On the eve of the newly reformed Bradford Northern's first game in the championship the *Telegraph & Argus* looked back over the previous eight months of the club's history. Its headline said it all: "New Northern – who said it couldn't happen?"

It went on to praise the efforts of all concerned in helping revive the club, but paid special tribute to Joe Phillips and Trevor. The report said of Trevor: "Foster was the driving force behind the plan initially and, but for his enthusiasm last winter, it is doubtful whether the club would exist today. Bradford Rugby League owes him a tremendous debt."

The club's first game against Hull KR on 22 August 1964 was a remarkable experience. The team was cheered every step of the way from the dressing rooms to the pitch by 13,542 fans. It was the first five figure crowd at Odsal for more than seven years and the team performed on the field in a way not seen by Northern fans in many a year. Although they lost 34-20, they did not give in and showed enough skill and effort to suggest that the team was heading for better things.

Three weeks later Northern won their first game when they beat Salford convincingly 20-12 at Odsal and went on to finish a respectable 17th out of 30 clubs in the table.

The Observer commented on the remarkable story of the fall and rise of Northern that year and noted: "The average age of the board is about 45, probably the youngest in the game. Players are no longer expected to touch their forelocks as a director walks by. Northern, while still keen on discipline, have swept away the vestiges of pre-war boardroom despotism. Chairman Joe Phillips often trains with the players and most of them call him 'Joe'."

The club was back on an even keel with a young, enthusiastic board of directors who would take it forward again. Two years later, his work at Leeds completed, Trevor was back in a coaching capacity with young players at the club he loved. The story could hardly have a happier ending.

Without Trevor, and other dedicated people playing a dynamic role in trying to save the old club, and then starting afresh, Bradford Northern would not have returned. Thankfully, they did not wait for others to act. Apathy is often the greatest threat to such ventures but Trevor and the committee succeeded in galvanising the city of Bradford and ensured the club would rise again. In a life of great achievements, this ranks as one of his greatest.

Bradford Northern 1944.
(Photo: Courtesy Trevor Foster)

Trevor with Ernest Ward.
(Photo: Courtesy Trevor Foster)

Dai Rees. The boots had been purchased from the
1947-48 New Zealand tourists at the
end of their tour.
(Photo: Courtesy Robert Gate)

Above: Billy Davies arrives at Odsal – with Harry Hornby & Dai Rees
Below: Bradford Northern January 1947
(Photos: Courtesy Trevor Foster)

Bradford Northern players relaxing at Ambleside
before playing at Workington in April 1948
(Photo: Courtesy Trevor Foster)

Action from the 1949 Yorkshire Cup Final: Bradford Northern versus Huddersfield
at Headingley. Bradford won 11-4. (Photo: Courtesy Robert Gate)

Trevor going forward against St Helens at Odsal, in the Challenge Cup, 15 March 1950.
Bradford won 11-0, but lost to Widnes in the semi-final.
(Photo: Courtesy Trevor Foster)

Bradford Northern 1951-52.
Bradford finished top of the league table with 57 points.
(Photo: Courtesy Robert Gate)

Above: 1953 Yorkshire Cup Final at Headingley: Bradford Northern versus Hull.
Trevor introducing the Lord Mayor of Leeds to Barry Tyler.
Below: Trevor holding the Yorkshire Cup after Bradford won 7-2.
(Photos: *Telegraph & Argus*)

11. Bradford: My community

When Trevor arrived in Bradford on an overcast Monday afternoon in September 1938 with Mr Harry Hornby, he was not to know that this northern 'city of wool' would quickly adopt him as a son of Yorkshire.

Over a period of six decades, he would become a living legend in Bradford, not only for his prowess and success on the rugby field but for his commitment and inexhaustible voluntary work for young people and many local charities. 'Mr Bradford Northern', as he became known, inspired and positively influenced the lives of many local people, particularly those who were to come into contact with him at the famous Bradford City Police Boy's Club, now the Bradford Police Club for Young People in the Girlington area of the city.

Whenever, there was a need to raise funds for a community good cause or support needed for a local charity, Trevor was always the first to volunteer his help. If that meant rallying people to form a working group or committee to organise events and activities or simply to stand in the pouring rain outside the local supermarket from eight in the morning until six at night with his collection box, then so be it.

Former Lord Mayor of Bradford, Councillor Bob Sowman recalled: "He would always be the first there to offer help, and his enthusiasm was infectious. Everyone from Lord Mayors, councillors and chief constables to schools, youth and sports clubs, churches and hospitals as well as the many official charity groups all turned to Trevor in their hour of need. He became the 'Charities Champion' in Bradford and one the city's greatest ambassadors".

First impressions and the war years

In his first weeks in Bradford, Trevor made it his business to learn as much as he possibly could about the city's history and its hopes and ambitions for the future. He settled quickly into his new digs at 1, Farcliffe Terrace in the Bradford 8 district and his landlady, Miss Norcliffe, was a great source of local knowledge.

He found a city whose prosperity was almost totally dependent upon the state of the international textile trade. A brief boom after the First World War could not disguise real problems for the economy of the local area; the most obvious of these was the unstable nature of the world market for wool. Most soldiers returning from war had reverted to their former jobs, often at the expense of the women who had been employed while they had been away. Trevor recalls his father having a similar experience: "I remember my father Richard telling me how he had returned to Newport in 1902 after serving in the Boer War in South Africa. He received a Distinguished Conduct Medal and Long Service Award, but would not have found employment in South Wales if he had not replaced a woman worker in the hospitality trade".

After a brief period of economic dislocation in the 1920s and early 1930s, employment levels had risen. However, in the early 1930s Bradford had failed to attract investment from the new scientific and technically based employment areas or the growing number of service industries which were dependent upon white collar rather than manual skills. When Trevor arrived towards the end of the decade, many jobs were being created in banking, insurance and building societies. Local government employment was also becoming an attractive alternative to work in the woollen mills.

Other local rugby league playing towns were more fortunate: Leeds had a wide spread of employment; Halifax had a machine tool and confectionary industry as well as textiles; and Huddersfield had a balance of wool and engineering.

Trevor recalls: "The worst situation was in the smaller villages around Bradford which were reliant on the local mills for their prosperity. When the wool trade contracted there was little alternative employment for people living there and they would often leave the area to look for work. One of the bigger and more successful Bradford-based employers at that time was Jowett Cars in Idle, who employed around 1,000 people. The Fattorini family was also very well known for its high-class jewellery and were changing the emphasis of their business to include 'mail order' which involved the creation of the Empire Stores and Grattan, and more job opportunities for local people. The printing trade was also on the up; the production of Christmas cards was becoming very big in Bradford."

Shorter working hours meant greater leisure time for people. There was an expansion and diversity in recreational activities, particularly in professional sport and the cinema. The local ice skating rink and dance halls were popular venues.

Around 20,000 new houses had been built in Bradford and the transport system, including environmentally friendly electric trolley buses, was expanding to allow people to travel to work from all parts of the city. For the more affluent, cars provided great personal mobility. Processed and packaged foods were becoming popular, including brands and shops such as Heinz, Crosse and Blackwell, Sainsbury's and Mac Fisheries, although the worst paid employees of all were the shop workers.

It was common for women to contribute to the family income, for example, a husband and wife both working in textiles could earn more than £5 per week between them. A single income was rarely adequate to support a family. A qualified male teacher could expect to earn around £350 per annum and his female equivalent approximately £260.

Trevor recalls: "My early memories of Bradford included the smoking mill chimneys, particularly the great Lister's Mill chimney which towered above the rest. I was told you could ride a horse and cart around the top of the chimney and that it could be seen from as far away as the Cow and Calf rocks on Ilkley Moor. There were many fine Victorian buildings including Kirkgate Market, where I always bought fresh fruit and vegetables for the digs, as well as a number of shopping arcades.

The City Hall, the Wool Exchange and Bradford Cathedral were other important buildings I visited. Another feature was the rows and rows of sooty terraced houses stacked high on the very hilly slopes radiating out of the city centre, towards some of the most beautiful countryside which surrounds Bradford.

I have happy memories of visiting Ilkey to attend British Lions reunions, Baildon to walk on the moors with my family and Otley Chevin, which was a venue for official rugby league summer coaching camps I organised for many years.

However, my very first task when setting foot on Bradford soil was to find a Catholic church where I could celebrate mass. I walked for miles up and down the hills around Bradford and found three Catholic churches: St William's in Girlington; St Patrick's not far from the city centre and St Cuthbert's in Heaton, where Monsignor O' Connor (the role model for G. K. Chesterton's Father Brown) was the parish priest. I was spoilt for choice and had also found a good way to keep myself fit."

Within 12 months of Trevor's arrival in Bradford, the Second World War broke out and he would follow in his father's footsteps to fight for the freedom of his beloved country. Trevor remembers: "Bradford was like home from home for me. I immediately felt the warmth of the local people. It was as if I had never left the land of my fathers. The people here have always been very good to me and I have always tried to put a little back. Unemployment in Bradford was very similar to Newport, it was quite high, and certainly In 1938 it was higher than the national average. One of the main reasons I had signed professionally for the Bradford club was to ensure a relatively secure future, barring any serious injury. However, the war was to have a significant effect on my rugby career".

But the war brought harder times. Trevor recalls "returning home occasionally on leave from my wartime duties to play rugby. I remember seeing injured officers being treated at the Bradford Royal Infirmary. Rationing was the order of the day, food was in very short supply, two ounces of butter was the weekly allowance and meat was scarce. You needed a special coupon to purchase clothes. People were encouraged to 'Dig for victory', by digging up their garden and growing vegetables. There was a tremendous community spirit in Bradford at that time. Neighbours were always in and out of each others' houses borrowing small items, including food parcels, and generally supporting one another. The local bobbie walked the beat and always seemed to be around the neighbourhood offering help and friendly advice.

There were two bombing raids I was quite close to. One bomb scored a direct hit on St Peter's Catholic Church in the Leeds Road area. I was within a few hundred yards. The other when I was in town shopping and Lingard's clothiers in Darley Street was hit and badly damaged by fire. There was a pie shop I often frequented on the same road and in fact, I had just enjoyed a crusty beef pie with gravy and mushy peas when the siren went off."

Education welfare officer

Walking the streets of Bradford was to become more than a fitness regime or a pastime for Trevor. Soon after he retired from rugby he was appointed as an education welfare officer (EWO) by the corporation. Never one to own a motor car or a motorbike, he spent 24 years literally walking thousands of miles visiting homes and schools around the district in his efforts to keep young people at school and out of trouble. There was no better way to gain the respect of local people and to keep in touch with what was going on than to keep his feet firmly on the ground.

Trevor became an EWO in 1957 after working on the ground staff at Odsal. His first duties included assisting and administrating applications for families with hardship who might have been eligible for free school meals and other needs such as clothing allowances and assisted summer holidays. Initially he was responsible for the Fairweather Green and Allerton districts and later moved to the Buttershaw area of Bradford.

Since 1938, Bradford has experienced changes as great as any in its history, with the impact of the Second World War, the continuing decline of the worsted trade, and then the influx of immigrants, initially from the east and south of Europe and later, in the 1950s and 1960s from India and particularly Pakistan to work in the wool mills.

The changes in the city were all to have an influence on Trevor's life and commitment to Bradford. For example, the contribution of the Asian community to Bradford's economic, social and cultural life and the needs of young people for education, sport and recreational activities would drive Trevor to embrace a much wider community in his voluntary work.

Family life in Bradford

Trevor is never happier, nor more at ease, than when surrounded by his family at home in Bradford. He married Jean Unsworth, the daughter of a former Bradford Police inspector at St Patrick's church in the city on 13 June 1949. Jean spent all her working life as a nurse in Bradford, both hospital and community-based, before going into nursing management. Although they separated in the mid 1970s, they have remained in contact through their children.

His son Simon is employed in further and higher education in the East Riding of Yorkshire. Trevor's first daughter Jane, like her mother before her, worked as a nurse at the Bradford Royal Infirmary. She was married and had three daughters when she died tragically aged 41, after a long and courageous battle against cancer. His second daughter Sara is a probation officer at Her Majesty's Prison Wakefield, an institution Trevor visited on a number of occasions in his playing and coaching days to give talks and demonstrations to inmates about rugby league and physical fitness training. One of these visits in 1973 was with Ian Brooke, the Bradford Northern coach, prior to the 1973 Challenge Cup Final against Featherstone Rovers. Trevor recalls: "We gave a talk and showed films which were appreciated by the prisoners. We promised to bring the cup to show them if we won the Final. One chap said that he would be there to see it whenever we won because he was 'bloody in for life'." Trevor's youngest daughter Bridget works as a nursery nurse at a primary school in Harrogate.

In the late 1950s Trevor and Jean fostered a young boy, Joseph. He lived with the family for more than five years when they were resident in the Heaton district of Bradford, in the parish of St Cuthbert.

Jane's premature death in August 1992 had a profound effect on the family. Trevor, in his grief, determined to devote even more of his time to those in need and particularly to those suffering through cancer. He became involved with several local cancer charities and continues to this day to work tirelessly on behalf of their fundraising efforts.

In recent times Trevor has followed with great interest the remarkable efforts of Jane Tomlinson, who is also suffering from terminal cancer. Jane has raised money for cancer charities through running marathons and other endurance events. Trevor and Jane have met at various fundraisers. Trevor says: "She is a quite remarkable lady and an inspiration to me."

The Foster family's annual picnic in Lister Park, Heaton is the highlight of Trevor's social calendar. The gathering of his children and nine grandchildren provides an opportunity for a family sports extravaganza. Trevor takes the lead, organising cricket, rounders, football and touch rugby competitions. He always scores the first try at rugby and demands that everyone 'play the ball' correctly. Lister Park has been one of Trevor's favourite haunts throughout his time in Bradford. Most summer Sunday afternoons prior to the Super League era he would sit overlooking the bowling greens, adjacent to the Cartwright Hall Museum with a brass band playing in the background and the towering shadow of Lister's Mill chimney. He was in seventh heaven, devouring his six or seven Rossi's ice cream cornets, and looking forward to his regular Monday morning swim.

The Bradford Police Club for Young People

Nestling in the suburbs amongst the bustling commercial retail centre which includes Morrison's supermarket and the deprived areas surrounding the then infamous former Sloane Square is one Bradford's jewels in the crown.

Founded by a group of Bradford City Police Officers in 1935, The Bradford Police Club for Young People, (formerly The Bradford Police Boys' Club) in Walker Drive, Girlington has earned its richly deserved reputation as a youth club with a difference. It has always provided an ethos of openness, challenge and belonging for young people.

Former club director Rob Powell says: "Our club gives a sense of belonging – we are an anchor agency within the community – people just turn up. Its strength is its ability to engage young people whatever their needs in a well-structured and supportive environment. An 'open all hours' policy provides a point of contact that is not subject to the constant changes young people experience in their schools, family life and through their social workers. It is like an extended family.

The importance of the quality of the staff cannot be over-emphasised. Trevor is the epitome of this. He is always supportive and non-judgmental. If there is anyone who has provided a more consistent and committed approach to the young members over the last 40 years than Trevor I would like to meet them. He has positively influenced the lives of so many at the club. Trevor is able to identify and communicate with young people in an effortless way. His enthusiasm and indefatigable optimistic outlook on life is infectious. Always the gentleman, with good manners, he has a marvellous sense of humour."

Trevor first started working at the club that has since become such a big part of his life in the early 1960s, soon after he had been appointed as a youth sports coach by the local council. He had previously assisted at the Central YMCA and the Sedburgh Boys Club, coaching rugby league to junior members. He then became resident assistant leader at the Police Boys Club. The club's leader at that time was Derek 'Skip' Machin. He was developing activities to include the increasingly popular sports options of rugby league, football and boxing. In Trevor he had found a genuine local sports star who would increase the profile of the rugby league section and provide much needed support for him as leader. The boxing section recruited veteran coach and boxing secretary Alec Allan, and this sport too went from strength to strength.

Alec Allan worked with Trevor both in the Boys' Club and as a teacher at Rhodesway School: "In the early 1960s I was asked to become year head at Rhodesway School as well as fulfilling my previous duties as head of the special needs department. It was then that I first became a friend and colleague of Trevor. He was an education welfare officer, although he was known by the children as 'the board man'. Because we were both heavily committed to, dare I say it, 'fostering' a right attitude in the children we called at the houses of absentees to sort out problems and sometimes met at the same doorstep.

One policeman asked me: 'Why are there far less Rhodesway pupils appearing in the juvenile court than those from other schools?' This could be attributed to Trevor's zeal and concern for wayward pupils, whom he coaxed or dragged onto paths of righteousness. Once I called at a house, the door opened, a dog dashed out, bit me and went back inside. Trevor seemed to escape such indignities and was highly respected by parents and children alike. What a formidable companion to have. After several years, we lost contact and I retired from Rhodesway.

In the mid-1980s we met up once more when I did voluntary work at Bradford Police Boys' Club as boxing secretary. When I started working under Rob Powell I found Trevor already well established and doing sterling work at the club. Trevor immediately offered to help and was timekeeper for the boxing rounds. He understood the needs of the children and his help during the training sessions, three times a week, was invaluable. Every time we held a tournament Trevor and Rob were on the door. No-one dared to sneak in. I believe we not only enjoyed ourselves, but contributed to giving children wonderful experiences and turning out good citizens to boot. Trevor is a considerate person. Despite his wonderful fame in the world of rugby and being renowned for good deeds he has time for everybody. He has never lived upon his past glory, but believes in the here and now. No-one could call him a yesterday's man, nor a seeker of fame. He is a true Christian, giving time to the needs of others. I am proud to call him my friend."

Trevor's interest in boxing is not well known. He outlines: "I have always been interested in boxing and belonged to an amateur club in my own district of Pill in Newport near my parents' pub. But my boxing career was a short one. I lost my first fight as a schoolboy in a local contest, but my next adventure with the gloves was a long time after when, 6,000 miles away in Cairo as a Staff Sergeant, I fought in a services tournament before a large body of people, military and civilians. I was opposed by a Bombardier of the Royal Artillery and managed to win a nice medal after a close contest. So my boxing career was a 50-50 affair: lost one, won one."

The presence and experience of the two charismatic and committed sportsmen helped to kick-start the club into a golden era. Their positive influence around young people of all ages, from all backgrounds and at all levels of ability was significant. The club's membership increased to well over 200. There were many boxing and rugby success stories, as both Trevor and Alec gave outstanding long service to the club. Alec became a legend in his own right and organised amateur boxing shows throughout the year. They were extremely competitive events, held at venues across the north of England and had tremendous support. Many of the boxers became notable achievers, some becoming amateur champions. Two who successfully turned professional were Frank Grant, a Lonsdale-belt winner, and Junior Witter, the British and Commonwealth light-welterweight champion.

In rugby league, Trevor's involvement ensured that any talented youngsters would also be given the opportunity to have trials with the junior team he coached at Bradford Northern. Two players who started out at the Police Boys Club later distinguished themselves at the very highest level of the game. Keith Mumby, who starred in all Trevor's Bradford junior teams, became arguably Northern's greatest ever full-back. Brian Noble, the current Bradford Bulls and Great Britain coach and former Northern hooker, captained Great Britain's tourists to Australia in 1984.

Brian recalls Trevor as a role model in his early days at the club: "Trevor had a massive influence on my career. He taught me three important things: how to behave as a sportsman, how to be a gentleman and, less importantly, how to play rugby league".

Brian has always maintained a keen interest in the work of the Police Boys Club, particularly since he served as a police officer in Bradford before taking up his post as a full-time employee with the Bulls.

Trevor recalls: "The club was very handy for Brian, who lived just up the road, close to the Drummond Road Swimming Baths. He loved all sports, as did his brother Jack who excelled at soccer at the time. I first encountered Brian when I was the local 'board man'. When I visited his home, I would be at the front door, and he was running out of the back door to dodge me. I eventually encouraged him to become a Police Boys' Club member. He shone at rugby, kept himself very fit and his qualities of leadership were very evident to me.

He was instrumental in forming the rugby league section at the club, became a committed member and introduced many new young players to rugby league. Two brothers I recall at that period were John and Joe Pitts, sons of a local businessman and greengrocer. John went on to play for Bradford Northern's first team and Joe often reflected to me that his time at the club saved him from a career in crime."

A typical weekly programme at the Police Club over the last 40 years offered a wide variety of activities:

Monday: Mornings: use of Gymnasium by Whetley Middle School. Evening: senior youth club, boxing, weight training, gymnasium, social areas, information and guidance point for young people.

Tuesday: Mornings: use of gymnasium by Whetley Middle School. Evening: work with girls and young women, football training.

Wednesday: Evening: senior youth club, boxing, weight training, gymnasium, social area, rugby training and athletics.

Thursday: Afternoon: Melville House (people with learning needs). Evening: weight training, social area, teens club, swimming pool visit, shooting range.

Friday: Evening: Kamyaab Keystone club, boxing, Girlington Youth Against Crime, drama group, football.

Saturday and Sunday: Morning and afternoon: homework support group, power hour – one hour's study and one hour's play, football and rugby competitions.

In 1972, when club leader Skip Machin moved on to take up an education management post in Scotland, Rob Powell was appointed club warden. He had previously worked at the club as a mature student and came from a school background.

His astute leadership and vision brought a refreshing new approach and complemented Trevor's involvement perfectly. Under his management the club prospered and continued to develop, embracing the growing local Asian community. Many new activities were introduced including drama, music and the very successful Saturday morning 'Power Hour'. This involved teenagers coming in to do an hour's study and then being free for an hour to take part in any activity they wanted from table tennis, pool, indoor football and shooting, to disco, art or chess. The take-up was quite amazing and demonstrated the need for young people in a disaffected area to be able to balance work and play. The club was also used as an attendance centre for young people on community service and shared its facilities in partnership with other organisations including Bradford City AFC.

Rob later became club director before retiring in 2000 to become the chairman of the Yorkshire Association of Young People's Clubs based at the Girlington Community Centre.

The club's structure has always differed from most of the big youth centres in the city. Being an independent organisation, it receives only part of its income from the local council. Rob recalled: "The club's independence and its long existence can be an advantage; however it is obliged to raise a considerable annual sum for running costs and this has become increasingly difficult. It relies heavily on fundraising and donations as well as applications to charities and other funding bodies. When I first arrived, Harry Ambler was the local chief constable and he was a great supporter. Fifty per cent of the staff at the time were police officer volunteers. Priorities change and recruiting sufficient voluntary help of the calibre required to support the club's ethos became increasingly difficult."

Paul Craven who took over the reigns from Rob is the current club director, and has steered it diligently through a time of financial restructure. He has great experience and expertise in making successful bids for youth related projects and has introduced many new activities.

Trevor still walks the mile or so from his home in West Park to the club on two evenings each week and is now the club's president and also a vice-president of the Yorkshire Association of Young People's Clubs. He takes both positions very seriously and with typical enthusiasm says: "I have several ideas and plans to help the fundraising efforts and to raise the profile of the club even more to local people.

I would like to organise a bumper open event involving past members, many of whom have been successful in life. The present Lord Mayor of Bradford was a member and, of course, we have Brian Noble and Junior Witter. I want to see the Bradford Bulls here with all their trophies and the Bradford City players, not forgetting the Yorkshire cricketers who are from the Bradford area.

The former assistant chief constable and loyal supporter, Harold Long, who once travelled to Australia to establish a link which still exists between the Bradford club and a police boy's club in Sydney, would be the guest of honour. Other former police officers who have supported the club in the past and all the civilian staff who have given great service over the years would also be invited. I feel sure local television and press would support such an occasion. Anything we can do to engage disadvantaged young people in sport and other recreational and educational activities, we must do."

Top: Wedding Day: 13 June 1949. Trevor and Jean with guests,
including Frank Whitcombe and Dai Rees.
Below: Family group in the early 1960s: From top left: Jane, Trevor, Simon, Sara, Bridget
and Joseph Elston, who lived with the family for eight years as a foster child.
(Photos: Courtesy Trevor Foster)

Trevor with the Super League trophy and some enthusiastic young school students
(Photo: *Telegraph & Argus*)

Award for 30 years service to clubs for young people

In 1998 Trevor received the prestigious Gold Award from HRH the Duke of Gloucester, in recognition of his 30 years' voluntary service to the National Association of Clubs for Young People. This is the highest award for voluntary service.

The Odsal 'Chalkboard'

When Bradford Bulls launched their award winning 'Chalkboard' partnership initiative from Odsal Stadium in the mid-1990s they were overwhelmed with its success. The innovative partnership involving Bradford Council's Education Department, the Bradford Rugby League Development Scheme, West Yorkshire Police and the Probation Service among others was groundbreaking and prompted an immediate and positive response from many local year 5 and year 6 pupils and their teachers. Its aims were to provide support for schools in addressing young people's personal and social development and to promote healthy living. Programmes were developed to include issues relevant to young people, for example, drug misuse, crime and citizenship and to incorporate National Curriculum subjects.

Groups of young people from participating schools spent two days per term in the Chalkboard classroom at Odsal Stadium where they have full access to the facilities and the support of the players, staff and a resident teacher.

Trevor was a natural choice for Chalkboard to provide an input covering the history of the club and to talk about his experiences of rugby around the world. A history and geography lesson all rolled into one.

He immediately volunteered and became an instant hit with the young children, delivering weekly classes to a host of local schools. Trevor's favourite session was to be interviewed by the children about the history of Bradford Northern, what it was like to live and play rugby in the 1930s and how a healthy lifestyle has kept him fit throughout his life.

The Chalkboard project has gone from strength to strength and has won a cluster of local and national community awards in recognition for making a real difference to the education of young people in Bradford.

Frances Batty from Swain House Primary School was full of enthusiasm for the project and recalls one particular Chalkboard experience: "It was on a Wednesday lunchtime that, as the Bradford Bulls mini-bus pulled into the Swain House Primary School grounds, there was a buzz of excitement that swept through the playground. Who and what was it? What were they here for? It was Trevor Foster MBE and the Bradford Bulls Community Team who, through a project funded by Age Concern, had come to talk to our year 6 children. Trevor's genuine enthusiasm and love of rugby guaranteed a truly inspirational afternoon for the children who were keen to ask him questions about a remarkable life. It wasn't just Trevor's sporting achievements that captivated his audience, but also his great love of Bradford. The session was made even more interesting as he brought along a selection of souvenirs and mementoes that he had collected over the years and that the children could not only look at but also touch – and, in one instance, wear too. As if this wasn't enough, the Bulls also brought along the Super League Trophy – a fabulous opportunity for all the children to appreciate what everyone at the Bulls had attained during the season and realise what can be achieved through determination, effort and teamwork. The sheer sense of civic pride that this experience has instilled in the children cannot be underestimated and we all look forward to another visit from the Bulls."

Trevor's work for education in Bradford also included the role of a 'bus supervisor' with the Special Services Division of Bradford Metropolitan Council at Allerton Schools, a part-time job that he enjoyed after retiring as an EWO. This involved using his considerable calming and negotiating skills to ensure pupils travelled safely and without misbehaving to and from school each day.

For many years through the long summer school holidays and during his time as an EWO Trevor was also employed as a Sports and Play Leader in the Bradford Parks. Hundreds of children took advantage of a variety of organised team sports he supervised. This was the forerunner of today's Summer School activities. Many of the youngsters were from families who could not afford to take a summer holiday away from home. Some of those people still recognise Trevor walking around Bradford today, and now in their 50s and 60s they always stop him for a chat and to wish him well.

Recognition and reward

Trevor is well renowned for his pro-active work for the people of Bradford in respect of the many good causes he supports. He has given many, many hours to help the needy and those less fortunate than himself. To list and describe in detail all those charities and good causes would not be appropriate in the context of this biography. However, it is important to highlight those which have, for many years, benefited from Trevor's determination and selfless desire to help others.

The Bradford Cancer Support Centre is a local independent registered charity which was set up in 1988 to provide support services to cancer patients and their families. Trevor has been involved with the charity for a number of years helping to raise funds through a series of talks he gives to clubs and organisations about 'his life'. He can always be found supporting the needs of the Centre. Also, he works for Yorkshire Cancer Research and Macmillan Cancer Relief on 'flag days' and other events.

The Lord Mayor of Bradford chooses a deserving local charity to support each year for the Lord Mayor's Appeal, which raises tens of thousands of pounds. Trevor is proud to lead the hundreds of volunteers in making collections at vantage points across the city and has never once missed an opportunity to support this annual event.

Trevor was introduced to the Friends of Bradford Royal Infirmary by his old pal Jack Bower, a lifelong Bradford Northern and Bulls supporter and fundraiser. He is a club life member who did sterling work for the supporters club after the 1964 reformation. Along with Trevor, he became a founder member of this organisation in 1988. The BRI has benefited greatly from Trevor's involvement. As a committee member he never misses a meeting. He organises the raffle for the autumn fair every year and carries out publicity for them all year round. He was particularly involved with the 'Bradford Heart and the MRI Scanner Appeals'. He is also a regular visitor to the hospital, taking time out to talk to the very sick and chronically ill on the various wards.

The Catholic Housing Aid Centre (CHAS) has been in existence for around 40 years and Trevor has been very closely associated with them, always very willing to help in their fundraising activities. Only recently he raised £1,000 for their Home for All Appeal.

The Bradford Society for Mentally Handicapped Children & Adults will soon celebrate its 40th birthday. Trevor has helped to raise money for this charity which is run entirely by volunteers. He has been an excellent supporter for their cause and is always only too happy to help with collections.

Whenever any drug-related initiatives require support in the city, Trevor is keen to offer his services. Either working from his home base at the Bradford Police Club for Young People or out and about giving talks and advice about lifestyle, health and fitness to voluntary organisations and drug users, he has always been extremely active.

Trevor is a deeply religious man and a confirmed Roman Catholic. He has supported his local church in Heaton with all sorts of fundraising activities including school fayres, coffee mornings and raffles. He has also led campaigns to raise funds for new buildings and restoration work. He has served as a governor of St Cuthbert's RC School. He has given long-term support to the St Vincent de Paul Society, which is devoted to helping the poor and homeless. He is always on duty at Sunday morning Mass selling the Catholic newspapers and church magazine.

Trevor was awarded the Benemerenti Medal by His Holy Father Pope John Paul II for his voluntary work for the church, at a special Vigil Mass at St Cuthbert's Church on Christmas Eve 2001. Of all his treasured possessions and many awards he considers this to be the greatest.

The visit of Her Majesty Queen Elizabeth II to Bradford Cathedral on Thursday morning 27 March 1997 to distribute the Royal Maundy was to be a thrilling and unique occasion for Trevor. He was one of two well-known Bradford Catholics who personally received from Her Majesty the traditional red and white purse including specially minted silver coins to mark the Queens 71st year. The recipients, 71 men and 71 women were chosen by Buckingham Palace in recognition of their Christian service to the community. It was the first time in the Bradford diocese's 76-year history that the monarch had visited the cathedral. Trevor recalls: "There were around 1,000 spectators packed into the cathedral. It was a very moving and dignified ceremony, where Her Majesty paid homage to her subjects. It symbolises the washing of the disciples' feet by Jesus Christ himself.

When the Queen handed me the Maundy Monies she noticed my Welsh Rugby blazer badge. I told her I had met her dad (King George VI) at the Wembley Rugby League Cup Final in 1948. She said 'How very nice'."

Trevor is continually in demand to give talks and presentations at various functions, including dinners, lunches and other events, to community groups and clubs across the city. He would love to see the reformation of the Bradford Sportsman's Society which was so successful in the 1950s and 1960s as a focal point to raise the image of sport in the community and as a facilitator for fundraising activities to support the needs of young people.

Dr Foster MBE

Trevor's remarkable dedication and long service for the community in Bradford has in recent years been officially recognised from all quarters.

He has never sought the limelight and remains the same quiet, unassuming gentleman. He is not one to promote his successes, but there is good reason to record them in his biography and if that brings acclaim to his favourite city and results in some community project or charity gaining greater support and profile in its hour of need, then he is a proud and happy man.

Councillor Margaret Eaton, the leader of Bradford MDC outlined Trevor's work for the city: "Being the first ever recipient of the Lord Mayor of Bradford's Lifetime Achievement Award was due recognition of the decades of dedication and commitment Trevor Foster has given to the city of Bradford.

Trevor has devoted over 60 years to the city as a rugby league legend, as well as endless work for countless charities. He has been actively involved in charities such as the Millennium Scanner Appeal, Bradford Police Young People's Club and Friends of Bradford Royal Infirmary

At Bradford Council we are particularly proud of the fact that Trevor is a former colleague who worked as an education welfare officer.

Best known throughout the world for his sportsmanship and fair play, Trevor Foster has given great service to Bradford Northern, now the Bulls, as player, coach, director, timekeeper, president of the Supporters' Club and chairman of the Floodlight Fund.

His 60 years unbroken association with the club is a wonderful and unique record: one that is unlikely to be repeated in modern day sport."

The National Museum of Photography, Film and Television, which is based in Bradford, staged a 'Bradford 100' Exhibition (the people who most make a difference to other people's lives without necessarily realising it). Nominations were sought from the population of Bradford, asking them to choose the city's unsung superheroes. 'A hundred people who represent the spirit of Bradford' included Trevor with the most votes of all the nominees.

In 1998, there was a Trevor Foster Tribute Dinner at The Norfolk Gardens Hotel, to mark his Diamond Jubilee – 'Celebration of a Legend', attended by Gerry Sutcliffe MP and organised by the Bradford Bulls. The £3,500 profits from the dinner went to Trevor's chosen charities including: Cancer Support Centre, Daisy Bank; Bradford Police Young People's Club; Lord Mayor's Appeal; Bradford Society for Mentally Handicapped Children & Adults and Friends of Bradford Royal Infirmary. Jack Bates, the former chairman and long-serving director of Bradford Northern, recalled Trevor's generosity: "I must mention Trevor as a philanthropist. The club arranged a testimonial dinner for Trevor at the Norfolk Gardens Hotel in Bradford when he presented every penny of the proceeds for various local charities. This from a man who was by no means rich, as during Trevor's playing days the wages for players, even at international level for Wales and Great Britain, were in tens of pounds rather than thousands."

Also in 1998, Trevor received the first ever Lord Mayor's 'Lifetime Achievement Award' from the Lord Mayor, Councillor Tony Miller in recognition of 60 years Service to the City'. The Lord Mayor's Tribute Dinner to mark Trevor's Diamond Jubilee in the city was attended by 100 invited guests. Trevor thought he was going out for a fish and chip supper with his family, instead he found himself arriving at Bradford City Hall to be greeted by a fanfare of trumpets and a Welsh Male Voice Choir.

In 2000, the *Telegraph & Argus* invited Trevor to an awards ceremony following his nomination as one of three in 'Best Community Sports Contribution' category. Trevor was the winner in this category and donated his cash prize to Temple Bank School for Partially Sighted. Also, Trevor was nominated for the Nationwide Awards for Voluntary Endeavour.

In 2001, Trevor received the MBE, which rugby league supporters thought he had deserved for a long time. He was included in the New Year Honours, and received a letter from Lieutenant Colonel Robert Cartwright, of St James's Palace, which invited him to the investiture to be held at Buckingham Palace on Friday 2 March. The MBE was awarded in recognition of his service to the community in Bradford. His children Simon, Sara and Bridget accompanied him to London. Trevor received over 100 letters of congratulation from all over the world.

There were many letters of support for Trevor to be awarded the MBE. One came from Cliff Morgan, one of Welsh rugby union's legendary figures, and a longstanding friend of Trevor's: "All his life Trevor Foster has believed sincerely in the fact that service is the rent we all have to pay for living on God's earth. He was a distinguished rugby international for many, many years and during his career brought great credit to sport and to his adopted city of Bradford in particular. Even today, Trevor is active in serving the community and his work for youngsters and the town of Bradford is immense. In fact, his whole life is given to helping people less fortunate than himself. He is dedicated to giving hope to others.

Very few people have devoted themselves and given so much of their time to charitable causes in the way Trevor has done. He would never ask for any recognition of this, but every one of his friends and colleagues would be delighted to see the name Trevor Foster in the Queen's honours list."

In 2002, Trevor was awarded an honorary degree of Doctor of the University of Bradford in recognition for his work and contribution to the City. His contemporary, Bulls hero Brian Noble also received an Honorary Doctorate in recognition of his contribution to the Bradford Bulls as first team coach.

Trevor has known Brian Noble since the current Bradford Bulls coach was at school. Trevor took him to the Bradford Police Boys Club. Trevor wrote this tribute to Brian Noble: "I knew Brian before he came to Odsal. He was a pupil at Hanson Grammar School and also a member of the Bradford Police Boys Club, where he enjoyed all the activities which gave him a stepping stone to the most wonderful honour: to captain a Great Britain Lions team to Australia and New Zealand."

Also in 2002 was the unveiling of Trevor Foster Way, a new road very close to where Bradford Northern played in their early days at Birch Lane and just a few hundred yards from Odsal Stadium. The idea was put forward by Councillor David Green, who represented the Odsal ward and was supported by Bradford Council. Councillor Green commented: "[Trevor] is a great ambassador for Bradford. This road is 100 yards from the Odsal Stadium, which will reflect his contribution to the local community and rugby league."

In 2004, Trevor was nominated for the National Award 'Living Sports Legend' sponsored by Help the Aged. Trevor and Simon attended the official function at The Dorchester Hotel in London. Trevor was runner-up in the category. The winner was marathon winner Arthur Keily. Also, he was nominated for The Yorkshire Sporting Legends and Heroes Awards alongside Jane Tomlinson; Trevor's own hero.

Trevor's contribution to the city is covered in *Bradford's Own*, a book written by Derek A. J. Lister, bringing together the extraordinary lives and achievements of those who were born or lived in Bradford. The book also includes cricketers Jim Laker and Brian Close, the Bronte sisters, David Hockney, Barbara Castle and J. B. Priestley. Now aged 90, Trevor still enjoys his community activities in the city that has been his home since 1938. It is a remarkable tribute to a very full and active life that he has been recognised as much for his community work as for his achievements in rugby league.

Above: Arthur Clues – a fierce opponent and long-time friend.
(Photo: Courtesy Robert Gate)
Below: 6 November 1966 at Headingley -
Trevor scores in a charity match. (Photo: *Rugby League Journal*)

Coaching: Top: On a course;
middle: At Odsal with Milam Kasonovic
and Jack Scroby;
bottom: with a successful Bradford
Northern colts team.
Photos: Top & bottom: Courtesy Trevor
Foster; middle: *Telegraph & Argus.*

12. Odsal

"Like a small piece of heaven on earth". An unusual description for a rugby league ground, but Trevor's comment shows what Odsal has meant to him during his time in Bradford. Coming north from Newport in 1938, the huge bowl of the stadium made an enormous impression on him. It was to be the scene of many great moments as a player, and was to become "literally my second home" in over 60 years involvement with Bradford Northern and then the Bulls.

Interviewed by John Ledger in September 2000 in the *Yorkshire Post*, he recalled his first visit to Odsal: "When I arrived I walked into the big room – it's now called the Trevor Foster Lounge, who would have though that? – and I looked through the window and saw all the terracing, the shingle, the railway sleepers and the mud, and thought 'What am I doing here?' But once I got out on to the pitch, I knew I had done right."

It was historically neat that Trevor tied together two of the great parts of his rugby life – Odsal and Wales - when he made his international rugby league debut for Wales on 23 December 1939. He played in a Welsh team that beat England 16-3 at Odsal.

He was offered work on the ground staff at Odsal before the war, and again worked there in the early 1950s, after leaving his coaching post with the Rugby Football League. He was on the staff when the famous 1954 Challenge Cup Final replay between Halifax and Warrington was played. The events of that day, when the official attendance was 102,569, but in reality probably around 120,000 were present, have been described elsewhere, in particular in *There were a lot more than that*. Interviewed by Robert Gate for that book, Trevor recalled: "I was closely concerned with the organisation and preparation for the replay. It was certainly a momentous event which created history for our wonderful game." Trevor recalled the "colossal queues" outside the ground as kick-off approached, and people pushing through the fragile fence by the car park entrance to get into the ground. He remembers after the game, Harry Hornby, the Bradford Northern managing director announcing that a new world record crowd had been set: "his face full of pride and shedding a few happy tears." Trevor also recalls being in the club offices the day after the replay, and taking phone calls from all over the world, asking about how so many people had squeezed into the ground to watch rugby league.

Odsal remained a central part of Trevor's life after he retired from playing in 1955, but continued his work for the club as a coach, then as a director, and later as timekeeper.

The name Odsal will always be associated primarily with rugby league. But other sports have been staged there – including speedway and stock car racing. Trevor remembers in 1948 when he had helped Great Britain win the Ashes, being taken to a speedway meeting at Odsal that evening after the match in the afternoon, and being given a great reception by the 20,000 crowd watching a very different sport.

In 1956 Odsal was put to another use, very different from rugby league or speedway. A Catholic pageant was held there, between 25 and 29 September, and gave Trevor an opportunity he would never have anticipated. In the programme for the event, he is listed among the Arena Cast, not even having a speaking part. But a few days before the event, news leaked out that he was to play the part of Christ on the cross, dressed only in a loin cloth. He had agreed to play the role two months before the event, but had asked that this not be publicised. Some young rugby league fans saw him being measured for the cross at the stadium and word soon spread. The newspaper report said that the organiser wanted "a man of religious conviction with a fine physique and in peak condition".

Mr Kearns, the producer, said that Trevor would be suspended for about 10 minutes. His feet would be on a rest, and he would have a belt that would be hooked onto the framework. His hands would grip strong wire, but he would have to hold almost the full weight of his body

– almost 14½ stones, with his arms and upper body. Another actor was to play Christ when he was not on the cross. Trevor said that he had not been in any dramatic presentation since he had left school, but said that he was "greatly honoured". He went on: "It will be a marvellous experience. I have a love of my religion, and when I was approached I could not say anything else but yes."

The development of Odsal

Almost from the time the ground opened in 1934, the subject of how to develop and modernise Odsal has been present – up to the current time. Trevor has been at the centre of this debate.

From the 1960s onwards, all rugby league clubs gradually faced pressure to improve and upgrade their facilities. The 1971 Ibrox disaster, when 66 football fans died in a crush on a staircase at the end of a Rangers versus Celtic football match, had made sports authorities more aware of the need for proper safety regulation, and while Odsal was a unique ground, with an atmosphere – and at certain times a climate – all of its own, it posed special problems for modernisation. Trevor has been at the forefront of raising money both to redevelop Odsal, and campaigns to keep the stadium open over the years.

The first started in 1977, when the need for new floodlights, which had first been used in 1951 but taken out of service in 1960, had become more pressing. Most professional rugby league clubs now had floodlights, and for one of Bradford Northern's status to lack this facility was no longer acceptable.

Odsal had been the first ground to stage floodlit rugby league in the north - London's White City had staged a season of floodlit games for London Highfield in 1933-34. On 31 October 1951, Bradford Northern played New Zealand with a 7pm kick-off. Subsequently, Trevor played for Wales against the Kiwi tourists that season under the Odsal lights, which had been adapted from the speedway lights.

However, by 1960, Odsal's lights were beyond use, damaged by the weather and the club not having the funds to maintain them properly. In 1977, Trevor led a campaign to bring floodlit rugby league back to Odsal. The club had considered a move back to its former home of Bradford Park Avenue in the early 1970s, but after it looked likely that the move would happen, the proposal collapsed and the club secured a new lease on Odsal from Bradford Metropolitan Council.

Trevor's appeal to raise £5,000 to help pay for the lights said that: "The time has now arrived when, with the excellent progress and improvement in the Stadium's appearance and amenities, we, as supporters, should make a wholehearted effort to introduce Floodlit Football to its original home". By this time, only seven other professional clubs apart from Northern lacked floodlights, and all the game's leading clubs had them.

However, there was still concern at the club's financial position. The Supporters' Club, at their meeting in August 1977, endorsed Trevor's proposals for the campaign, but it was agreed that the Supporters' Club would keep the money raised until a contract had been signed by the club for the new floodlights to be installed.

By November, £500 had been raised and in June 1978, the original target of £5,000 was passed. Trevor wrote at the time: "During the past nine months much hard work and dedicated service has been given to this project by the Bradford Northern Supporters Committee and the response to the appeal has been magnificent". By 27 November 1979, when the club celebrated the first match – against St Helens – under the new lights, more than £8,000 had been raised. The total cost of the new lights was £42,000.

140

Trevor was given the honour of switching on the new floodlights. It was the first floodlit match at Odsal for 19 years. Club chairman Jack Bates said that a "mountain of work" had taken place since the new lease on the ground had been signed three years earlier, culminating in the new floodlights. When asked to write about Trevor for this book, Jack Bates recalled his work for the floodlights campaign. Coach Peter Fox said at the time that "the modern high-power lighting system will just crown the whole stadium", after describing the other improvements that had been carried out. However, he was not sure whether the club should enter the BBC2 Floodlit Trophy, as it would involve extra fixtures.

Writing in the match programme, Trevor recalled playing in the game 28 years earlier against New Zealand. He went on: "There has been a need for lights at Odsal for many years. Looking at the towers it certainly enriches the stadium. This is a major step forward in the development of our vastly improving facilities at Odsal towards the 'Super Stadium' which we all dream about. Floodlight football to me was an enjoyable experience in which the ball and players seemed to move that much faster."

Despite some success on the pitch in the late 1970s and early 1980s, when Peter Fox led the team to consecutive championships, Northern continued to struggle financially. However, in 1986, the club's financial adviser wrote to people who had supported the club, saying that the financial position was improving, after "several years' horrendous losses", and that the club had been in profit in 1983-84 and 1984-85. In 1985-86, the Odsal Lifeline Society was organised to help raise money for the club. Trevor was the chairman, and in December 1986 wrote to members about the progress the operation was making. The society had supported the signing and contract payments of various players, including Steve Barnett, Wayne Race and Paul Grayshon. Wales and Great Britain winger Phil Ford was working to promote the society and new recruit from rugby union Terry Holmes was also involved.

As well as supporting the club, the society was holding a Christmas Party for children from the Lindley House School, which was for children with learning difficulties. Trevor's letter outlined that Grattan, the mail order company, had donated the toys, and that Holmes was to be Father Christmas. Barrie Stamper, a successful local businessman, who had sponsored the club on a number of occasions, became involved behind the scenes. His financial acumen was very helpful to the club.

Another responsibility Trevor took on in 1986 was to become the official timekeeper for the club, taking over from Jack Senior, a referee and Bradford amateur rugby league official, who had done the job for just one season. Trevor is still timekeeper for the Bulls, which has included carrying out this role in Challenge Cup Finals, Super League Grand Finals and World Club Challenge matches. In 2004, his fellow timekeeper at the Super League Grand Final against Leeds Rhinos was his long time friend, 78-year-old Billy Watts. His involvement with Leeds dates back to 1938, when he first watched a match at Headingley. He has been Leeds' timekeeper since 1975. John Woodcock interviewed both of them for the *Yorkshire Post* a couple of days before the match, and their friendly rivalry shone through in the article. Watts said that "whatever our respective teams are doing on the pitch, we know we have a serious job to do", while Trevor said it was "a privilege to be involved."

In 1987, a new financial crisis put the future of Odsal under threat. In a feature in the *Telegraph & Argus*, headed 'Shame of Odsal', the paper's rugby league writer, Brian Smith outlined some of the problems facing the stadium. He said that it now had "superb terracing" but "Odsal has now lost its identity and seldom can so much money have been spent on ensuring that so many people get wet. At least there was some character about the place before they pulled down the old stand, but now it's a stadium without a soul and has a stand

1964 Resurrection campaign: Top: The Bradford Northern Development Committee.
Below: The public meeting at St George's Hall. Joe Phillips speaking, Trevor sitting behind him with his hands behind his back. (Both photos: *Telegraph & Argus*)

Left: Joe Phillips – a great player for Bradford Northern, and also a key figure in the 1964 resurrection campaign.
(Photo: Courtesy Robert Gate)

Above: The agenda from the St George's Hall meeting. (Courtesy Trevor Foster)

which is as useful as half an umbrella." He went on to say that the £3.5 million spent on it by the local council had left Odsal as a "rather more stylish hole in the ground".

Coming two years after the devastating fire at the city's Valley Parade football ground, when 55 people were killed, once again the issues of safety and the need for modern facilities were coming to the fore. Trevor defended Odsal, saying: "In my heart of hearts I believe that the council is concerned about Odsal and that they would like to transform this historic stadium into a place which everyone can visit in comfort to enjoy first class facilities." He said that the Council seemed to have spent money to improve the stadium for the 1985 World Speedway Championship, but had not continued to improve it. He argued that a multipurpose stadium would be best. Trevor concluded that the fans would return to Odsal if the development of the ground continued.

It was clearly a controversial issue. Another supporter, former Northern vice-president Eric Jowett, said he would not go to Odsal while the fences put up to segregate supporters when Bradford City played there after the Valley Parade fire, were still present. He said that the Council "spent £3.5 million on speedway and hundreds of thousands of pounds on Bradford City but they will not spend a penny piece for the regular rugby league supporter." Even Trevor's comments had acknowledged that a move away from Odsal was a possibility, with Park Avenue an alternative, where the club could have their own facilities.

The debate was still going on in 1988, when the *Telegraph & Argus* reported that Trevor was urging all the Council's political groups to work out a financial package for Odsal. He said: "The stadium has already been improved immensely with ratepayers' money and a final push is now needed to put the obvious things right. The character of Odsal must be restored because now we have a good rugby league team which will go on to greater glory and attract bigger crowds." He concluded that there would be problems if the club had to move to Valley Parade.

In April 1989, Trevor's name was mentioned as a possible trustee as a new consortium challenged the existing board for control of the club. By the start of the new season, current chairman Chris Caisley had taken over. But, the problems of Odsal in the modern era continued. In the autumn of 1990, the debate about a possible ground share at valley Parade was still ongoing. One Northern supporter wrote to the *Telegraph & Argus* saying: "No-one can dispute that fickle supporters will be put off attending a match at Odsal in bad weather. However, these are the same fans who tend only to follow a winning team." But he was clear that he would not attend matches at Valley Parade, describing it as "cramped" with a poor view of the pitch.

The arguments over Odsal's future continued in the early 1990s. In 1991, Trevor was contacted by the Save Odsal Stadium Campaign, which was arguing for gradual redevelopment of the stadium, its development as a national stadium for the game and against the idea of sharing Valley Parade. The campaign was organised by local members of the Rugby League Supporters Association. Trevor attended the campaign's first public meeting, and campaign organiser John Drake remembers him speaking passionately in favour of staying at Odsal. The idea of a ground-share with Bradford City FC at Valley Parade was eventually dropped.

Three years later, in 1994, planning permission for a National Superdome at Odsal was being sought. Trevor was invited by Bradford Council to an exhibition and meeting at Odsal in the Trevor Foster Room about the proposals. Trevor was also contacted by the architects, who said that their plans included a new Trevor Foster Lounge. Trevor had been honoured by the naming of the lounge after him, but always found it ironic that a lifelong teetotaller should have a bar named after him.

Odsal had been a burden for the club and the Council, and had obvious problems when staging winter rugby league, with its cold open spaces. However, it turned into a major asset

144

for the club when summer rugby and Super League started in 1996. Northern became the Bulls, and although some older or more traditional supporters were shocked at the changes to their game, Bradford Bulls developed the concept of Super League arguably better than any other club. Once the terraces of Odsal had been windswept open spaces, often sparsely populated, now they were teeming with families enjoying the fun. The success of the Bulls on the pitch was undoubtedly a major factor – whether the singing and dancing would have attracted the same crowds to watch a losing team is debatable.

There was a feeling at this time that the game's history was being forgotten. Rugby league still lacks a museum, and at this time the game's Hall of Fame was on display in a pub in Oulton, through a sponsorship deal. Trevor wrote to the RFL's then chief executive, Maurice Lindsay, proposing that it be relaunched, and moved to Odsal. He said that it could be developed with a rugby league museum, and mentioned the '100 years of rugby league exhibition' that had been recently staged in the city's museum. But his ideas were not taken up by the RFL, and although the Hall of Fame is now situated at the entrance to the game's headquarters at Red Hall, there is still no official museum to remember the game's past in all its glory.

However, the need for a viable redevelopment plan for Odsal was still present. In December 1996, proposals for a superdome seemed to have collapsed, and Trevor called for "a partnership [to be] formed with the Council to make improvements on a smaller scale. We now have summer rugby so the stadium could be made comfortable for a fraction of the price. I would be loath to see us leave Odsal."

The millennium was marked throughout the country in many different ways. The Bulls showed that they had not forgotten their history by inviting Trevor, Jeff Grayshon and Tommy Smales among a group of Bradford's great stars in September 2000 to receive medals after they had been named in the *Telegraph & Argus* Millennium Masters Team.

But at the end of September, the Bulls did finally move to Valley Parade, so that Odsal could be redeveloped as a new 22,000 all-seat modern stadium.

The move to a football ground across the city was not popular with supporters. However, it was tolerated as long as redevelopment of Odsal was in sight. However, by early 2002, it was clear that further problems were apparent with the redevelopment proposals. The Bulls' success on the pitch – they had won Super League in 2001 and won the World Club Challenge in February 2002 – was not being matched by the creation of a new modern home. The government's decision to order a public enquiry into the development was the final straw for the project's developers.

Space does not allow for a full account of the issues around the Bulls' return to Odsal. But Trevor was once again to the fore in the campaign. Just after the World Club Challenge triumph, he said in the *Telegraph & Argus* that the new stadium "would be the dawn of a new era for the club and the city... If it does not go through, it will be the worst blow of my life." In a letter to *League Express*, he called for Bradford supporters to continue to support a return to Odsal. He wrote: "Odsal is the home of the Bradford Bulls and always will be for me." As part of the campaign, he had become President of the Bradford Independent Supporters Association (BISA), and worked closely with them.

Vicky Woodcock, the then BISA chair, acknowledges the role Trevor has played in BISA: "Trevor is the honorary president of Bradford Independent Supporters Association and, as with everything he does, Trevor puts his heart and soul into it. It was at one of the meetings in the first year of BISA that he captured the hearts and minds of everyone who attended the meeting. Bradford had moved out of Odsal in 2001 in readiness for the stadium to be developed, but it [the proposal] had been called in by the government [for a planning enquiry].

It looked likely everything was going to fall through, with the possibility of never returning to Odsal. BISA was campaigning to stop this and Trevor was adamant we would go back home regardless of what it took. Trevor stood up and told us of his love for Bradford Bulls and the ground on which he played. He said even if it meant he had to walk from Bradford to London [for the enquiry] we would go back to our spiritual home.

That evening you could have heard a pin drop in the room. The passion with which he spoke and the determination in his nature was clear. Everyone that night would have followed Trevor to the end of the Earth. He is an inspiration to all of us."

Sam Grundy, BISA's current chair, commends Trevor's work for the club: "When BISA was set up in 2002 we were overjoyed to get the support of Trevor Foster MBE. Trevor kindly agreed to be our honorary president and has been a stalwart supporter ever since. In the 65 years Trevor has been involved in rugby league he has become a legend not just in Bradford but also throughout the rugby league community. Nobody has contributed more to the game of rugby league in the past 65 years.

We are so lucky to have such a kind, thoughtful and hard-working man as our honorary president and his presence at our meetings is always a pleasure. Trevor is always eager to help out and make time to talk about rugby league to anyone. Without him there would probably be no Bradford Bulls today."

Return to Odsal

A compromise was reached with the Council that allowed the Bulls to return to Odsal for the 2003 season, without an immediate development programme, but with a long-term lease and effective control over the stadium's future. A new stand was built at the old speedway pits end, but Bulls fans were clearly glad to be back on their familiar terraces, even if they still got wet at times.

The return to Odsal in March 2003 was an emotional occasion. Trevor led a group of former players back onto the pitch and symbolically kissed the ground. To mark the occasion, the club staged a legends match, organised by the Past Players' Association. Trevor played, along with Keith Mumby, Karl Fairbank, Paul Medley, Brendan Hill and Roger Simpson. The players changed in the old changing rooms, under the Trevor Foster Lounge, and walked onto the pitch down the terraces, through the crowd, as in the old days. Bradford Northern had reformed for one final match. Trevor's delight at the club's return to its spiritual home was clear for all to see.

The programme from the Life of Christ pageant in September 1956.
Trevor played the part of Jesus Christ. (Photo: Courtesy Trevor Foster)

Rugby League — First Division

First Floodlit Match

BRADFORD NORTHERN

VERSUS

ST. HELENS

* Match Sponsors to-night
Rawson Bacon Supplies
Phone Bradford 390919

TUESDAY
27th November, 1979
Kick-off 7.30 p.m.

* To-night's
MITRE MATCHBALL
Sponsored by
Greenbank Construction Co
Building Contractors
Phone Bradford 34415

Souvenir Programme 20p

New floodlights at Odsal in 1979.

Above: Trevor and Charlie Ebbage present
a cheque on behalf of the Supporters Club
to Jack Bates for the floodlight fund.
(Photo: *Telegraph & Argus*)
Left: The match programme from the first
match under the new lights. (Courtesy
Bradford Bulls RLFC)

148

THE RUGBY FOOTBALL LEAGUE

At a meeting of the
Rugby League Council

Trevor Foster

was unanimously elected a

Life Member of the
Rugby Football League

in recognition of his outstandingly
meritorious service to the game
over many years.

Chairman

Leeds
Secretary   *Greg Mc Call*

The certificate presented to Trevor by the RFL to mark his admission to life membership.
(Courtesy Rugby Football League)

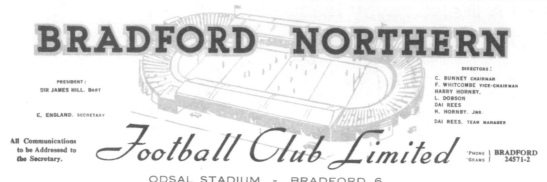

BRADFORD NORTHERN

PRESIDENT:
SIR JAMES HILL. BART

E. ENGLAND. SECRETARY

DIRECTORS:
C. BUNNEY CHAIRMAN
F. WHITCOMBE VICE-CHAIRMAN
HARRY HORNBY.
L. DOBSON
DAI REES
H. HORNBY. JNR.
DAI REES, TEAM MANAGER

Football Club Limited

All Communications
to be Addressed to
the Secretary.

PHONE } BRADFORD
GRAMS } 24571-2

ODSAL STADIUM - BRADFORD, 6

28th January, 1958.

Trevor Foster, Esq.,
39, Spring Gardens Road,
BRADFORD 9.

Dear Mr. Foster,

This may seem a very formal letter to you, but is a
very necessary form of address under the circumstances.

On behalf of the Directors, I have much pleasure in
inviting you to join the Board of the Bradford Northern
Football Club. Our Articles of Association allow us to
co-opt a fellow Director, and we unanimously and sincerely
trust you will be able to accept.

I would be grateful if you would let me know if it
will be convenient for you to attend our next meeting which
takes place at Odsal Stadium on Tuesday next, 4th February.

With all good wishes,

I remain,

Yours sincerely,

C. Bunney.

The letter from Bradford Northern that offered Trevor a place on the board of directors.
(Courtesy Trevor Foster)

13. A Welsh rugby league legend

Trevor's playing career coming to an end coincided with a decline in the profile of rugby league in Wales. The Welsh international team was disbanded in 1953, as Great Britain were to enter the 1954 World Cup, not separate England and Wales teams. The Welsh amateur league collapsed in 1955, and apart from occasional exhibition matches, rugby league was not played in Wales in any serious form until 1975. Rugby union players continued to 'go north' to play rugby league, although the economic post-war boom meant that there was less economic pressure on players to change codes compared to the 1920s and 1930s.

In 1968, the Rugby Football League relaunched the Wales international team. An interview with Brian Bearshaw in the *Manchester Evening News* in 1969, when the Wales rugby league international team was in the process of being resurrected after 15 years in abeyance, illustrates Trevor's passion for the Welsh cause. Trevor had been in the Welsh dressing-room a couple of months previously, prior to an international against England, expecting to experience the Welsh fervour that had always been present in his playing days.

He told Bearshaw: "There was no atmosphere. It was very sad. I was in the dressing-room to rub one or two players down. I felt cold. There seemed a lack of enthusiasm among some, and two of the players weren't fit. The two substitutes... were itching to get on the field. They badly wanted to play, yet they had to sit on the bench for the whole match. It was said the Rugby League couldn't find a team manager for our international side. But this is ridiculous. There are many of us about who'd be only too happy to take it on. The importance seems to be going out of these matches, unfortunately. Let's build them up again, get the players together, get Welshmen together, organise meetings and restore interest".

It was not until 1975 that the team played in Wales. The RFL had so little confidence of being able to attract a crowd in South Wales that matches were played mainly in Lancashire. It was surprising that Trevor was never offered the role of team manager for Wales – surely he would have been the ideal candidate. Trevor worked in a voluntary capacity with the Welsh team when Roy Francis was coach, and assisted with training sessions. He became President of the Welsh Players Association in the 1980s and was time keeper for Wales in this period.

Jonathan Davies recalled Trevor's support for the Wales team: "Trevor is a legend down in Wales. My abiding memory of him is as the President of the Welsh Rugby League Players Association when he used to travel with the Welsh team to international matches. It was in my earlier days in rugby league, we were in the dressing room before a big match at Swansea. I looked down to see Trevor then in his late 70s acting as the teams physio and giving my legs a "rub down" with liniment in the warm up. His passion and his pride in Wales rubbed off on us all. Trevor has that special quality of being able to lift the mood of the occasion simply with his presence"

Cardiff Blue Dragons

The successful launch of Fulham RLFC in 1980, the first new professional club in the Rugby League since 1954, gave the game a wider vision, and more confidence to take the code into new areas. Following the Fulham model of playing on a football ground, and with a close relationship with the host club, Cardiff City RLFC (the Blue Dragons) were launched in 1981, with former Wales rugby union and Salford rugby league star David Watkins at the helm.

The RFL marked the occasion of Cardiff's first game, against Salford on 30 August 1981 at Ninian Park by inviting past Welsh rugby league heroes to the game. Trevor was invited to the game, and was welcomed onto the pitch with the other Welsh legends before the game.

Cardiff survived for three seasons, never quite able to win promotion to the First Division. A final season move to Bridgend, when they struggled to field a team, seemed to have finished professional club rugby league in Wales for the time being. And in 1984, the RFL had put the Wales international team into hibernation again.

Then, in 1989, after various clubs had tried to tempt him north, Doug Laughton and Jim Mills persuaded Jonathan Davies, the Wales rugby union captain, to 'come north'. In a similar move to that of David Watkins 20 years earlier, the recruitment of Davies by Widnes had an immediate impact on rugby league's fortunes in the principality. The rugby union side was at a low ebb at this time, and other high profile union players headed north. John Devereux, David Young, Kevin Ellis, Adrian Hadley and Allan Bateman all headed up the M6 in Davies's wake, and in 1991, the Wales team was launched once more, on a memorable night in Swansea.

Once the team had established itself, an immediate target on the horizon was the 1995 Rugby League World Cup, to be held in England. The 1989 to 1992 tournament had culminated in Great Britain narrowly losing to Australia in the final at Wembley.

But despite the obvious attractions of a Welsh team, with the former rugby union players giving a strong and dynamic nucleus, the Rugby League authorities decided to have a Great Britain team, and exclude Wales from the tournament.

Trevor wrote to Maurice Lindsay, then chief executive of the RFL, in June 1993 to protest at this decision. He had become President of the Wales Rugby League Players Association and wrote to the RFL on their headed paper. He said: "It was with great sadness that I received the new of the planned exclusion of the Welsh Rugby League from the 1995 Centenary World Cup Competition. I wish to put on record my deep and genuine sorrow for this quite astonishing decision which smacks in the face of the tremendous development (initiated by the RFL) regarding the Welsh national side over recent years. As a former Welsh rugby league international, also captain of Wales, and currently president of the Welsh Players Association, I am writing to express my concern at this policy decision, and to ask for an immediate reappraisal.

To suggest that the principality and the famous Welsh jersey will not be represented at arguably the most prestigious event in the history of our great game, is an affront to all those supporters, players and officials who have worked so very hard over the years to establish and enhance its international progress. Wales may not have the playing resources at their disposal in comparison to Australia, New Zealand or Great Britain, but have proved over the last two years that they are able to compete on level terms with any nation, and certainly are capable of competing in any seeded or 'pool' competition which would involve France, Fiji, Tonga and Western Samoa, for example."

He went on to outline the support that existed for the game in Wales, the work done already, including in the student game and the opportunity the World Cup offered to build the game in Wales. Trevor's letter was also published in the rugby league press.

In his reply, Maurice Lindsay said that development of the game in Wales was important, but he was not sure if the playing squad was strong enough, as it was not possible to use amateur or student players in a predominantly professional competition, as it would put their amateur status at risk if they wanted to play rugby union.

Trevor had copied his letter to the All Party Parliamentary Rugby League Group and to Neil Kinnock MP. On behalf of the group, David Hinchliffe MP replied to Trevor, offering their support, and saying that they had raised the question with Maurice Lindsay.

Fortunately, the matter was resolved satisfactorily, and a newspaper report said that "Trevor Foster is smiling again, having campaigned successfully to ensure Wales a World Cup place in 1995." Wales made a magnificent contribution to the 1995 World Cup. Their match against Western Samoa at Swansea was a superb game, and 7,000 Welsh fans headed to Old Trafford for their semi-final against England.

Rugby Union

Before the World Cup, in 1994, Trevor had written to the Welsh Rugby Union, the Rugby Football Union and the Committee of Home Unions to propose a rugby union versus rugby league challenge match for charity. This was a year before the events of August 1995, when rugby union became 'open', accepted professionalism, and the 'Berlin Wall' that had stood between the two rugby codes for 100 years, came down. The distinguished gentlemen writing replies to Trevor, some of whom had played against him during the War, were unaware that in less than two years, Wigan and Bath would be playing a 'cross-code challenge' and Wigan would be winning the Middlesex Sevens at Twickenham.

Dudley Wood, on behalf of the RFU, said that they enjoyed "good relations with the Rugby Football League and we fully acknowledge their position as a professional sport... Rugby union football remains a sport for participants in full employment who play as a recreation in their spare time. In my view, it would be completely inappropriate to attempt to stage a match between amateur players playing for fun and professionals playing for financial reward..." For the WRU, Edward Jones said "The Welsh Rugby Union does whatever it can on all occasions to help charity but a match against a rugby league team would not be acceptable." He also denied that the rugby league authorities had applied to stage a match at Cardiff Arms Park.

However, there was better cross-code co-operation in May 1995, when the Wales Rugby League Players Association informed its members that "after gentle persuasion by our chairman, Jim Mills, Cliff Morgan CBE has agreed to be the guest speaker at our annual dinner." Trevor had been friendly with Cliff Morgan for a long time.

The improved relationship between the codes helped rugby league in many ways in Wales. Young players could play league without fear of being ostracised in union, and rugby league had access to the major rugby union stadiums for the Challenge Cup final when Wembley was being rebuilt. In September 1999, Glanmor Griffiths, the chairman of the WRU, wrote to Simon Foster, confirming that two complimentary tickets were to be supplied for Trevor to attend the Wales against Western Samoa Rugby Union World Cup match at the Millennium Stadium on 14 October. Less than 10 years before, the WRU had banned Jonathan Davies from going onto the pitch as a BBC commentator because he was a rugby league player. Now one of Wales's greatest rugby league players was to be a VIP guest of honour. How times change.

Simon Foster, who had arranged the visit, commented: "To return home to Wales and be a special guest of the WRU; to sit in the stands at the new 'Cardiff Arms Park' and sing the Welsh National Anthem, will make my father a very proud man." But it was not a completely rugby union weekend, the next day Trevor attended the Wales versus Ireland rugby league international in Swansea.

South Wales

Trevor is the only surviving member of his immediate family in South Wales. Elder brothers Leslie and Edward (Teddy) and sisters Madelaine, Eileen and Freda are all deceased. He keeps in touch with his many relatives back home through his niece Stephanie. She lives in the Pontypool area and has a keen interest in rugby. The weekly telephone contact brings Trevor up to date on news, including family and rugby gossip. Stephanie has been known to give her uncle the occasional hot tip on local junior rugby talent that may have potential for league up north. Several of these leads have been followed up by scouts in the principality.

In 2003, the Challenge Cup final was staged at the Millennium Stadium for the first time. It was a Yorkshire Derby – Bradford Bulls faced Leeds Rhinos, and, of course, was a repeat of Trevor's first Wembley final in 1947.

In recognition of his lifetime's work for the Bradford club, Trevor was given the honour of leading the Bradford team onto the pitch. Bradford chairman Chris Caisley magnanimously gave up his position – it is usually the club chairman who has this privilege. Once again, much of the press coverage focussed on Trevor. In *The Observer*, Andy Wilson interviewed Trevor and fellow Welsh legend Lewis Jones. Trevor told him: "It's going to be a really special day, because the Welsh people have been a great part of rugby league since it started in 1895. There have been problems, but there is also a great affinity, and I know they love their rugby league down there. It's a tremendous, wonderful thing to be going back to Cardiff, 12 miles from my home, with Bradford, the club and city I love. It will be one of the greatest days of my life." And Trevor was satisfied with the result as well, Bradford winning by two points to take the cup home.

Trevor is delighted to see amateur rugby league thriving in South Wales. On a recent visit to Cardiff over the 2004 Challenge Cup Final weekend he took the opportunity to call in at Pill Harriers Rugby Club in Newport, whom he had played for in the 1930s and was surprised and elated to see that they now host a successful rugby league team, Newport Titans. Trevor presented Pill Harriers with a Bradford Bulls shirt, and was given a white Pill Harriers jersey in exchange. The team played in white when Trevor played for them in the 1930s.

Trevor commented: "I have great optimism about the future of rugby league in South Wales. There is obviously a need to establish a super league presence down there soon. The amateur game is certainly established and is played to a high standard. There is a real structure taking shape and the foundations are secure. We have never had such an opportunity to capitalise on the pioneering work of 'Mr Perpetual Motion' Mike Nicholas and his many supporters and helpers.

Mike's commitment to the development of rugby league in South Wales through so many knock backs and adversity has been quite extraordinary. He deserves every encouragement and the full support of the Rugby Football League".

Also during the 2004 Challenge Cup final weekend, at a dinner in the City Hall, Cardiff, Trevor was inaugurated into the Welsh Sports Hall of Fame, along with snooker player Terry Griffiths, footballer Ivor Powell, cricketer Tony Lewis and posthumously footballer Bryn Jones and gymnast Arthur Whitford. One of the original 10 Hall of Fame members, Wigan and Great Britain legend Billy Boston was present at the reception. The Hall of Fame was set up in 1980, and from then until 2003, 73 sports people were added to the roll of honour. Rugby League is well represented, with Billy Boston, Willie Davies, Lewis Jones, Gus Risman, Jim Sullivan, David Watkins and Jonathan Davies all being included. The Hall of Fame carries a great deal of prestige in Welsh Sport. The Chief Executive of the Sports Council for Wales said that the annual dinner had become "the foremost [event] in the Welsh sporting calendar."

A rugby league legend

In 1988, Trevor celebrated 50 years in Bradford, and involvement with Bradford Northern. Among the tributes to Trevor then was the presentation of the Arthur Brooks Memorial Trophy at the Rugby league Writers Association dinner. The award is for service to the game.

Since then, his service to rugby league, both in Bradford and in the wider game, has been recognised in many different ways. Ten years later, a report on 'Bradford's tribute to its greatest servant' referred to Trevor's 60 years with Bradford Bulls: 'The army of support that is currently behind Bradford Bulls owes most to Foster for being the driving force behind the re-formation of the Club in 1964 after it had folded and was on the verge of disappearing'. A tribute dinner was held for Trevor in Bradford, with Ray French as the guest speaker.

Two years later, in 2000, Trevor received a letter from the Rugby Football League, saying that it had 'unanimously agreed that your exceptionally meritorious service to the game should be recognised and rewarded with the grant of Honorary Life Membership of the RFL'. He was congratulated on this by the Lord Mayor of Bradford, Councillor Harry Mason, at an official reception at Bradford's City Hall. Later, Trevor became a life vice president of the RFL.

Richard Lewis, the executive chairman of the RFL, wrote the following tribute for this book: "Trevor's enthusiasm for the game of rugby league is legendary within the Rugby Football League. We have only to celebrate any connection with Wales or Bradford Bulls and Trevor's smiling face is guaranteed to add both warmth and the human touch to what ever we are trying to achieve. That is a rare quality and one that all of us at the Rugby Football League very much appreciate.

One wonderful example of Trevor's still fiercely held enthusiasm for rugby league came to light when we staged a media event at Cardiff's Millennium Stadium in January 2003 as we prepared the way for the introduction of the Powergen Challenge Cup Final at the stadium later in the year.

Somebody from the media asked if Trevor would mind symbolically placing the ball over the try line for the television cameras. Instead he ended up running; yes, a grand old man of 88 running, to score a try in the corner of the Millennium Stadium pitch.

His last 'playing' appearance in Cardiff made the television news in Wales that night. Besides helping raise still further rugby league's profile among the Welsh public, it brought a huge smile not only to the assembled media but also to both Trevor and the Welsh public. That's Trevor Foster: a Welsh-born, rugby league treasure."

British Lions

In 2001, Trevor was voted 'Lion of the Year' at the British Lions Reunion Dinner, organised by the British Rugby League Lions Association. Trevor has always been a supporter of players' associations, both at Bradford, for Wales and for the British Lions. In May 1987, Trevor was involved in a new initiative, organising the first Bradford Northern Players' Association Annual Dinner, and is still involved in the association today, as its president.

Former British Lion and current Sky Sports rugby league expert Mike Stephenson remembers a Lions reunion tour to Australia: "I consider Trevor as one of my dearest friends and one of the all time greats of rugby league. His attitude to life and our game is a credit to him for he has touched so many hearts along the way and no doubt there are hundreds of young players and fans who can proudly say they have had the pleasure to have met such an icon of the greatest game of all.

They do say the way to a man's heart is through his stomach. So, in that case Trevor Foster has the largest heart in the world. I do recall a British Lions reunion tour to Australia in 1985. My family in Sydney had the pleasure of being hosts to Trevor and former Great Britain and Wigan hooker Joe Egan. Obviously we were expecting men with healthy appetites; but these guys could eat for Australia. They ate us out of house and home. I've never seen so many potatoes devoured at a single sitting.

When Trevor had settled into his new lodging, his first mission was to circumnavigate the area to find a Catholic church. He was away for a long time and giving some cause for concern. Eventually after a few hours there was a knock at the door... It was Trevor who said he had found the church, but had spotted a game of rugby league in the local park and stopped to watch the entire game, so typical of the man.

It was a privilege to drive him all over the rugby league heartlands. We had many adventures, not least a return overnight journey from Canberra through a horrendous tropical storm which took nine hours. Yet we hardly noticed the weather or the danger as we reminisced about our rugby playing experiences. Trevor just sat there throughout, calm, cool and collected in collar, tie and jacket, smart as ever. A perfect gentleman."

Johnny Whiteley also remembers a visit to Australia with Trevor in 1980: "It has been my privilege to know and be associated with Trevor for over 50 years. A big man with a big heart who played rugby with a passion. He was a hard opponent on the field and a gentleman off it. His love for being involved in community work with youngsters in Bradford is well documented.

Trevor and I toured Australia in 1980 with the former British Lions team. The team would often sit around the hotel and listen to his wonderful stories which were so articulate and humorous. Trevor Foster is a great ambassador for sport. He has a love for the game of rugby and all the people who are involved in it."

Two other former British Lions have fond memories of Trevor. Ray French, the current BBC rugby league commentator and distinguished writer about the game recalls: "In the April of 2000 BBC Television *Grandstand* viewers were treated to a stroll down memory lane ahead of the screening of the Bradford Bulls versus Leeds Rhinos Challenge Cup Final clash at Murrayfield in Edinburgh. For older Bulls' supporters the sight of former second row, Trevor Foster, strolling over the try line in the 72nd minute for what proved to be the match clinching try in Northern's 12-0 triumph over Halifax in the 1949 Wembley Cup Final no doubt stirred the emotions. Over 51 years later the live television shot of the genial Welshman with his finger poised over the hooter and ready to call time on another Bradford success, encapsulated all that is best about rugby league and its heroes: devotion, loyalty, integrity and honesty. Yes, Trevor Foster has displayed them all and more."

Former dual-code British Lion Bev Risman wrote for this book: "Living in the London area for many years, I had not seen Trevor for what seemed an age, although our paths had crossed fleetingly at Lions reunions, until he appeared as the timekeeper for Bradford Bulls in a match against my club, London Broncos, and was amazed to find that he was 84 years old and still looking as fit as a fiddle.

I've met him frequently since then and we have had time to chat, and I have heard him tell his rugby stories time and again with such fervour and passion that you could almost believe he was still playing. Trevor played at the same time as my father Gus, both with and against him and they were great friends. They were together in the War and played rugby union in the Armed Forces teams for Wales and Trevor was in the 1946 Tour party to Australasia which my father captained. His influence in rugby league and his devotion to his beloved Wales, is now legendary and it is wonderful to see that his efforts are at long last bearing fruit with the expansion of the game there."

Parliament

Also in 2001, Trevor received a special award for services to rugby league presented by Minister for Sport, the Right Honourable Richard Caborn MP, on behalf of the All Party

Trevor with Welsh rugby union legend Cliff Morgan.
(Photo: Courtesy Trevor Foster)

Four Welsh rugby league Lions: Trevor with Jim Mills, Billy Boston and John Mantle.
(Photo: David Williams)

THE RUGBY FOOTBALL LEAGUE.

Tel: 41238.
Telegrams: 'Norfu' Leeds.

180 Chapeltown Road,
LEEDS 7.
15th December 1939.

Dear Sir,

ENGALAND v. WALES, at Odsal, Bradford, December 23rd,
kick-off 2.30 p.m.

The following teams have been selected to represent
ENGLAND and WALES, in the International Match at Odsal,
Bradford, on behalf of the Red Cross Fund.:-

ENGLAND: W. Belshaw (Capt.)
        E. Batten   A.J. Croston   J. Lawrenson   O. Peake.
              H. Goodfellow   T. Kenny
        L. Thacker   T. Armitt   H. Dyer
              R. Roberts   C. Booth
                   E.H. Sadler

Reserves to travel: S. Brogden and F. Gregory.

WALES: J. Sullivan (Capt.)
        A. Bassett   C.H. Evans   A.J. Risman   A. Edwards
              D. Jenkins   W.T.H. Davies
        F. Whitcombe   C.D. Murphy   D.M. Davies
              T. Foster   J.E. Orford
                   A. Givvons

Reserves to travel: D. Madden and H.W. Thomas.

Referee: Mr. P. Cowell (Warrington).

The Chairman of The Council (G.F. Hutchins, Esq.)
is in charge of the England team, and A.A. Bonner, Esq. in
charge of the Wales team.   Players must report in the
dressing rooms at Odsal not later than 1.30 p.m..

The remuneration will be £1 per player, plus 10/-
extra for expenses, plus fares.

This is recognised as an official International
match, will count in records, and as one for presentation of
Caps.

Please bring all the gear you require, except jerseys,
pants and stockings, which will be provided.   Other items such
as garters, laces, belts, knee and ankle bandages, etc. must
be brought.

You are to make your own arrangements for travelling
to and from Odsal.   As you know, rail and 'bus services have
been severely curtailed and you should take steps to ensure that
any trains and 'buses you intend to use are actually running.

Rail ticket is enclosed herewith.

Should you be unable to accept this match, or
should you be injured or unfit in the meantime, please wire or
telephone me at once so that the reserve can be called up.

Yours faithfully,

John Wilson

Secretary.

Mr. T. Foster.

Letter from John Wilson, the RFL secretary, to Trevor inviting him to play for Wales against England at
Odsal in December 1939 – his first international. (Courtesy Trevor Foster & Rugby Football League)

Parliamentary Rugby League Group at an official dinner in Trevor's honour held at the Houses of Parliament.

The Group was set up in 1988 to be a voice for the game in Parliament. David Hinchliffe MP has for many years been one of its leading members, and is a Wakefield Trinity supporter. He wrote: "I well remember the first time I met Trevor Foster. He was a man who was starring at Wembley before I was born, the only man ever to score six tries against Wakefield Trinity in the same game, a genuine legend of The Greatest Game and as we shook hands, he called me "Sir". Trevor is a classic example of what impresses me most about top rugby league players. Despite achieving so much and gaining the plaudits and admiration of thousands of the game's followers over many years, with very few exceptions, their feet remain very firmly on the ground. They rarely forget where they came from and those who helped them on the way.

It never ceases to strike me as well how men who mixed it in the hardest of sports with the hardest of opponents - and there were few harder than Trevor's old oppo Arthur Clues - can, off the field, espouse the most decent of values in their personal lives. There can be few better examples of this than Trevor Foster.

Trevor achieved everything in rugby league, but has continued to contribute to our game - even in the humblest of roles - long after the end of this playing career. His marvellous life is a model for all of us. It is a privilege to know you, 'Sir'!"

Lord Lofthouse of Pontefract is also one of the Group's stalwarts. He also has many fond memories of Trevor's involvement in the game: "I was aged 13 and in my last year at the local secondary school in Featherstone where rugby league was our bible and Post Office Road was our citadel. I suppose it would be the very early season of 1939 when I think I first saw Trevor. It was the season just prior to the commencement of the war and I recall that season commenced with the arrival of the New Zealand tourists who only played two matches and had to return when war broke out.

Bradford's first match [of the wartime emergency league] was at Featherstone. At that time the Featherstone players were my heroes, one of them being Vic Darlison who introduced me to him. Vic was later to move to Bradford and join Trevor in that great pack of forwards who would grace the Wembley Final on three occasions directly after the war. I was privileged to be present on each occasion. The highlight for me was I think after the second final, Vic Darlison took me along to the celebrations in London that particular night and again introduced me to that great forward Trevor Foster. From that day my affection and respect grew for him and I have valued a growing friendship since that time. I once recall Vic Darlison saying: "He is too nice a chap to be playing with us lot". The occasion I shall always recall was the Rugby League Challenge Cup Final at Twickenham when the television had a shot of him stood alone and what appeared to be a statue of one of the finest exponents of rugby league I believe the game has ever seen. My sporting life and my love of rugby league has been enriched by my friendship with Trevor Foster and I shall always be grateful to the late Vic Darlison for introducing him to me."

Two of the game's leading administrators also have fond memories of Trevor. Harry Jepson OBE, former Hunslet club secretary outlined: "Trevor Foster's last league game for Bradford Northern at Odsal was in 1955 and Hunslet provided the opposition. That day, as I watched Trevor being carried off the field in honour on the shoulders of Hunslet's captain – the legendary Australian Arthur Clues – I never in my wildest dreams imagined that, almost half a century later, Trevor would still be playing an active role on the Odsal stage. But that is, in fact, the case.

In the interim Trevor has played many parts in the service of the club he joined from Newport in 1938. In the dark days of 1964 he was a beacon of light and hope in the rebirth of the famous old club and now, as he nears his 90th birthday, he is rightly basking in the glory of his beloved Bradford Bulls' current triumphs. Add to this his rugby league deeds for Wales and Great Britain, plus his active service during the Second World War, and you have the quintessential club man, surely unparalleled in any sport."

Maurice Oldroyd, who has given a lifetime's service to the game, remembers: "My first view of Trevor Foster was soon after the war, when I was an avid Fartown man. He and Arthur Clues were probably the two outstanding second-row forwards of their time. I particularly remember him playing for Bradford against Huddersfield in the third round of the Challenge Cup in 1953, which produced a staggering 69,429 attendance at Odsal. Fartown went on to beat St. Helens at Wembley 15-10. I also distinctly remember the headlines in the Saturday night *Green Final* [in 1948] when he scored an amazing six tries out of eight against Wakefield Trinity. Trevor transcended all boundaries and eras. He played in the first inter-code representative games during the war and he was still involved in our game over 50 years later, when the next inter-code games between Wigan and Bath took place.

Trevor was a leader of men, who worked quietly behind the scenes on community work in his beloved Bradford and he was a leading light with the Bradford Police Young People's club, who played in the local youth leagues. Two of its most famous products were Brian Noble, current coach of the Bulls and Great Britain, and Keith Mumby, who made a record number of appearances for Bradford.

What is most obvious is his love, enjoyment and passion for the game which shines like a beacon. He can still make a good speech and stimulate enthusiasm and perhaps his humbleness is personified that even now, after his 90th birthday, he is still the Bulls' official time-keeper. Surely a man for all seasons."

The modern game

Trevor attends every Bradford Bulls match, carrying out his duties as timekeeper. Unlike some former players, he appreciates the modern game, recognising the changes from his own playing days. He also enjoys attending the game's big occasions, in particular international matches against Australia. On 15 November 2003, Great Britain lost narrowly to Australia at Hull's KC Stadium. Another series defeat against the old enemy. Trevor and Alex Murphy, two elder statesmen of the game, reflected on the occasion. Both had beaten Australia as players. "To win against Australia is the lifelong ambition and pinnacle of a rugby league player's career" exclaimed Trevor. "We came so close, but failed again to execute the very basic skills of rugby league at the highest level and under extreme pressure" replied Murphy. "It is not just about the pre-match and tactical planning, the level of fitness or the pride in the jersey", responded Trevor. "Great Britain have all of that. But Australia have learnt infinite belief and self discipline. They also combine their natural athleticism and flair with a tough mental approach and God's gift of patience. This is a winning formula in modern-day international rugby."

Alex Murphy nodded in agreement, beads of perspiration across his furrowed and frustrated brow. "Trevor", he said, "I wish you and I could return to our prime. We'd give those Aussies something to think about." The two wise men continued to debate the issues long into the night in their efforts to come to terms with Great Britain's defeat.

"For my sins", said Trevor, "I was at the Boothferry Park massacre in 1982 [Australia won 40-4], when the gap in class between these two international teams was as wide as the River Humber. Today, things are very different, we are much closer to their level of performance. I am very optimistic for the future. I have great faith in the Rugby Football League, our young players and the home-grown coaches to find the winning formula again. We have much to look forward to."

Of the recent Bradford players, Trevor has great respect for Robbie and Henry Paul, who have both played a crucial role in the rise of the Bulls. He wrote about them: "What a tremendous impact these two brothers had on the game of rugby league football, as many of their countrymen from New Zealand such as Mike Gilbert, George Harrison, Jack Mclean, Bob Hawes, Joe Phillips had before them – bringing wonderful rugby skills to the famous Odsal Stadium. They all, along with Robbie and Henry, proudly wore the red, amber and back colours. Robbie and Henry have achieved great success both on and off the field. They are always ready to make themselves available for the supporters of the game in so many ways. They are a great example of the New Zealand sporting culture with their outstanding and warm-hearted outlook on life. They have made wonderful contributions to rugby league football. They are great entertainers. Robbie loves to score tries and is always looking for the break to open out the opposition and to dart through to the try line.

The Bradford supporters have adopted him as a proud citizen of Bradford. Henry in the same vein has showed the sporting world his outstanding talents by also making an impact in rugby union. Robbie has now become the articulate captain of our great club."

Trevor selected two all-time select teams of players he has seen and played with or against for this book. Both include players from all his period in the game:

Great Britain (post war): Martin Ryan, Eric Batten, Gus Risman (captain), Neil Fox, Billy Boston, Roger Millward, Alex Murphy, Frank Whitcombe, Joe Egan, Brian McTigue, Phil Lowe, Andy Farrell, Johnny Whiteley.
Subs: Ellery Hanley, Paul Sculthorpe, Stuart Fielden, Ernest Ward, Jonathan Davies or David Watkins.

Bradford Northern and Bulls: Keith Mumby, Eric Batten, Ernest Ward, Paul Newlove, Jack McLean, Billy Davies, Tommy Smales, Frank Whitcombe, James Lowes, Jimmy Thompson, Trevor Foster, Jeff Grayshon, Ellery Hanley.
Subs: Robbie Paul, Henry Paul, Ken Traill, Karl Fairbank.

We will allow Trevor to select himself in the second row of his Bradford team. There is no dispute that he is there on merit.

Chris Caisley

It is appropriate that the last tribute in this book is from Chris Caisley, the current chairman of the Bradford Bulls. He became club chairman in 1987, and says that the name Trevor Foster is synonymous with the club: "Since I became a member of the board of directors of the rugby club then named Bradford Northern in 1987, there have been a number of people who have given a lot of years of valuable, continuous service, paid and unpaid, to the club. This is not necessarily surprising because the club now known as the Bradford Bulls has at its core a philosophy built on hard work, innovation, quality of performance, togetherness, loyalty and, above all else, a belief that these things can go hand in glove with a true sense of enjoyment.

That in Trevor Foster we have someone who not only possesses these attributes, but who has also been with Northern and the Bulls for more than 65 years is quite remarkable. It is also undeniably the case that had it not been for Trevor's efforts in the 1960s there would not have been a club in existence today, let alone one that has been as successful as the post-Super League Bulls.

Over the years there have been many changes, some good, others bad, in the sport of rugby league. We have entered into full-time professionalism, the commercial world of sponsors, big television contracts, merchandising and all manner of inventions which go to make up the modern game. Trevor has never been in the slightest bit fazed by change and whatever has come to pass he has remained steadfastly loyal to the sport and to the club into which he has put body and soul since moving north from Wales in 1938.

The term 'legend' is overused and overhyped these days, but to many Bradfordians in and around his adoptive city, whether young or old, men or woman, boys or girls, Trevor is a true Bradford legend who is regarded with affection by all those who have come across him over the years. I hope the success the Bulls have achieved from time to time has given him enjoyment and some reward for all the hard work he has put into the club, numerous charities and the community in general. To everybody at the Bulls and their supporters the name of Trevor Foster is synonymous with the club. He is their 'Mr Reliable', and as he is now in his 91st year, long may that continue."

90 not out

Saturday 4 December 2004 was a big day for Trevor when he celebrated his 90th birthday with family and friends at the famous Bradford Police Club for Young People.

The Young People's Club proved the ideal venue, since Trevor has spent many long and happy hours there as a volunteer and rugby coach, just a few minutes walk from his home.

One hundred people attended the surprise party for Trevor who was 'gobsmacked' when he arrived to find many old friends and former colleagues as well as family who had travelled from all parts of the UK. Guests included his former playing partner Frank Whitcombe's family, Robbie Paul's family, the Bradford Bulls coach Brian Noble, former Lord Mayors of Bradford and his local parish priest. All had come to pay tribute to Trevor's coming of age.

A feature of the event, which included a nostalgic look back at his colourful life, presented by his son Simon, was an amazing 14 piece cake weighing 14 stones and 2lbs.(Trevor's playing weight in 1938). The cake, decorated in red, amber and black was designed and baked by lifelong Northern and Bulls supporter Peter Le-Talbot.

Trevor said: "I had never expected this. I knew that a few of my family were coming to my house for tea. What a wonderful reception. Another great kindness has been given to me in this great City. I still feel young and pretty fit and have offered my services to Brian Noble should he be one short in the first fixture of the new season".

We will finish this book with a phrase that Trevor uses when he writes to family, friends and colleagues: **'Wales Forever'**.

Appendix 1: Statistics and records

Trevor Foster's playing career
Compiled by Robert Gate

Bradford Northern

	A	T	G	P
1938-39	23	11	1	35
1939-40	25	8	-	24
1940-41	25	13	-	39
1941-42	25	13	-	39
1942-43	19	9	-	27
1943-44	15	8	-	24
1944-45	13	3	-	9
1945-46	7	1	-	3
1946-47	24	7	-	21
1947-48	41	22	-	66
1948-49	29	3	-	9
1949-50	37	11	-	33
1950-51	19	4	-	12
1951-52	32	5	-	15
1952-53	34	4	-	12
1953-54	35	5	-	15
1954-55	29	3	-	9
Overall totals	**432**	**130**	**1**	**392**

Debut   29 October 1938 versus Hull (H), lost 14-20
Last game 20 April 1955 versus Wakefield Trinity (A), lost 12-31

Note: These figures differ slightly from those published in 1986 in Robert Gate's *Gone North* (Vol 1), subsequent research throwing up certain anomalies. The figures are taken from the Rugby League Record Keepers Club publications and also take into account work done by Nigel Williams, the Bradford Northern statistician.

Representative appearances

Tests (3)
10 August 1946	Great Britain 8 New Zealand 13	Auckland
9 October 1948	Great Britain 23 Australia 21	Leeds *2 tries*
6 November 1948	Great Britain 16 Australia 7	Swinton

Internationals (16)
23 December 1939	Wales 16 England 3	Bradford *try*
9 November 1940	Wales 5 England 8	Oldham *try*
18 October 1941	Wales 9 England 9	Bradford
27 February 1943	Wales* 9 England 15	Wigan
26 February 1944	Wales 9 England 9	Wigan

24 March 1946	Wales* 7 France 19	Bordeaux *try, goal*
12 October 1946	Wales* 13 England 10	Swinton
16 November 1946	Wales* 5 England 19	Swansea
18 January 1947	Wales* 5 France 14	Marseilles
23 November 1947	Wales 21 France 29	Bordeaux
6 December 1947	Wales 7 England 18	Swansea *try*
20 March 1948	Wales 12 France 20	Swansea *try*
10 April 1949	Wales 0 France 11	Marseilles
22 October 1949	Wales* 5 Other Nats 6	Abertillery
1 March 1950	Wales* 6 England 11	Wigan
7 December 1951	Wales 3 New Zealand 15	Bradford

* Captain

Other representative matches (7)

23 March 1940	Yorkshire XIII 13	Lancashire XIII 10	Barrow *try*
4 May 1940	1940 Tour Probables 29	1936 Tourists 21	Salford *2 tries*
21 March 1942	Northern Command 22	Rugby League XIII 18	Halifax
10 October 1942	Northern Command* 14	Rugby League XIII 10	Hull *2 tries*
18 December 1943	Army XIII* 4	Rugby League XIII 11	Halifax
7 October 1944	Northern Command* 23	Rugby League XIII 27	Huddersfield
20 February 1946	Whites 18	Colours 14 (Tour trial)	Leeds *try*

* Captain

1946 tour games [excluding tests] (9)

22 May	Great Britain 36	Southern Division 4	Junee
1 June	Great Britain 14	New South Wales 10	Sydney
2 June	Great Britain 12	South Coast Division 15	Wollongong
13 July	Great Britain 34	Toowoomba 5	Toowoomba
16 July	Great Britain 53	North Coast Division 8	Grafton *try*
27 July	Great Britain 24	South Island 12	Christchurch
29 July	Great Britain 8	West Coast 17	Greymouth
31 July	Great Britain 32	Maoris 8	Wellington
7 Aug	Great Britain 42	South Auckland 12	Huntley

Career record

	A	T	G	P
Bradford Northern	432	130	1	392
Tests	3	2	0	6
Wales	16	5	1	17
1946 tour	9	1	0	3
Representative	7	6	0	18
Overall totals	**467**	**144**	**2**	**436**

Appearances in major finals

Challenge Cup finals (4)
22 April 1944	Bradford N* 8	Wigan 0	Bradford (second leg)	
	(Bradford won 8-3 on aggregate. Trevor missed the first leg)			
3 May 1947	Bradford N 8	Leeds 4	Wembley	*try*
1 May 1948	Bradford N 3	Wigan 8	Wembley	
7 May 1949	Bradford N 12	Halifax 0	Wembley	*try*

Championship finals (5)
18 May 1940	Bradford N 21	Swinton 13	Swinton (first leg)
25 May 1940	Bradford N 16	Swinton 9	Bradford (second leg)
12 April 1941	Bradford N 17	Wigan 6	Wigan (first leg)
14 April 1941	Bradford N 28	Wigan 9	Bradford (second leg)
18 April 1942	Bradford N 0	Dewsbury 13	Leeds
8 May 1948	Bradford N 5	Warrington 15	Maine Road, Manchester
10 May 1952	Bradford N* 6	Wigan 13	Leeds Road, Huddersfield

Yorkshire Cup finals (6)
5 April 1941	Bradford N 15	Dewsbury 5	Huddersfield *2 tries*
6 December 1941	Bradford N 24	Halifax 0	Huddersfield *try*
27 November 1943	Bradford N* 5	Keighley 2	Bradford (first leg) *try*
4 December 1943	Bradford N* 5	Keighley 5	Keighley (second leg)
30 October 1948	Bradford N 18	Castleford 9	Leeds *try*
29 October 1949	Bradford N 11	Huddersfield 4	Leeds
31 October 1953	Bradford N* 7	Hull 2	Leeds

* Captain

Yorkshire League Championship (3)
Bradford won this competition in 1939-40, 1940-41 and 1947-48

Appearances in major war-time rugby union services internationals (7)
7 March 1942	Wales 17	England 12	Swansea
28 March 1942	Wales 9	England 3	Gloucester *try*
7 November 1942	Wales 11	England 7	Swansea
20 March 1943	Wales 34	England 7	Gloucester
20 November 1943	Wales 11	England 9	Swansea
8 April 1944	Wales 8	England 20	Gloucester
25 November 1944	Wales 28	England 11	Swansea *try*

Newport RFC

1937-38: 34 appearances, 12 tries.
1938-39: 1 appearance.

Appendix 2: Trevor Foster testimonial souvenir brochure (1955)

(N.B. We have not 'modernised' the punctuation or presentation of this booklet, which is therefore in a different style from the rest of this book. We have also not included the statistical section, which is covered by Appendix 1 above.)

FOREWORD

Sixteen or seventeen years ago, whilst on a trip to South Wales, I called, as was my usual practice, on an old Northern player who had then, and still has, the interest of Bradford Northern at heart, namely Bill Morgan, who at once said: "I want you to go with me on Saturday to see a lad at Newport. I think he is a coming star." How true were his remarks!

During the next twelve months I saw a lot of this lad and steadily and persistently tried to persuade him to come to play for Bradford. Finally one fine morning I met him up at Pontypool bus station, and brought him North. He thereby carrying out his given word, although all the Newport papers on the previous Saturday night had banner headlines stating: "Trevor Foster refuses very tempting offer to go North." Frankly I admired that lad that morning because I knew what a wrench it was to him to leave his club mates, his blind father, his mother and all his family and friends, to come North with me, almost a stranger to him.

During the intervening years that admiration has grown highest regard one man can have for another, and that regard for him is only in line with that of countless thousands who have had the pleasure of making his acquaintance throughout the world. Lip service has been paid to his exceptional qualities as a gentleman as well as a footballer wherever Rugby Football has been played.

Now you are given the opportunity of showing, in a practical way your sincere regard for him. Trevor's name will go down in history as one of Rugby's greatest and cleanest players, and our duty, as far as I see it, is to make it crystal clear to the world that the Testimonial which we shall eventually present to him is worthy in every way of the loyal service, the sacrifice, and the pleasure he has so willingly given us.

Sincerely yours,

Harry Hornby

Harry Hornby

The Trevor Foster Testimonial Fund

THE Committee of the above Fund wish to extend Hearty Congratulations to Trevor on achieving every possible honour in the Rugby League Code. We have formed this Fund as a tribute to Trevor for his outstanding character of which you all know him. He always serves us with the artistic and classical polished type of Football, which is always a delight watch, and is always a feature of any game he plays. Given the support of his many admirers a Grand Cheque from this Fund to make the Benefit a real bumper for Bradford Northern's Welsh and Great Britain International of whom we are all very proud.

WHAT OTHERS THINK ABOUT TREVOR FOSTER
(Some comments from Press Reports)

"Sunday Graphic"
"Brilliant forward play by veteran Trevor Foster was the inspiration behind Northern's win. Running and handling like a back, covering up his defence with the speed and agility of a player half his years, Foster was the spearhead of almost every attack that began from the play-the-ball."

"The People"
"Trevor Foster worked like a Trojan among the forwards, but was not well supported on most occasions."

"Yorkshire Sports"

"Oldham faded under the inspiring lead Foster gave his Bradford forwards. The ball was as heavy and slippery as it could be, yet Foster never missed a pass nor gave other than a perfect one."

"Daily Herald"

"When youngsters talk of forwards in the days to come, the old 'uns will talk of Trevor Foster - one who had hands as misleading as a gifted halfback; one who kept his head when the going was fierce and gave science preference when strength alone might have been just as successful; one who was universally admired as the shining example of the scheming and spectacular school as compared with the 'bull-at-a-gate' type."

"The Times"

"Trevor Foster was the best forward on the field by a very long way, and at times played with the skill and speed of a three-quarter."

"News of the World" (Jim Sullivan)

"It must have been disappointing to many of the stars in this match - Wales v. England at Odsal in 1942-that they realised that but for the war they could have been playing themselves into the touring team to go to Australia in April. Trevor Foster would have been a certainty for the second row. Powerful, fast and intelligent, he is one of the finest players who ever left my native country."

"Sunday Chronicle"

"The English forwards had a scrum advantage, but the Welsh pack was never subdued. In fact, they had in Trevor Foster the best forward on view. He gave a great display."

"The Irish Times"

"The individual hero of the day was Trevor Foster. While the Irish defence could perform wonders in stopping the opposing backs, they could not cope with Foster, an enormous forward who could travel for 20 yards as fast as any man on the field, shake off tackles, swerve and sell the dummy.

"Two of the British tries were scored by Foster all on his own, and on his two appearances here at Ravenhill he must rank as high, at least, as any of the great wing forwards of Rugby history."

"Swansea Argus"

"Famous Rugby Union exponents have gone North from time to time and distinguished themselves in their new environment. Many great names come to mind, but surely there have been no greater players in the professional sphere than Jim Sullivan and Trevor Foster."

I felt greatly honoured to be asked to contribute to this testimonial brochure.

From the Rugby League playing fields at the season's end there will be no Trevor Foster of Bradford Northern and to me the fact is as sad as it reads, for he is one of the greatest forwards of his position it has been my pleasure to watch and to play against.

The best advice I could give to young forwards of today is go and watch Bradford and model your style on that of Trevor Foster, one of the greatest of our time. As a sportsman there is none better.

Our game will be the worse for his retirement. Why he should retire I do not know for his display at Warrington last October was nothing short of the season's best.

So well did he play that some of our young players remarked: "He must have been good when he was younger." My reply was easy: "Yes, he was great."

If Trevor can model a Bradford pack on his own style there will always be good football at Odsal.

"Au revoir" to a great player and a gentleman.

CES MOUNTFORD
(Warrington manager and former Wigan and New Zealand half-back).

Rugby League followers in general, and those of Bradford in particular, will remember Trevor Foster long after he has ceased to play as one of the best second-row forwards who ever came from Wales.

They will remember him not so much for his try scoring feats, although he has got his share, but for his ability to hold the ball until he could part with it to advantage and to take the tackle if such was inevitable, rather than let a colleague do so.

But most of all they, and I will remember him as a man who played the game in the true spirit of Rugby; who did not consider that every knock that came his way was deliberate and intended, and consequently never retaliated.

He has been an ornament to his club and to the Rugby League game, and will take with him into his retirement from active football the well-earned and deserved reputation of a sportsman and a gentleman.

MR. JOHN WILSON
(former Rugby League secretary).

Trevor Foster's career with Bradford Northern was nearly cut short by eight years. Australians can spot a genuine article when they see it, and during the 1946 tour Trevor was the target of many tempting offers to settle "down under" as a player-coach - even though injury prevented him from showing his best form and kept him out of the Tests against Australia.

Trevor's conduct has always been held up as an object lesson for young footballers.

He has never had much to say for himself, but it was astounding how by sheer quality of character, the "Old Gent" as Frank Whitcombe affectionately dubbed him, could wield authority and command respect among a bunch of high-spirited tour players.

The Rugby League game will lose a model player when he retires. I only wish we could look forward to the recruitment of another 100 players even half as good.

ALFRED DREWRY ("Yorkshire Post")

"To know anyone you must live with them," goes the old saying, and if that is so then I know Trevor Foster well, for I lived up with him for six months.

Yes, I was a travelling colleague of Trevor's in the 1946 Great Britain tour to Australia and New Zealand. There I learnt to appreciate some of the finer qualities of Foster the gentleman as well as the Foster forward.

Throughout the whole tour Trevor's calmness and fine outlook on things had a great bearing towards its success.

But Foster the forward had made his impression felt on me in a personal way in 1941.

As manager of Dewsbury, it was Foster the forward who, at least temporary, cost me my first Cup thrill and ambition. With the immortal Sullivan at full-back, Dewsbury expected to beat Bradford in the Yorkshire Cup final. A minute before half-time Sullivan had a chance to give us the lead with a penalty under the posts. The ball hit the upright and we turned round with a point deficit.

During the interval I told the players: "Foster is our only real danger, keep him in check." But the wish was more than the accomplishment, and instead of Dewsbury winning the Cup, Bradford did, thanks to a superb Trevor Foster effort.

Glowing tributes from all quarters will be showered on Trevor in this his benefit year. May I add to all these: "It has been good to know you. Trevor."

EDDIE WARING
("Sunday Pictorial" Columnist and B.B.C. Commentator)

It is always regrettable when one learns of a decision by any person to pass from the scene of many triumphs particularly when it applies to someone who is such a colourful personality as Trevor Foster.

During my career as a referee I officiated on many occasions both in club and representative matches when Trevor participated, and, in addition, was with him in some of his activities on behalf of the game to which he dedicated himself.

As a player he has been outstanding, in his efforts unsparing on and off the field, with a readiness to protect, help and advise those desiring to progress, but probably not so well gifted as himself.

I do not recollect him being responsible for anything unsavoury whatever the provocation; he is modest in success and magnificent in defeat.

The game can't afford to lose such a man and I am sure there is a niche he will be able to fill, but what better memory can any man leave when he can be truly described "As a Sportsman - one out of the bag."

MR. A. S. DOBSON
(former Rugby League Referee)

What a wonderful game this Rugby League of ours would be if the general type of forward play was based on the ethics Trevor has expounded to our enjoyment since he left Newport in September, 1938.

What a perfect example he has set in gentlemanly deportment in all things.

Unlike Tennyson's Brook, footballers do not go on for ever. The irreparable loss to the game, which Trevor's retirement means, will I hope be minimised by long and successful service as a coach.

Would that he could train countless others to play the game with the same skilful artistry and in the same sporting spirit which has given us so much pleasure during the years.

Rugby League would stand higher in prestige if it had more Trevor Fosters. Unfortunately it has only possessed one.

TOM LONGWORTH
("News Chronicle")

It gives me particular pleasure to be invited to contribute to this brochure because my association with Trevor goes back many years. It began on the Rugby Union field early in the war! Trevor was a Welshman and in the Army. I was English and a "R.A.F. type." Both of us were back-row forwards. It was, therefore, inevitable that we should meet!

At that time I remember being impressed with Trevor's superb handling ability and his sportsmanlike style of play. This early impression has been confirmed since seeing him in action in Rugby League football.

Knowing how much Trevor's heart is in the game, I realise that to retire was a hard decision for him to make. However, with his coaching ability and his roots in the game he will be around and about for many years to come.

If he can rear young players to emulate his own standard of sportsmanship and rival his own ability he will do a further great service to the game.

MR. W. FALLOWFIELD. M.A.
(Secretary, Rugby Football League)

TREVOR ANSWERS YOUR QUESTIONS

What was your greatest thrill?

Playing my first game for Wales at Odsal in November, 1939, with Jim Sullivan as my captain. Receiving a pass from Gus Risman, I managed to score a try and up came Jim Sullivan to shake my hand. My father, who was totally blind, was listening to the broadcast of the game, and it gave him some happy memories.

What was your happiest memory?

Winning the Cup at Wembley on our first visit. ...Our opponents were Leeds, and Northern were considered as second favourites. It was a happy moment walking to the Royal Box to receive a winning medal from the Duke of Gloucester.

Have you any regrets?

None.

Have you any hints for the younger players?

Yes. Enjoy your football. Give thought to your games and be alert at all times. Rugby is a great team game, and all youngsters should take part. Train well and you will play well. Be a clean sportsman.

Who are the best players you have opposed?

The best back is Willie Horne (Barrow). He is a great ball player who could win a match on his own. A genius with his quickness off the mark, deceptive running and exceptional kicking ability. His tactical moves are excellently conceived and the bigger the occasion the better he plays-an inspiration to any team.

The best forward is Arthur Clues, Hunslet and former Leeds second-row man. I first played against him on the famous Sydney cricket ground in 1946. He impressed me from that first game. His speed and agility for a big man is remarkable. Always dangerous near his opponents' line, he is a tower of strength and a potential match-winner.

Have you had any amusing experiences?

There have been many, but one stands out. It was during a Rugby League international between France and Wales at Bordeaux. A member of the Welsh team was having a fight with a Frenchman. The Welshman struck his opponent on the jaw, and a few seconds later repeated the dose. When asked why he had done it, He said the Frenchman was interfering with his play. When he hit the Frenchman he cried: "Merci" "I thought he was calling me a fancy name so I hit him again," added the Welshman.

If you could pick a team from all the Northern players with whom you have been associated, what would it be?

This is a difficult one to answer, but I think my choice would be: Joe Phillips; Eric Batten, Jack Kitching, Ernest Ward, Alan Edwards; Billie Davies, Donald Ward; Frank Whitcombe, Vic Darlison, Herbert Smith, Barry Tyler, Sandy Orford and Ken Traill.

One of the most interesting public houses in Monmouthshire is the Church House. Portland Street, Newport - the place where Trevor lived before he came North.

A plaque on the wall outside reveals that W. H. Davies, "Tramp Poet" was born there, while inside tile walls are covered with souvenirs of Army and Rugby Football occasions.

Trevor's father, Mr. Richard Foster, who died about two years ago, was the licensee for 40 years and Mrs. Foster is now in charge.

The Foster family have been steeped in Army tradition. Trevor's grandfather joined the 41st Foot (now the Welsh Regiment) when he was 17 and served in the Crimean War. Later he went to India where his three sons were born.

In 1885 Trevor's father joined the regiment. He served throughout the Boer War as a colour-sergeant and was awarded the D.C.M. and the Queen's and King's South African Medals.

A few years ago he was presented with the Meritorious Service Medal and an annuity of £10.

In 1910 he took over licensed premises at Maesteg and a few years later he and his wife moved to Church House which was formerly kept by Mrs. Foster's mother.

All the Rugby souvenirs on those walls do not belong to Trevor. The cap his father was awarded while playing for Cardiff in 1897 has a place of prominence, too.

Trevor, who has two brothers and three sisters, was married to a Bradford nurse. Miss Jean Unsworth, daughter of a former Bradford Police Inspector, in 1948.

Recently they have removed from Bolton to Bradford Moor and have three children Simon Richard (four), Jane Ann (three), and Sarah Elizabeth (18 months).

By "The Oracle" of the "Telegraph and Argus" and the "Yorkshire Sports"

"FOR WHEN THE ONE GREAT SCORER COMES TO WRITE AGAINST YOUR NAME, HE MARKS - NOT THAT YOU WON OR LOST – BUT HOW YOU PLAYED THE GAME."

How many of us will score maximum points when, in the words of Grantland Rice, the day comes for our cards to be marked?

I know one who should have a place at the top - Trevor Foster, whom we hope will have a bumper benefit to mark his last season as a player.

This brochure, the proceeds of which will help to swell the testimonial fund, is full of praise from people in all walks of life, who have known Trevor either on or off the field, and every word of commendation that has been written is worthy of this brilliant sportsman.

I doubt if anyone has ever commanded more respect throughout the game's history, and he has won that rare honour because of his great love for the code, his modesty, sincerity and faithfulness to his club.

Mention is made among the tributes about an offer from Australia, in 1946, which Trevor almost accepted, but this is only one of many - all tempting - which he has turned down because he has always been happy at Odsal.

WANTED BY OTHER CLUBS

Hull, Hull Kingston Rovers, Huddersfield, Barrow, Workington, Wigan, at one time or another- have made enquiries about him - not only as a player but as a coach.

They are recognisant of the fact that many great footballers have graced this game of ours, but few - if any - have his talents to develop and instruct youngsters in the finer arts.

He must have spent thousands of hours, particularly when he was appointed Director of Coaching, with young players, and he is still called upon by headquarters because of his unsurpassed skill and knowledge.

Nobody has criticised Northern's management and players in recent years more than I have done, and as I study the many words of complaint showered on them I cannot find any concerning Trevor Foster, because, at all times, he has given of his best.

Not only that, but he has held a Northern pack together that, on many occasions, looked like the best in the Rugby League, although, individually, few were ready for international recognition.

I have paid countless tributes to his qualities, and, as this brochure is full of them, I will concentrate on telling you something of his life story.

UNUSUAL CHRISTIAN NAMES

Trevor John French Foster was born at Newport, Monmouthshire, on December 3, 1916. How did he get those other two Christian names?

Well, in that same year Sir John French was created a Viscount, and Trevor's mother added them as an expression of her admiration for the famous soldier.

He started his Rugby Union football as a schoolboy at Holy Cross, Newport, and he filled the full-back position. He was not long before he won a place in the Newport schoolboys' team, which won the Welsh championship.

Already there were signs of a potential star in the making, but it seemed as if the game had lost a promising youngster when Trevor left school to help in the family hotel because of his father's gradual loss of his sight.

There was no football for four years, but once the family affairs became more settled Trevor found more time to devote to the handling code.

He went along to Phil Harriers, a noted Monmouthshire side, and spent two years with them - as a wing forward.

WHEN HE CAME NORTH

At this period Trevor was quickly developing into an outstanding forward, and in 1937 he switched to Newport. He had only one season there, but he was the side's leading try scorer, and his skill soon brought the Rugby League scouts in search of him.

But before he was tempted by an offer from Bradford Northern, in September, 1938, he had toured Devon and Cornwall with the famous Captain Crawshay's side, under the captaincy of the inimitable Billy

172

Davies, and had been chosen as first reserve for Wales against Ireland at Swansea.

Rugby was not his only sporting interest, and while in Wales he had taken part in many first-class baseball games and was a competent amateur boxer.

Although Trevor had already made a name for himself in Rugby Union circles, there was no fanfare of trumpets to greet his debut for Northern against Hull, at Odsal on October 29, 1938.

The hard-boiled Yorkshireman does not acknowledge anyone until he has seen for himself the qualities and ability of a player.

HIS FIRST "HAT-TRICK"

Northern's supporters had not long to wait. Trevor opened his scoring account with a "hat-trick" of tries against Bramley that Christmas, and he was the leading try scorer among the forwards at the end of the campaign.

Long before his first season had finished, however, those who knew anything about football realised that Northern had made one of their best signings.

It was the start of a gradual team-building policy. The next close season Billy Davies was persuaded to come to Odsal, and Mr. Harry Hornby and Mr. Dai Rees decided to build the team around these two brilliant Welshmen.

What a tragedy to the management and players, now showing football, the likes of which had never been seen before in Northern's history, when war started.

Trevor was robbed of many honours, including a tour to Australia, during the hostilities, but Northern, against sides that were recruiting "guest" players from other clubs, became one of the leaders.

Trevor was appointed captain, and he led his side to many successes - but he was in uniform now.

JOINED THE K.O.Y.L.I.

Early in 1940 Trevor Foster joined the King's Own Yorkshire Light Infantry, and the following year passed out as a sergeant instructor in the Army Physical Training Corps.

The Army soon started to appreciate his footballing ability. He was appointed captain of the Northern Command Rugby Union and Rugby League sides; made many appearances for the British Army in Great Britain and France; and played for Wales in both Rugby Union and Rugby League internationals.

Then came an overseas posting to the Middle East, and while in Cairo and Palestine Trevor captained the Welsh team. He was now a staff sergeant and devoted much of his time in remedial and hospital work, helping to get troops back to fitness.

He took up basket ball, winning several prizes, and participated in Army boxing contests.

One of his treasured possessions is a parchment certificate of merit for outstanding service, signed by the Commander-in-Chief of the Home Forces.

One of the secrets of Trevor's success story is that he has always insisted in keeping in first-class physical condition and on his return he quickly fitted into Bradford Northern's side.

He handed the captaincy over to Ernest Ward, but he was still the planner among the forwards, and he played a notable role in the side's rapid rise.

THAT SIX-TRIES FEAT

Not a season passed without at least one trophy being won by Northern, who were feared just as much in Lancashire and Cumberland as they were in Yorkshire.

One of his most outstanding feats, and there have been many, was the remarkable game against Wakefield Trinity - a side that usually has a good set of forwards. But in April, 1948, Trevor made them look like amateurs as he scored six tries in a 28-16 victory.

Then came the gradual breaking up of this brilliant combination. In 1949-50 Northern slipped to the twenty-first position - the lowest they have occupied since their very first at Odsal - but Trevor was still there to give accomplished performances, although there was little support for him.

Another team-building policy was started. This time players were bought to fit in with the longest-serving members Trevor and Ernest Ward. More successes came Northern's way, particularly in scoring power, and, once again, it was Trevor who shaped the play of the pack.

Times are hard again now, but he still continues to give the right lead, and the benefit Ken Traill has gained from playing alongside him ("No one could wish for a better partner," says Ken) may help to overcome the terrific problem which will face the management at the end of this season, when the man who has provided so much of the very best entertainment the code can offer puts his football kit away for the last time.

When I was asked to contribute to this brochure my mind began to go back over the years - quite a few since the day Rugby League football was graced by the presence of Trevor.

What did I remember most?

The war-time clashes between Wigan and Bradford, the international clashes between England and Wales when we were still on opposite sides, or the Cup Final between Wigan and Bradford in 1948.

No. I found myself recalling the 1946 tour of Australia when we were both members of that side.

There is an old saying and a true one - "You have to live with a person before you know him." Living with Trevor for six months puts me in a position to say he was what the Rugby League authorities would refer to as a perfect tourist. His character was at all times reflected on the field of play; none played the game as it should be played more than him.

League followers everywhere will regret the retirement at the end of this season of Bradford's last playing link of their brightest days.

JOE EGAN
(Leigh manager and former Wigan international hooker)

Nothing pleases me more than to pay tribute to one of the grandest players to grace the Rugby League. Trevor Foster is one of the gentlemen of the game.

I had the pleasure of having Trevor with me on the 1946 Tour of Australia, and it is no exaggeration to say that he was the most popular member of the party. He never said a wrong word, and always offered a helping hand to other members of the party. Coming immediately after the war, it was a trip with plenty of trials and tribulations to tax any man's patience. Trevor would always come up smiling.

I also played Rugby Union with him during the war. He was always the same, right on top of his game all the time, and could be relied upon always.

I think Trevor Foster is a model for any budding player to look up to, and if he decides to stay in the game when he retires, he will most assuredly become one of the best coaches in Rugby League football.

We salute you, Trevor. It is too much to hope that all future players in the game could become like you in play and temperament. If that was possible, Rugby League would have nothing to worry about for years to come.

Wishing you every success for the future, and a big bumper benefit.

GUS RISMAN
(Britain international and former Workington player-manager)